30 YEARS OF

'ALLO 'ALLO!

The inside story
of the hit TV show

BY

RICHARD WEBBER

CARLTON
BOOKS

DEDICATION

To Paula,

I definitely couldn't have finished this one without you. With all my love.

ACKNOWLEDGEMENTS

I would like to thank everyone who helped in whatever way to make this book possible, including Clive Eardley; David Hamilton; Helen Molchanoff; Jeff Walden at BBC's Written Archive Centre; my agent Jeffrey Simmons; Roland Hall at Carlton; Nicki Edwards; David Barton at the BBC; Aaron Brown, editor of the British Comedy Guide (www.comedy.co.uk) and my lovely wife, Paula, who stepped in to help when the deadline loomed. Of course, the book wouldn't have been possible without the help and generosity of the cast and crew, all of whom gave up time to chat about their memories of working on the sitcom; some even generously provided photos for the book. I'm grateful to you all, especially Gorden Kaye, Vicki Michelle, Sam Kelly, Guy Siner, Arthur Bostrom, Kim Hartman, Kirsten Cooke, Francesca Gonshaw, Richard Gibson, John D. Collins, Nicholas Frankau, Sue Hodge, Roger Kitter, Sarah Sherborne, Paul Cooper, Estelle Matthews, Carole Ashby, Moira Foot, Phoebe Scholfield, Richard Cottan, Robert Katz, Mike Stephens, Shelagh Lawson, Bernadette Darnell, Charles Garland, John B. Hobbs, Mike Stephens, Chris Wadsworth, David Buckingham, Martin Dennis, Peter Farago, Paul Adam, Roger Harris, Colin Gorry, Stephen Lucas, Roy Moore, Simon Spencer and, special thanks to Robin Carr, Roy Gould and the lovely Susie Belbin. Particular thanks, though, must go to Jeremy Lloyd and Ann Croft. I hope you enjoy reading the end product!

THIS IS A CARLTON BOOK
Published by Carlton Books Limited
20 Mortimer Street
London W1T 3JW

ISBN 978-1-78097-207-7

Printed in Great Britain by CPI Group (UK) Ltd, Croydon CR0 4YY

CONTENTS

———

FOREWORD BY JEREMY LLOYD

Who would have thought, 30 years on, I would be writing this foreword to Richard Webber's remarkable tribute to *'Allo 'Allo!*. I am overwhelmed, having read this book, to see that the show still has such a warm place in the national psyche. Still shown in over 40 countries on television, it seems that on top of such a loyal following, there is a new generation now in love with all these familiar characters.

About three years ago I stood at the back of a theatre on the coast watching a new cast perform the show and the audience, old and young, enjoying shrieks of laughter. I hadn't been sure a stage version without the original actors would be a success, particularly at such a time of hardship for so many families, but was delighted to find that demand extended the initial run, up and down the country, for a further six months. Vicki Michelle – the only member of the original cast – joined this tour and I was thrilled that this new group of actors captured the essence of all these well-known favourites so well. As a comedy writer there is no greater tribute to your work than hearing laughter fill a theatre and seeing the audience have a great time. It seems that familiar family fun is what is needed in difficult times.

According to those who publish the amateur rights to *'Allo 'Allo!*, it is one of the most successful of their shows both in the UK and internationally. It amazes me when I think that groups as far away as Texas (I "Googled" it!) are still dressing up, laughing and trying to find that *Fallen Madonna With The Big Boobies*.

Talking of its wide appeal, *'Allo 'Allo!* has fans from all walks of life. I am constantly reminiscing with taxi drivers and even my friend the guitar god Jeff Beck – who has a hilarious sense of humour – proudly admits he has recordings of every show.

Reading Richard Webber's words reminded me of the elaborate structure and attention to detail involved in the making of the pilot episode of *'Allo 'Allo!*. I started by outlining the basics of the idea and creating the first episode with David Croft – and then I shoved off on holiday to Spain unaware of the hive of industry I had left behind!

I can honestly say I've never enjoyed working with any writing partner more than I did with David; we seemed to have the uncanny knack of blurting out the same line or scene at the same moment – that is unless one of us had a mouthful of Ann Croft's splendid mid-morning treats.

I find it hard to believe that 30 years have passed since I first suggested the idea to David. Richard Webber's book is a mine of information of what went on under the surface of this brilliantly Croft-crafted show, which appeared to run so seamlessly from one episode to the next.

I am extremely proud to have had such a greatly talented friend and collaborator as David Croft and I miss him greatly, but this book is like a diary I wish I had kept. Now having read it, including the fascinating interviews with those involved, I realize just how exciting and bonding those years were. We were a tight group and show family – I felt a bit of a writing orphan for a while when it all finished. What a great run we had.

How lucky to be involved in a wonderful adventure of the mind. Thank you Richard Webber – you have painstakingly reminded me of a wonderful ten years of my life.

Jeremy Lloyd, August 2012.

LISTEN VERY CAREFULLY, I'LL TELL YOU THE HISTORY ONLY ONCE

In an age when there is a dearth of genuinely funny sitcoms, it's only right that we treasure the true classics of the genre. After tirelessly entertaining viewers for years, one could excuse Jeremy Lloyd and David Croft's classic wartime offering, *'Allo 'Allo!*, for appearing jaded and ragged around the edges; but like other examples from that small band of vintage comedies which march relentlessly through the decades, it remains as fresh today as when it first graced our screens – and in the case of the pilot episode, that is 30 years ago in December 2012. Just a handful of plot devices ran through the sitcom but from them emerged a heady mix of physical and visual gags, dollops of innuendo and plenty of real farce.

Quintessentially British in its style of humour, the evergreen Second World War sitcom, set in France during the occupation, attracted over 17 million viewers at its peak and sold to more foreign markets, including France and, eventually, Germany, than previous exports. In fact, it needs little explaining; after all, why would you be reading this page if you weren't a fan or, at the very least, aware of this accessible sitcom? But it's intriguing to consider why some sitcoms endure the passing of time unscathed while others drop over the precipice into obscurity.

Examining the elite of the genre, there are marked similarities in each show:

in addition to top-flight scripts, solid ensemble acting and a polished style of production, there are plots which, although laughter-inducing, are founded in a sense of reality and contain sufficient threads of conflict from which humour can stem; it doesn't take long to realize *'Allo 'Allo!* – which extended to 85 episodes between 1982–92 – scores highly in each of these categories. Take the sense of realism: yes, the show was high farce at times and one assurance from a script written by Messrs Lloyd and Croft is that every page will be brimming over with laughs. But permeating through the comedy, the setting and basic scenario couldn't have been more real.

Once a sleepy town in Northern France, Nouvion's streets and its citizens lives changed forever the day the Germans marched in; the peaceful pavements were now pounded by armed soldiers and the local watering holes, including Café René, frequented by the enemy. The poor owner, René Artois, the self-proclaimed coward who became an unwitting hero, was pulled from pillar to post: not only was he blackmailed by the German officers to hide the treasures and valuables they had plundered – including the famous painting, *The Fallen Madonna With The Big Boobies*, by the fictional Van Klomp – but his establishment was chosen by the local French Resistance to become a safe house for downed pilots of the Allied Forces until they were repatriated. So, one can see that the sitcom had more than its fair share of conflict from which humour could be mined. Realism, albeit portrayed through comedy, is a fundamental element of *'Allo 'Allo!* and explains why David Croft – who not only co-wrote but produced and directed the lion's share of the episodes – kept reminding the cast of the setting's danger before each episode was recorded.

The deadpan seriousness, a striking trademark of the series, was one of the secrets behind the sitcom's success. The writers never tried to hide the exigencies of the war and requested a seriousness whenever necessary. Arthur Bostrom, who played Office Crabtree, a British intelligence agent, from Series 2, says: 'That was the house style. You may have been talking about something which seemed ridiculous on the surface but David always said before each episode, "Don't forget there is danger here, you could be shot at any moment; you could be found out and killed – this is real." That is why it worked: it wasn't sent up, it was performed seriously.'

Authenticity is another symbol of a David Croft-produced show. There were no shortcuts taken; yes, it was a comedy and the primary objective was to entertain the masses. However, being comedy didn't mean one could cut corners or be any less diligent when it came to getting details correct: everything from costume and make-up to sets and props had to be in keeping with the period reflected in *’Allo ’Allo!*. Prop buyer Roger Wood, who now resides in Australia, remembers the efforts involved in finding a particular item to be used by Rose Hill, a.k.a. Madame La Fan, in the pilot. He says: ‘Something I searched high and low for was a French ear trumpet for the old lady. Originally, David Croft wanted a horn like a cow’s horn but they didn’t have things like that in France back then so I finally found an old, silver French version in Portobello Road.’

David Croft played a proactive role in ensuring apposite props were being used, particularly on location. Simon Spencer, now a freelance producer/director, started working on *’Allo ’Allo!* as a floor assistant. He recalls: ‘David’s location filming was like making a mini feature: with a large main cast, supporting actors and dozens of extras playing German soldiers, French peasants and, of course, Resistance workers, it was an epic and exciting experience.

‘David instilled a solid foundation for me in all areas of production. He taught me the importance of a solid script, thorough pre-production and a disciplined shoot – but always with a sense of fun and a twinkle in his eye. If the crew were happy and enjoying themselves, then so would the actors and somehow that added to the magic of the performances on screen.’

Simon’s first location shoot as an assistant floor manager meant he was responsible for props; one episode involved Carmen Silvera playing a bus conductress. ‘The script called for a ticket punch and in London I had talked this through with our prop buyer. Early on the morning of shooting, David would go through the props needed for the scenes that day. I showed him the ticket punch but it was the wrong type.’

Calmly, David asked Simon to source the correct ticket punch as soon as possible – not an easy task. ‘It was 7.30 in the morning, in the middle of a Norfolk field. The period double-decker was driving down the road and shooting was due to start at 8. The only way to get a 1940’s ticket punch was to courier one from London, but it wouldn’t be on location until lunchtime; I was in a complete panic, but David wasn’t. He told me to dispatch the prop buyer and they’d start filming without it. David adjusted his shooting schedule which enabled shooting to go ahead for the entire morning.

‘When the ticket punch arrived from London that afternoon, he took a single shot of Carmen with the machine around her neck. When the scene was edited, no one could tell during the majority of the scene there was no ticket punch! Neither David nor the lovely Carmen Silvera made a fuss. I learned an important lesson about the importance of checking seemingly simple props and also how much you can learn when working with such consummate professionals.’

’Allo ’Allo!, was the brainchild of Jeremy Lloyd, who, together with David

Croft, had written, among others, the long-running department store sitcom, *Are You Being Served?*, and the less successful sci-fi comedy, *Come Back, Mrs Noah*. Highly proficient writers in their own right, their individual attributes meant they were able to form a rich, fruitful and lasting working relationship. Reflecting on why the Lloyd-Croft partnership was so successful, David's wife, Ann, who was a top London actors' agent before retiring, says: 'Basically, David pulled the scripts together from a structural point of view. He was a very sensible, quiet man who thought things out very carefully. Jeremy is probably the greatest one-liner this country has ever produced and has the most marvellous turn of phrase; he would come up with some brilliant ideas which David would put into a readable form. That's why they were a great team and worked so well together.'

The idea for *'Allo 'Allo!* was conceived in Jeremy Lloyd's kitchen – under the kitchen table, to be precise. Lloyd was working with Croft on a programme idea but making little headway. Not enjoying the experience, he headed back to his London home one afternoon intent on finding an alternative project with brighter prospects. 'I lay under the table, which I do when I want to think of something,' explains Jeremy, who agonized for ages before dreaming up a new idea. Although it was nearly midnight, Lloyd rushed to the phone, keen to share his thoughts with his co-writer. 'I said: "What about doing something concerning the war, perhaps with the French Resistance?" David replied: "It's a marvellous idea, we'll start tomorrow." We abandoned what we were doing and within days had written the first script.' In fact, in David's autobiography, *You Have Been Watching* ... , he recalls the pilot script being penned at lightning speed – in two and a half days.

The following day, Jeremy and David continued their discussions at Croft's London home. Soon, ideas were flowing, a clear sign that perhaps after having abandoned their last two projects – one involving characters from the *Are You Being Served?* set-up being shipwrecked on a desert island after holidaying on Young Mr. Grace's yacht – they had found an idea with legs. 'I'd seen lots of films about the French Resistance and felt it was an ideal subject for our new series. When David asked where I thought the setting should be, we got a map of France and a pin; closing our eyes, we stuck the pin in the map and landed on Nouvion,' smiles Jeremy, who claims he wasn't influenced by the BBC's wartime drama, *Secret Army*, transmitted between 1977-79 and spotlighting the history of the Belgian Resistance movement. 'I hadn't watched the drama because I'd been in America working on a *Whodunnit!* series – which we'd had great success with on Thames Television. *'Allo 'Allo!* was a spoof, really, of all the movies and TV series depicting the war.'

There were, however, striking similarities between *'Allo 'Allo!* and *Secret Army*, something noticed by the cast and crew of the drama. But the setting of the sitcom wasn't one of those likenesses. There was a discernible charm about the French town, close to the coast, viewers visited each week; it became an important part of the show's fabric. Subconsciously, viewers almost believed that life existed in the screen town, thinking that Café René opened its doors each day. All the sitcoms that David Croft wrote with his writing partners Jeremy Lloyd and Jimmy Perry were character based and audiences quickly became familiar with them, virtually second guessing what each would do. There was almost a soap quality to the show with the characters' lives being played out in front of us, a hopeful portent.

Pilot: The British Are Coming

Michelle explains to Rene that his café is to be the next safe house for escaping airmen.

MICHELLE: You are about to perform a great service for France. The escaping airmen will hide here until you give them the forged papers.

RENÉ: Where will I get forged papers?

MICHELLE: A man will live here in your cellar; he is an expert forger. He will forge the papers and give them to you.

RENÉ: Oh well, could I not just post the papers to wherever the airmen were before they came here – save them a journey? I mean it's no trouble, I would even pay for the stamp.

MICHELLE: If the letter was intercepted it would be traced back to you and you would find yourself in the town square, dead!

RENÉ: Your way is best.

After penning a pilot script, David Croft called upon the services of one of his toughest critics: his wife, Ann. In his autobiography, he stated that she was 'usually rather less than enthusiastic' about their efforts. This time, though, Ann would surprise her husband. She says: 'I read it and came back with tears running down my face. David and Jeremy asked what I thought and I said it was the funniest thing they'd ever done. Jeremy raised his eyes to heaven, saying, "Oh my god, that's the kiss of death." Usually, with shows like *Are You Being*

Served?, I was always tutting about it in a pompous fashion but I found *'Allo 'Allo!* extremely funny, particularly the first script with the classic "Matches" scene.' Fortunately, the BBC hierarchy were just as passionate about the script and greenlighted the making of a pilot episode.

James Gilbert, BBC's Head of Light Entertainment until September 1982 and the incumbent when the pilot was commissioned, says: 'David would have come in and said what he was going to do. He always had projects on the go, which he'd tell you about. I'd simply say things like, "Let me know when you're ready to have a go at that one." David had a remarkable success rate and I trusted his judgement. He only came unstuck once, with *Come Back, Mrs Noah*, which didn't work.'

Gareth Gwenlan, BBC's Head of Comedy between 1983–90, concurs with Gilbert and held David in high esteem. 'He was responsible for a large percentage of the department's output. I'd ask him how many episodes he could deliver of a particular programme, he'd tell me, I'd give him the money and he'd get on with it. He was the mainstay of the Comedy Department for 20 years and always delivered quality.'

So with the backing of his bosses, David Croft's attention turned to casting the pilot episode. Now, it's impossible contemplating anyone else playing the screen characters we've grown to love, but other performers were considered, as the original production file held at the BBC Written Archives, near Reading, Berkshire, proves. However, there was only ever one person Croft wanted for the role of René, the lugubrious, put-upon café owner. Gorden Kaye made an impression on Croft while playing a cantankerous soldier in *It Ain't Half Hot, Mum*; he impressed further as Nicky Manson in the ill-fated *Come Back, Mrs Noah* and in three episodes of *Are You Being Served?*. Croft, in his memoirs, stated: 'These he played with gusto, not being in the least daunted by the presence of all the famous and experienced TV stars around him. Jeremy and I wrote *Oh, Happy Band!* with him very much in mind for the leading role.' The premise of the show was a village community battling to prevent a proposed airfield wiping it off the map; much of the resistance and anger was expressed via the village's brass band; it was the role of the band leader that Croft had earmarked for Kaye.

Unfortunately, the threat of industrial action at ITV, for whom Gorden was contracted to appear in a show, precluded him from accepting the role. Although he would be available for the pilot, it was unlikely he could commit to a series. David wrote: 'This of course was not acceptable, so on the Wednesday before going into rehearsal on the Monday, I found myself without a leading man.' Facing the prospect of cancelling the series, Croft phoned various agents and discovered that Harry Worth, with whom he'd previously worked, was free to take on the lead role; sadly, though, the comedy didn't progress beyond the solitary series. But David remained determined to find a vehicle for Gorden Kaye and *'Allo 'Allo!* was that show, becoming his big break in the world of TV comedy. After discussing the role with Gorden's agent, Croft wrote to the actor on May 20, 1982, enclosing a copy of the script for his consideration.

The programme production files at BBC Written Archives reveal David Croft's thoughts when considering thespians for the remaining roles. Recorded against each character's name are those performers Croft considered, however briefly. While deciding who would play René was a fait accompli, it wasn't the case for many of the others. For René's wife, Edith, two actresses considered were Doremy Vernon, who played the canteen manageress for David and Jeremy in *Are You Being Served?*, and Anita Carey. Although it's unclear if either was contacted regarding an audition, Carmen Silvera put her name in the frame by writing to Croft on July 13, 1982. Silvera was performing in the repertoire season at the Theatre Royal, Haymarket, London. Also in the company was Gorden Kaye. In her letter, Carmen states that it was Kaye who suggested she dropped David a note about the upcoming TV series. Carmen stressed she'd be delighted to work with David Croft again – having played the role of Fiona Gray in 'Mum's Army', one of *Dad's Army*'s most poignent episodes – and wondered if she would be suitable for the role of René's wife or any anything else in the sitcom. She closed her letter with a touch of humour, writing, 'Perhaps I could come and see you for vanity's sake, really, as I'm told I look better than I did ten years ago! You might not agree but it would be lovely to see you again anyway.' David needed no reminding of the qualities of Silvera's acting and she was duly recruited for the role.

Jennifer Browne and Geraldine Gardner – who had appeared in episodes of *Dad's Army* and *Are You Being Served?* respectively – were considered alongside Kirsten Cooke for the role of Michelle, leader of the region's French Resistance; Gardner was unlucky because her name was also pencilled in alongside Vicki Michelle's to play Yvette, the hard-working waitress. Helping Yvette in the café was Maria, played by Francesca Gonshaw. But several actresses, including Tracey Childs, were put on the list of possibles for this role. In August 1982, however, David made a formal approach to cast Swedish-born Mary Stavin, a former Miss World, in the role. Deemed a foreign artiste, Croft applied to the Department of Employment for permission to employ her. When describing the role she would be expected to play, he wrote, 'Waitress, who is also a part-time prostitute and – in later programmes – a German agent. She has a good

French accent with German undertones.' Becoming a German agent presents an interesting insight into how the character could have developed.

When asked which British artistes or foreign artistes not requiring permission to take employment had been considered for the part, Croft's lengthy list included Diane Hardcastle, Martine Copeland, Imogen Bickford-Smith and, interestingly, Koo Stark. A month later, Croft received bad news when the Department of Employment declined his request: it was felt that if a more extensive search was conducted, a suitable actress could be found. Before long, that person arrived in the shape of Francesca Gonshaw.

While Rose Hill was the only actress considered for Edith's bedridden mother, John D. Collins was the sole name jotted down for Flying Officer Fairfax, although the character was originally called Flying Officer Adamson. For the other flying officer, John Sessions' name is noted as well as Nicholas Frankau's. The other character introduced to help the airmen escape Nazi Europe was Monsieur Leclerc, a role brought to life by Jack Haig, although Cyril Shaps was also considered.

CATCHPHRASES

"Oh 'eck!"
(René)

When it came to the bumbling Germans, prolific character actor Norman Mitchell was seen as a possible alongside Richard Marner for Colonel Von Strohm while Tony Aitken and Sam Kelly's names were those in the pot for Captain Geering. David Troughton, son of the late Patrick Troughton of *Doctor Who* fame, had just played Sergeant Pritchard in an episode of *Hi-De-Hi!* and was another consideration for Gruber while Imogen Bickford-Smith, cast as a doctor in *Are You Being Served?*, and Helen Gill, whose credits included an appearance in *Secret Army*, were alongside Kim Hartman's name for the role of Helga.

Finally, John Clegg, so often used by David Croft – most notably as Gunner Graham in *It Ain't Half Hot, Mum* – was a name to be mulled over for the role of Otto Flick. But that piece of casting was settled when Croft found his man at his daughter's wedding, as detailed later in the Richard Gibson profile. Ann Croft, however, remembers a conversation with David on that sunny afternoon. 'We were just going in the front door when David turned back. He looked at me and said: "Do you know, Richard would be the perfect casting for the Gestapo officer." I replied, "Don't be so ridiculous, I just can't see that." David told me to turn around and look at Richard because he thought he had the most perfect Germanic face. He couldn't be too old because the character was Himmler's godson so had to be in his late twenties; David was convinced it would work – and it did.'

David Croft wasted little time writing to Gibson, penning a missive on August 3, 1982. But remembering his wife's surprise after floating the idea of Gibson playing Herr Flick must have been in his thoughts when he wrote, 'It may seem strange, way-out casting but I would like to talk to you about the possibility of playing Otto Flick … as you will probably gather having read past the first paragraph, the show is a send-up of the *Secret Army* type of production.'

One actor who appeared in the pilot, albeit briefly in the closing scene, was Richard Cottan. He played Claude, an onion seller arriving at the café, and was originally intended, says Robin Carr (a member of Croft's production team), to become a regular character who would pass on secret information to René. When it was decided this task was to be allocated to Leclerc, played by Jack Haig, the character got the chop and was never seen again.

Missing out was unfortunate for Richard Cottan – now a successful writer whose credits include the TV series, *Wallander* – because the same thing had happened on *Hi-De-Hi!*. In the pilot, Cottan was cast as Marty Storm, a bad Elvis impersonator, and was supposed to be a regular character. But he was dropped when the writers couldn't find anything for him to do so wrote a storyline in which Storm secured a recording contract and left the holiday camp. Robin Carr says Croft always felt guilty. 'I'd worked with Rick Cottan years ago at the Belgrade Theatre, Coventry, and for a time shared a flat with him. Feeling guilty, David said he'd put him in something when he had the chance. Come *'Allo 'Allo!*, he got Rick Cottan in to play the onion seller in the pilot. He was going to be a regular in the series but when Jeremy and David sat down to write it, Leclerc ended up doing everything the onion seller was going to do. So they didn't need the onion seller so Rick Cottan was written out again. He was the only actor to have played two different parts in two different pilots and not gone on to play the actual series!'

Richard Cottan wasn't aware that it was intended for the onion seller to become a regular. He did, however, write an undated letter to David Croft, which is retained in the BBC archives, mentioning his misfortune in *Hi-De-Hi!* and offering his services, which could have played a part in him being offered the onion seller. He wrote: 'About 400 years ago, I played Marty Storm in the first couple of episodes of *Hi-De-Hi!* In spite of the fact that this was a performance that captured the hearts of millions, summed up the dreams, hopes and fears of a nation, and gave my old mother a good deal of pleasure as she whiled away her dotage, Marty Storm is now a name doomed to the eternal obscurity of the BBC Missing Characters Bureau. Should you have any other characters requiring unobtrusive extinction, I'm your man.'

Casting is, of course, a critical stage in any TV programme: a good script can be ruined by poor performances, which explains why David Croft often returned to tried and tested thespians, many of whom had worked on his previous programmes; the same applied to the production team assembled for a show. David liked gathering around him people he trusted and could rely on to deliver the job to the exacting standards he expected.

Croft was also keen to engender a family atmosphere in his programmes; this was always in the forefront of his mind when sitting down to cast a show, as Robin Carr, who worked in Croft's production team before becoming a producer, experienced first hand. 'David liked people attending auditions with him, simply for a second opinion, and I sat in on some for *'Allo 'Allo!*. After one actor left, David asked what I thought. I told him he seemed fine. But that wasn't what he'd meant, so he replied, "I'm not talking about the acting, anybody can act, what was he like as a person? The thing is, we're not casting actors, we're casting a family; we're making friends for life – as pretentious as that may sound. These people are working in each other's pockets so we need those who'll get on. We only rehearse for four days, we haven't got time for histrionics." I'll always remember that conversation.'

Croft clearly didn't believe in histrionics, preferring to create a sensible, mature, convivial atmosphere within his team. Not wanting to stifle and never exigent, he always allowed those working for him to take responsibility and execute their jobs without the worry of making a mistake looming over them. The director exuded a sense of calm and, in return, his team did their utmost to repay him, investing 110 percent effort to make the show a success. David Croft, who had an unerring sense of timing and comedy, was respected and adored by cast and crew alike, his working methods a shining example of how to make a television series.

Sue Hodge, who played Mimi from the third episode of Series 4, jokes, 'He was like God, really, very quiet but moved in mysterious ways. He always got what he wanted without having to do or say too much. That's what I found incredible about all his castings: he just seemed to have the Midas touch.'

'Socially, he was fun and very gregarious,' says Richard Gibson. 'When it came to filming, he may not have spoken many words, but those he uttered were very good. He was very together and assembled teams he could trust to do the job. Once he'd found people who worked in the way he did and were reliable, he'd keep using them.'

Kim Hartman, who played blonde German private Helga Geerhart, acknowledges the family atmosphere which existed. 'There were times when it was hard work but it was always good fun. David and Jeremy were an exceptional combination and you always got a feeling of support from both. David knew exacty what he wanted so there was never any hanging around. He was a lovely man and commanded this tremendous respect; no one would ever dream of rolling up two minutes late for rehearsals, messing about or reading a newspaper while someone else rehearsed; we all enjoyed watching what was being created and wanted to please because we respected him so much.'

The Great Un-Escape

Whilst in disguise, Herr Flick is mistaken for a real priest by a passing young woman.

WOMAN: Please, Father, I have sinned. I have joined a house of ill-repute where many wicked girls cavort in scanty clothes and are naughty with men.

HERR FLICK: Well, what am I supposed to do about it?

HELGA: Father, you must give to this wicked girl a penance.

HERR FLICK: I see. Go home and say one hundred Heil Hitlers.

HELGA: You let her off very lightly, Herr Father. Usually you are much more severe.

It wasn't just the cast who were motivated by Croft's avuncular manner. Roy Gould joined the production team in September 1982, the week rehearsals started for the *'Allo 'Allo!* pilot. It was the same week as David Croft's surprise party to celebrate his 60th birthday at the BBC's North Acton Rehearsal Rooms. 'Everyone popped out from behind a screen and wished him happy birthday.

He laughed, then looked at me, saying, "Hello, who are you?" That was my introduction to David.'

Roy, who also worked on *Are You Being Served?*, *Hi-De-Hi!* and *You Rang, M'Lord?*, points out that all of David's shows were cheerful affairs. 'He always believed in running a happy ship. He knew what he wanted and how to get it in a pleasant way; there was never any shouting or screaming, everything was said calmly.'

Roy's comments are echoed by Susan Belbin, another member of Croft's production team who subsequently climbed the ladder to become a director. 'They don't come more charming than David Croft. He was of the old school and a true gentleman. He knew about television, actors, what was funny and what worked. He was also a fine writer. He trusted his team and was a delight to work for. Mind you. if someone played up he wouldn't stand any nonsense.'

Up on the fourth floor of Television Centre, Room 4045 was a hive of activity as David's team, known affectionately as 'The Croft Empire', toiled on preparations for the pilot episode. An important element of any show is the theme music and David, being musically minded, enjoyed playing an active role in crafting an atmospheric tune.

For *'Allo 'Allo!*, like he did for other shows, including *Hi-De-Hi!*; *Oh, Happy Band*; *It Ain't Half Hot, Mum*; *You Rang, M'Lord?* and *Oh, Doctor Beeching*, David turned to composer, arranger and writer, Roy Moore. 'David had an idea for the music so we got together at BBC's rehearsal rooms at North Acton. He wanted a pastiche French tune played on an accordion. Being very musical, he always briefed you very clearly because he knew exactly what he wanted. He was wonderful to work for.' After half an hour in the rehearsal room, Croft left Moore to polish the basic tune. 'I changed the harmonies and other bits and pieces before David returned, listened to the music and signed it off. It was done and dusted in an hour.'

The theme tune, christened simply *'Allo 'Allo!*, was recorded in a small studio, normally reserved for speech broadcasts, at BBC's Lime Grove. It turned out to be one of Moore's favourite tunes, but wasn't his only musical involvement with the sitcom. Whenever anyone was spotted tinkling the ivories – or appearing to do so – at Café René, Roy could be found behind the set playing the instrument. Any piano in the set, meanwhile, was usually stripped of its innards meaning the actor could pretend to play by pressing the keys without any sound being heard.

Some scenes saw Edith Artois attempting to sing, but rather than entertaining her customers, invariably they rushed for the door or stuffed cheese in their ears to block out the infernal din she tried passing off as her singing voice. 'She couldn't find any key you gave her,' smiles Roy. 'But there was an occasion when she accidentally found it and we had to change it because David said, "We can't have that!"' Edith never sang in tune, which was just as well because singing certainly wasn't Carmen Silvera's forté.

Edith's dreadful singing had comedic value and was exploited time and again, as Susan Belbin recalls. 'I'd worked with Carmen at Glasgow's Citizen's Theatre, my first theatre job, and she was lovely. While we were recording one episode, there was a technical problem. I was then production manager and told her that we'd have to do the song again. She wasn't happy but being a pro knew there was no choice. The truth of the matter – and she wouldn't mind me saying it – was that Carmen couldn't sing, which was a gift from heaven for David because he could exploit it for laughs.'

Unfortunately, the technical hitch meant the scene being recorded in front of the studio audience had to be re-taken several times; on each occasion, Carmen had to sing. 'On the third time, so as not to embarrass her, I told the audience that it was very difficult for such a good singer to have to do this off-key all the time. I made out that she was good, for which she rewarded me with a big hug afterwards.'

A Bun In The Oven

Gruber and the Colonel have been listening to a Spanish lesson on the gramophone to help in the event that they flee to Spain, when General Klinkerhoffen arrives.

GENERAL: Gramophone records? I hope you haven't been wasting your time listening to popular music?

GRUBER: No, General, we were looking for one of the Führer's speeches.

COLONEL: To boost our morale.

GENERAL: So, you *have* been wasting your time.

Another component needing to be addressed for the pilot was sourcing suitable locations for filming any outdoor scenes; sometimes, the region chosen, perhaps for accessibility or monetary reasons, was nowhere near the actual setting in the scripts. But for *'Allo 'Allo!*, David Croft wanted to explore the possibility of staying true to the scripts and filming outdoor scenes in France. Shelagh Lawson, who joined the BBC in 1975 and was an acting set designer when appointed to the pilot programme before becoming a fully-fledged designer in the mid-1980s, headed for France with a location manager on a recce trip. They were tasked with hunting down suitable locations in Normandy, including an avenue of trees and a building to represent the Bastille, for a scene showing Monsieur Leclerc, played by Jack Haig, breaking out of prison.

In preparation for filming across the Channel, Penny Thompson – a member of the 'Croft Empire' – wrote to several of the cast, including Haig, confirming that they would be travelling to France on Tuesday, August 24 and returning Friday, August 27. However, the plans were quickly dropped. 'It didn't work, quite frankly,' admits Shelagh. 'They would have had to be fantastic locations to warrant taking a whole unit there to film small inserts for a pilot. We didn't find anything suitable, so I had to go back and tell David that it would be a terrible waste of money when suitable locations could be found in the UK – which they were.'

Ultimately, the scene showing Monsieur Leclerc escaping from prison was shot outside Wapping Sports Centre, off Wapping High Street, London, on August 26, 1982, while the unit and actors involved in any remaining outdoors scenes, such as the two airmen cycling along an avenue of trees disguised as onion sellers, rendezvoused at Richmond Arms Hotel, Goodwood, West Sussex, where filming took place in and around the area between August 24 and 27. Once the filmed scenes were in the can, studio rehearsals began at Rehearsal Room 101, North Acton, on September 1, with the episode's interior scenes recorded in front of an audience on Saturday, September 11, 1982, in Television Centre's Studio 3.

Before the pilot was transmitted, David Croft showed the episode to his father-in-law; Ann Croft recalls the reaction. 'He would have been about 80 and sat in our television room watching it alone. He had a deep, rich voice and we could hear his laughter from afar. When we went into the room he was lying flat on the floor. I thought he'd had a heart attack and asked if he was OK. He replied, "I'm absolutely exhausted, I haven't laughed so much in years." We thought that was a good sign.'

The pilot episode was screened on December 30, 1982, attracting an audience of 8.1 million. It also received plenty of criticism, with viewers venting their anger by writing not only to magazines like *Radio Times*, but also to the BBC. People questioned whether the scriptwriters were being irreverent to those directly involved and who suffered as a result of the Nazis occupying this corner of Europe.

Among the complainers to the *Radio Times* was a viewer from Leigh on Sea, Essex, who classed the pilot as 'offensive and insulting to the intelligence of viewers and to the Royal Air Force, the French Resistance and German army. There is no excuse for such bad taste.' A viewer from Felsted, Essex, regarded the programme as 'in the worst possible taste'. Among letters written to David Croft and Jeremy Lloyd, which arrived at the production office, was one from a woman in Rutland who stressed that 'your so-called comedy was to me so offensive that I have already telephoned my first reaction to the Complaints Department, but want you, as the perpetrators of this horrible show, to know first hand just how appalling I think it is.'

But not everyone putting pen to paper was aghast with what they saw. One writer from Banbury, Oxfordshire, wrote: 'I watched one of the funniest spoofs I have ever seen ... it was one of the Beeb's greatest successes so far as making me roll about the floor (literally!).' And a couple from Henley-on-Thames, aware of the similarities people might make with a certain drama, wrote: 'There will, no doubt, be complaints about the obvious take off of *Secret Army*; pay no attention, we loved it and thought the casting perfect, too. Here's to more of the same.'

Newspaper reviews were mixed, but among the positive critics was Lucy Hughes-Hallett in the *Evening Standard*. Writing on December 31, 1982, she felt that the pilot 'already displays the ingredients necessary for a very popular series in that it reinforces all the prejudices beloved of the British. The most important of these is that all foreigners are funny.' In summing up the programme, she regarded it as a compilation of McGill-type picture postcard scenes, adding, 'Jeremy Lloyd might not write with the innocence of Jimmy Perry, but he does have a very clear sight of that broad theme of happy vulgarity which is so much a part of British humour.'

Having served in North Africa, India and Singapore with the army during the Second World War, David Croft was fully aware that the sitcom may court criticism, admits Ann Croft. 'But he was cheered up by a letter received from the widow of "White Rabbit".' This was the codename given to Wing Commander Yeo-Thomas, of British Special Operations Executive, who spent much of the Second World War behind enemy lines and was instrumental in organising the French Resistance. 'His widow wrote, giving some wonderful bits of information and saying how much her husband would have loved *'Allo 'Allo!*,' says Ann. 'Even when he was in a concentration camp they ran concert parties and there was always humour to be taken out of the most terrible things; it rather cheered David up.'

Another factor which helped reinforce the positiveness Croft felt about the sitcom – which was even the subject of a heated TV debate on *Day To Day*, fronted by Robert Kilroy Silk in 1986 – was organized by Air Commodore E. S. Chandler A.F.C., who was employed as technical adviser on some early shows. Chandler was a retired air commodore, a former Korean War fighter-pilot who rose to command a fighter station in the Southern counties. He held the coveted Air Force Cross and helped Croft in a host of ways, including arranging for the producer-director to meet former members of the Resistance. In the *Sunday Mirror* on November 17, 1985, David recalled: 'I was reassured when I met them. They thought the programme was hilarious. They understand that we are sending up not the real people but the ridiculous stiff-upper-lip portrayal of them in post-war films.'

Fortunately, there wasn't any significant resistance within the BBC concerning the subject matter; after all, fun was made of every nation involved – no one was singled out as the butt of the jokes. The stereotypical images of those being represented were ridiculed not the actual people who carried out those dangerous deeds.

Jeremy remembers David reassuring him about any criticism received. 'He told me to forget it because you can't please everybody all the time – and he was right. If you could, you'd be writing for the lowest common denominator and we weren't doing that.' We were knocking everyone, including the British and Germans – it wasn't just the Resistance,' says Jeremy. 'In fact, there wasn't anyone we weren't knocking. Luckily, the show was very funny; if it hadn't have been, then it would never have sold around the world and the BBC wouldn't have ordered more episodes.'

Arthur Bostrom, who played the ineffective Officer Crabtree, understood why some people may have initially held reservations about the subject matter but thinks they missed the point. 'It was bound to be a sensitive subject but the same criticism was levelled at *Dad's Army* as besmirching the memory of the brave Home Guard and what they did. But in time that totally mellowed and now people regard the show so warmly. I think that's the case with *'Allo 'Allo!*. It wasn't about sending up the war effort, the Resistance or anything.'

While partaking in a radio phone-in a few years ago, Arthur thought he was in for a stern talking to when a former member of the Polish Resistance came on the line. He was, however, pleasantly surprised and felt reassured. 'He said that he'd seen many programmes depicting the work of the Resistance and felt our programme showed it more realistically because they were often making it up as they went along, doing the best they could, in terribly dangerous circumstances and there were horrendous cock-ups. They would never have managed to do what they did without, somehow, retaining a sense of humour.'

Despite the criticism, the BBC spotted the potential of *'Allo 'Allo!*, realising that in their hands they were holding another potential gem from the pens of Jeremy Lloyd and David Croft. Eventually, three months after the pilot's transmission, a series of seven episodes was commissioned.

Although there would be an extended delay before the first season was recorded, Croft was keen to retain his performers, all of whom were eager to know if the programme was progressing beyond a solitary pilot episode. On March 24, 1983, he wrote informing them of good and bad news, stating: 'Thank you for your patience regarding *'Allo 'Allo!*. First, the good news – we plan to do seven new programmes. Now the bad news – we don't plan to produce them until 1984.' However, he was able to close with a further positive: production dates were already fixed with location filming commencing April 9, 1984 and continuing for at least three weeks. Studio rehearsals would then begin on May 7, with the recording four days later, and subsequent Fridays, up to and including June 22, 1984.

The gap between pilot and first series was due to David Croft's busy schedule. As he explained in his autobiography, he knew that his burgeoning timetable would result in a lengthy delay but wanted to plough ahead with the pilot regardless. He wrote: 'I thought the *'Allo 'Allo!* idea was very hot and there was a great danger of someone tumbling upon it. I was, therefore, very keen to send out a pilot to establish our ownership, so to speak.' And it worked.

With seven new scripts to write, Jeremy Lloyd and David Croft settled down to begin work, alternating between their respective London homes. 'We'd never go to the Beeb, it was always a house because you could get food, felt comfortable and were free of interruptions,' explains Lloyd.

Every writer has a different method of working: some write in total isolation, others prefer background noise or company. In the case of writing partnerships, such as David and Jimmy Perry, they would discuss plot ideas before heading off to write scripts separately. But when David wrote with Jeremy, they worked together in a relaxed fashion. 'Initially, we'd both jot down plot ideas. Then, I'd go through my half a dozen or so, David would go through his and we'd pick one,' recalls Jeremy. 'But before starting work, we'd have a coffee break. Then, not even thinking how the script would end, we would just start writing and see what turned up. Taking turns with the paper and pen, we'd normally work from ten until four, breaking for lunch. We could write a show in less than a week.'

Various threads weaved their way throughout the 85 episodes, including the continual efforts to repatriate the doltish airmen and the constant arguing over ownership of the *The Fallen Madonna With The Big Boobies*, a priceless masterpiece by the fictitious painter, Van Klomp. The Germans based in Nouvion had pillaged valuables, including the work of art, from the local Château, before blackmailing poor René into concealing it inside the café when Herr Flick, the Gestapo officer, arrived in town intent on retrieving the painting and passing it to Hitler. During the sitcom, the painting – originally concealed in a Knockwurst sausage – was passed from pillar to post and, at times, got rather confusing. The writers had problems keeping up with its whereabouts, too, as Jeremy explains. 'Yes, the hardest problem we had was remembering after, say, show 45 where the bloody sausages containing the precious paintings were; we had to have a chart on the wall detailing where they were so we didn't make a mistake.'

Hitler's Last Heil

René is very worried because a message for him from General de Gaulle has been transmitted for everyone to hear.

EDITH: You should try to relax a bit more.

RENÉ: Relax? How can I relax when a message to me from General de Gaulle has been transmitted throughout the whole of the district from a hearse? I'm a nervous wreck.

EDITH: Oh, do not worry, René, Michelle of the Resistance will find the hearse. Monsieur Alfonse needs it today.

RENÉ: And I will be needing it tomorrow if the Germans have heard that broadcast.

Sometimes, David Croft would even ring his office at the BBC to double-check. Roy Gould, a member of the production team, recalls: 'David would ask things like, "At the end of the last series, where was the Fallen Madonna?" You'd tell him it was in the café cellar or wherever and he'd be grateful; it was difficult keeping up with its location at times.'

Frequently, the writers laughed their way through the script writing. 'There were more jokes per page in *'Allo 'Allo!* than any other show we'd written. David generously called me a near-comedy genius. I don't know why he had to put "near" in!' laughs Jeremy. Together, they created an exceptionally long-running serial rather than a series, the format they had employed in previous sitcoms. Being a continuous plot, partly adopted to mirror the on-going nature of the war, an exposition – adeptly delivered by Gorden Kaye – was used at the beginning of each show to provide a recap of what had happened in the previous episode. These long speeches were a valuable part of the show and always presented word-perfect by Kaye.

When the writers had the basis of a script, David took it away and started moulding it into a workable form for his production team. Next, he'd read the script, in character, into a dictaphone machine and send or deliver it to his office at Television Centre. 'There were four or five of us crammed inside the 4th floor room, including the production manager, Susie Belbin, the production assistant, Bernadette Darnell, and two assistant floor managers, such as myself and Robin Carr; David was rarely in the office during set up,' explains Roy Gould.

'David would send the handwritten script through the post or bring it in. But his handwriting was like a demented spider, so you'd receive the dictaphone tapes, too, which the production assistant, such as Bernadette, would transcribe. While reading the script into the dictaphone, David would perform the parts and read out stage directions. I'd usually be in the office while Bernadette typed it up so would make notes of anything we'd need, such as guns or explosions; it was a quick way of keeping ahead.'

Once the scripts were typed up, the content rarely changed, unlike other shows where alterations aplenty can occur throughout the rehearsal period. Robin Carr, who first met David Croft while directing in the theatre, switched to television and began learning the trade as an assistant floor manager; bumping into Croft at Television Centre led to him joining his production team. Carr acknowledges few script changes took place, but can recall one occasion. 'There was a line for Officer Crabtree which went something like, "I was just pissing by your café", and David had second thoughts about it, thinking the audience weren't ready for it. Several episodes down the line, it reappeared. I remember Roy Gould and myself falling about laughing, saying, "I knew they'd get this back in!"'

With David being not only co-writer but producer and director, too, he visualized everything he wrote or dictated into his recorder. 'Everything in the script showed exactly how he wanted it done, so our job was relatively straightforward,' says Roy. 'If he said a scene was at a crossroads in the countryside with a church on the corner, that's what you looked for when finding locations.'

With a series now commissioned, more locations were needed and Susan Belbin, production manager for the pilot and first series before subsequently directing episodes, was responsible for sourcing suitable locations – and these turned out to be tried and tested spots as far as David Croft was concerned. Stanford Training Area at West Tofts, Norfolk, was used, just as Croft had done when filming *Dad's Army*, and part of Lynford Hall Estate, near Thetford, Norfolk, was hired to create Nouvion's town square. Built in the mid-19th century, this neo-Jacobean country house, set amongst acres of parkland and forest, is now run as a hotel and conference centre. But back then, some unused areas within the estate proved ideal for *'Allo 'Allo!*.

The café interiors were recorded in the studio at Television Centre using sets designed originally by Shelagh Lawson. Although she only worked on the pilot, it was her designs which set the tone for the rest of the series; although others following – such as Janet Budden and David Buckingham, set designers on Series 1 and Seasons 2–5 respectively – may have tweaked established sets, such as the café, Lawson was responsible for originating their style. 'There were lots of doors going hither and thither, rather like a stage set where people are coming in and out. It was based on traditional French cafés of that period, which I'd have researched at the large BBC library, flipping through books to check café designs, inside and out, and getting a feel for their character,' explains Shelagh, who highlights the details involved in set design. Thinking back to the pilot show, she recalls making a prison cell window used for the breakout scene whereby Monsieur Leclerc is rescued by the French Resistance. A suitable location had been found in Wapping but a barred window was required. Shelagh had to design a polystyrene brick window surround which was planted on the wall; then there was a cut-away to the studio where a controlled explosion took place, with stuntman Stuart Fell doubling for Jack Haig.

In the scene, there is a minor error, as Shelagh explains. 'When you see the scene showing the window being pulled out by a lorry, the camera shot went too wide and you just see the edge of the scenery. I was up in the gallery at the time and mentioned it but, for some reason, we couldn't take the shot again and couldn't edit tight enough. It's one of those things you cringe at when you see it happen but often the audience don't realize.' Usually, items such as the polystyrene window are ditched when the episode is complete but Shelagh rescued it. 'I kept it on my garden wall for years; it meant I looked out of my kitchen onto a prison window.'

Those lucky enough to work for the seasoned producer, David Croft, never felt restrained or restricted whilst carrying out their duties; he actively encouraged his staff to take on responsibility – whether behind or in front the camera. 'Those in his office basically set up the show,' says Roy Gould. ' He might ring and say, "I'll be in Thursday, let's go through what you've got so far." He'd arrive in the morning, we'd go through everything, ask any questions we were unsure about and then have lunch. David was fabulous to work for, a very generous man. He knew exactly what he wanted and was no fool; he didn't suffer fools gladly, either.'

He was willing to listen, something everyone appreciated. 'The good thing about him is that he always let you try things,' says Vicki Michelle, who played waitress Yvette in every episode. 'If something worked and wasn't detrimental to the script, he'd let it go.'

The atmosphere created meant everyone was willing to give their utmost and prepared to pitch in to help, like the time production assistant Bernadette Darnell doubled for Francesca Gonshaw in a hearse scene while Simon Spencer and Arch Dyson – who began in junior production roles within the team – clambered inside a pantomime cow outfit for a re-take after a technical hitch. 'The light-hearted location experience saw us standing in for the British airmen,' says Simon. 'Rushes of the scenes shot with the actors inside the cow outfit had gone to London and there had been some technical problems. David needed to re-shoot some scenes again but the actors – John D. Collins and Nick Frankau – had already returned to London. So myself and Arch Dyson, another AFM [assistant floor manager], were asked if we'd wear the costume and recreate their performance – in a field of real cows! I like to think we did a good job.'

A jovial atmosphere always existed whenever the cast and crew headed to Norfolk to record exterior scenes at the beginning of each series. For the period they were in East Anglia, the George Hotel, Swaffham, was their base. With everyone in high spirits, fun was had by all – and pranks weren't uncommon. Richard Gibson, Kim Hartman, Vicki Michelle and John D. Collins were among the worst perpetrators! 'Location filming was particularly fun,' enthuses Simon Spencer. 'Gorden was a wonderful storyteller, Carmen great for dirty jokes and Vicki, Kim and Richard Gibson always the pranksters – even bursting into my hotel bedroom for a late-night pillow fight. Such fun permeated its way onto the screen. My time working on 'Allo 'Allo! was a professional and personal delight.'

Sue Hodge, who joined the cast in the third episode of Series 4, remembers making an instant impression – although she's not sure if it was the right one – on her first time away in Norfolk. 'We'd all gone out to dinner and on returning to the hotel, I decided on a nightcap. But deciding to take it up to bed, I climbed the stairs and suddenly had a great desire to jump on the banister and slide down. So I put my drink on the floor and slid down. I was fine at the top but lost control on reaching the bottom and fell onto the floor in a heap. Just at that moment,

David came out from the bar and stepped over me, saying, "Good night, Hodge, see you in the morning on the end of a crane." He was referring to a scene I had to film. That's all he said.'

But the pranks weren't confined to days away in Norfolk. Richard Gibson and John D. Collins were involved in some high jinks at the North Acton Rehearsal Rooms – one occasion involving a revolting dummy. 'There were five floors of rehearsal space for BBC studio programmes of all kinds – from *Play School* to classical drama,' says Richard. 'One week, the *Juliet Bravo* police series team were working in the room below us, when John D. Collins passed their room, looked through the glass panel on the door and saw the cast in the middle of an intense note session. The director had his back to the window, with the cast facing it. Not long before, Gorden Kaye had been beheaded in a Shakespeare production, and brought in his bloodied dummy head to amuse us. Naturally, we had been looking for an opportunity to have some devilment with it, and John saw this as the moment. He ran up to our rehearsal room, marshalled stage management to find some rope, tied it to the head and lowered it out of the window, with a note attached that read: "I ain't got no body."

'A few of us went below to watch the reaction, and could see the director getting more and more agitated as he lost the attention of his cast. Twenty minutes later, in the middle of a scene that we were doing, the swing doors burst open and four people in balaclavas ran in with a headless dummy and a First Aid kit, dumped them in the middle of René's café, and ran out. Attached to the body was a note that read: "Dr Finlay on the way." One of the masked raiders was rumoured to be Stephanie Turner – Juliet Bravo herself.'

Recalling another occasion, John D. Collins says: 'Richard and I used to fly paper aeroplanes off the roof of BBC's Acton Hilton. We were on the seventh floor and would hum the Dambusters' march very loudly while throwing the aeroplanes off the roof.'

Once outdoor filming for a series was complete, rehearsals began on a Monday with a read-through at North Acton attended by cast and members of David Croft's production office. By Tuesday afternoon, Croft would return to TV Centre to complete the camera script for that week's episode, providing instructions to his camera team regarding what shots were required for each scene.

On Wednesday, the cast ran through the script again, this time in front of technicians, including representatives from the lighting, sound, costume and make-up departments. This enabled the various departments involved in the recording to watch and pre-empt any potential difficulties. 'If there were any problems they'd be sorted there and then, we didn't want any surprises on the night,' says Roy Gould. 'It was very rare that we rehearsed again after lunch; David didn't believe in over-rehearsing.'

Thursday involved a further script run-through before the production team returned to Television Centre to check on the progress of sets, although often these were built overnight. In the world of television even the smoothest of shows experienced occasional hiccups, like the occasion in April 1984, during the making of Series 1, when Susan Belbin, then production manager, was left with no alternative but to fire off a memo to the General Manager of Design and Scenic Services.

The sets for that week's recording were to be built during the day but weren't completed until 7pm on Friday 27th, an hour before the recording. Belbin blasted: 'A number of very inadequate reasons have been given – none of them hold water.' She listed three 'reasons', citing the last as probably the most likely reason, being 'at 1600 hrs. on the setting day (Thursday) my assistant went to the studio to see how things were "coming along". They were not! According to him, "there was a pile of scenery and a number of men standing about scratching their heads".' Belbin closed her memo by pointing out, strongly, that 'should there be a re-occurrence I doubt very much if we would be willing to rehearse under such conditions again.' Thankfully, such incidents were rare.

Fridays in the rehearsal schedule involved moving in to the studio, if the set had been erected. Further rehearsals took place, this time using the cameras to see how each scene looked through the lens. 'That took us to about 3pm. We'd have a break and resume at 4.30 for the dress rehearsal which was, basically, the show in full but this time, in costume,' says Roy Gould. 'Afterwards, everyone sat in the audience seating within the studio while David gave performance and technical notes before sending everyone away.'

After taking supper, the performers returned for make-up and costume while Felix Bowness, often engaged for the warm-up, got the ball rolling before introducing Gorden Kaye, who proceeded to talk to the audience for up to ten minutes, after which the show began.

'David always tried shooting the episode in 60-90 minutes,' says Roy. 'The seats in Television Centre were very uncomfortable and he always believed that performance was king over technical matters. So if the performance was good, even if there had been camera wobble or a boom slightly in view, it never worried him because he said the audience didn't notice most of the time.'

When possible, recordings took place on Fridays, partly because David Croft didn't believe in working weekends. Also, he didn't agree with cast members undertaking other projects, such as stage work in the evenings. 'He always said that the last thing he wanted was the walking remains of an actor turning up on Monday mornings,' says Roy Gould.

Firing Squashed

Louise from the Communist Resistance has just been in the café telling René, in a rather forceful way, of her undying love for him. Unfortunately, Yvette had been watching.

YVETTE: Oh! Oh, René! I saw everything through a crack in the door. How could you embrace that horrible girl. I thought you loved only me and our child?

RENÉ: I do love only you, Yvette. Oh please, she forced me to hold her, it was horrible. I could feel her live hand grenades pushing into me.

(Edith spots them through the door)

EDITH: René! What are you doing with that serving girl in your arms?

RENÉ: You stupid woman! Can you not see that I am suffering from nervous shock after being held at gunpoint by that ugly Communist Resistance girl? I would have fainted if Yvette had not supported me.

YVETTE: This is absolutely true.

EDITH: Oh, I am sorry, René. I did not realize the strain you were under.

RENÉ: I must go upstairs and lie down for a bit, dearest.

EDITH: I will come up and lie down for a bit as well. My soothing words and gentle hands will take away your anxieties.

RENÉ: On second thoughts, a brisk stroll around the square is what I need.

EDITH: (To Yvette) How quickly he recovers.

YVETTE: It must have been your soothing words, Madame Edith. You will have to go and lie down for a bit alone.

EDITH: So, what is new.

During the first series, the actors settled quickly into their roles and the writers were soon penning lines with the respective actors in mind. The comedy characters started to evolve – and so did the catchphrases, which became a prominent part of an *'Allo 'Allo!* script. But Lloyd and Croft never set out to create myriad catchphrases, they were simply lines which elicited laughter from the studio audience and clicked with the viewers; such utterances were seized upon by the writers who exploited them further in subsequent scripts. Some catchphrases became so popular that they entered the national vocabulary. 'I'll never forget Teresa May quoting at the despatch box, "Listen very carefully, I'll say this only once," Michelle's catchphrase, in the House of Commons; she even used a French accent!' laughs Jeremy Lloyd.

'Allo 'Allo! had its fair share of catchphrases, from René's 'You stupid woman!' and 'Oh, 'eck!' to Leclerc's 'It is I, Leclerc' and Officer Crabtree's hilarious 'Good moaning!'. But not every line which become associated with a particular character had the same impact as, for example, Michelle Dubois' 'Listen very carefully …'. The Italian captain, Bertorelli, began using the phrase, 'What a mistake-a to make-a' but it failed to take off and was one of the weakest catchphrases in the show.

Most of the primary characters had a phrase with which they were associated, but in the case of Vicki Michelle, she manufactured her own by increasingly emphasising the line, 'Oooh, René!', which is explained later in the book. Vicki kept pushing David Croft for her own phrase but the producer-director felt enough existed in the show. But the tenacious actress seized her chance while completing a scene directed by Robin Carr.

'We used to run the recording like a theatre, moving from one scene to another. If you could go through the whole half-hour without stopping to move cameras and microphones, David would have been delighted – but you rarely did that,' admits Robin. 'We had a long scene to do in General Klinkerhoffen's office, which was a big set, and it used all five cameras. All the German characters were in that room while all the French were in the bar ready for the next scene.

'David wanted these two scenes to run on. As a director, that meant having to stop using camera five in the General's office so that it could move to become camera one in the bar, ready to shoot. The others could then hurtle across to pick up the action as soon as they had finished being used in Klinkerhoffen's office. I asked David for a break but he wanted me to make it work. I told him that I could only achieve it if we could do a bit of comedy business in the café with Yvette and René, to which he agreed. So I had Vicki hiding behind the bar and told her to say something like, "René, bet you can't find me." But she didn't do that, she came out with an elongated, "Oooooooh, René!", which gave me time to get the cameras in position, ready to carry on filming the scene. So her catchphrase was created because of a big camera move.'

CATCHPHRASES

"This is of utmost urgency"
(Michelle)

One of the main strengths of 'Allo 'Allo!, in line with most other David Croft-produced shows, was the sterling cast. One of Croft's skills was being able to assemble a disparate group of performers and create an atmosphere which encouraged them to live their characters to the full. 'David used to say, "I don't hire stars, I make them,"' recalls Guy Siner, who played Lieutenant Gruber. 'While that might sound a rather self-important thing to say, it was actually true because when he started a new series he didn't get a big star in order to sell the show, he would simply write something genuinely funny, cast it perfectly and then allow the actors to flourish.' And flourish they did.

Reflecting on her time working with the actors, Susan Belbin, who went on to direct – among others – *Only Fools And Horses*, *Bread*, *Life Without George* and *One Foot In The Grave*, says Gorden Kaye was 'an absolute delight'. She adds: 'Vicki Michelle was a delight, too, a consummate professional. She played it for real, although slightly heightened for comedic effect. Nothing I ever asked of her was too much, she intuitively knew what was required. When she talked about the wet celery and egg whisks, you wondered what on earth she was talking about. But Vicki made it sound naughty and sexy which takes some doing when you're speaking gobbledygook!' smiles Susan.

'Kim Hartman threw her heart and soul into the part, too, and was perfect for the role. The chemistry between her and Richard Gibson was wonderful. Kim was never any trouble: she'd come in knowing all her lines and just get on with it.'

Sam Kelly, Richard Marner and Kirsten Cooke were other actors Susan Belbin applauds for throwing themselves into their roles. As for Rose Hill, she remembers her being 'great fun', adding: 'David and Jeremy were very clever because everyone had their little trademarks. I love the idea of hiring an actress and saying you're bed-ridden: you don't get out of bed, you don't really go anywhere, although occasionally you might be seen in a wheelchair; then to tell her she only had a handful of lines and most of the time would be banging on the floor with a walking stick. It was brilliant. But, again, for an actress in the twilight of her profession – perfect.'

Vicki Michelle is quick to point out that she learnt much from the actors around her. 'Gorden was a perfectionist and very clever at what he did. When you were watching him he'd put little nuances in so you were learning all the time; you respected him in what he did.' She also learnt from Rose Hill. 'In the script, she'd have a line like, "Oh, the flashing knobs" but Rose, a former opera singer, used to highlight and turn almost everything into a musical score. At the time, I thought it was very funny but, of course, it's longer camera time, especially when you haven't got much dialogue. She was brilliant but now I realize just how clever she was. Same with Ken Connor. He could have a scene involving a couple of lines but by the time he'd finished, it had become an epic. But being in rehearsal with these people meant you were learning from the masters.'

'If you read a Rose Hill script before seeing her do it, you'd think the scene would last 30 seconds – but I guarantee it would last two or three minutes,' laughs Robin Carr. 'It seemed impossible to elongate every vowel you spoke and be understood, but she managed it – not that David minded.' And with the character of Madame Fanny being an ex-burlesque performer, going over the top in her delivery typified the kind of character she was portraying.

A smile spreads quickly across Susan Belbin's face whenever she thinks about Jack Haig, alias Monsieur Leclerc. 'He could be a nightmare, but it worked. Sometimes, Jack took his performance to a music hall level; actors of a certain age who have to play older characters sometimes go over the top with all the quivering and shaking. And if there was one actor who would dare question David, it was usually Jack Haig.'

Ann Croft remembers working with Jack at Tyne Tees. 'He was a character. He was terribly deaf which made it difficult because he couldn't hear any of the cues so you had to pinch or tap him or something. But David said he was one of the best comedians he'd ever dealt with. Yes, he was erratic but had a natural gift for what the audience was reacting to. As a young man, everyone was tipping him to be the next Tommy Trinder.'

Whenever a scene was penned for Rose Hill and Jack Haig, Roy Gould admits that he and his colleagues would often 'cringe'. 'She was very pernickety about her lines, but always word perfect. Jack was the opposite: he'd talk around a speech. I remember once they had to play a scene together in the bed. Jack was meant to appear from underneath the covers and say a line or two, but in the dress rehearsal said something else. Rose didn't say a word. Staring at her, he said, "Come on, it's your turn." She replied, "You haven't given me the cue line. Are you going to do that tonight?" He said, "I dunno, I'll say something like it." They were so very different.'

Rose Hill and Jack Haig would occasionally bicker, says Charles Garland, who joined Croft's production office and worked, initially, on *Hi-De-Hi!* before moving across to *'Allo 'Allo!*. 'He'd always complain that she was very ponderous with her lines. Once, he said, "Cor, blimey, you could eat a ham sandwich halfway through her sentence!" She kept saying how he was mean to her – it used to go on.'

Robin Carr concurs with his colleagues' comments on Jack Haig. 'There were times when the cameraman would point at a particular space, which should have had Leclerc in it, and he wasn't there. I'd have to say to the cameraman, "Find him, please!" So he'd pan around and locate him in the wrong place completely. But as long as we got the shot no one knew he was in the wrong position. Also, he did paraphrase a bit and, occasionally, David would say, pointing at the script, "No, that's the line." Because the Jack version wasn't funnier.'

'I thought the casting, especially at the beginning of the show, was absolutely spot-on; they all fitted in beautifully,' says Ann Croft. 'For example, Carmen was the pro to end all pros. She was wonderful. Not only was she so professional about everything she did, she didn't mind poking fun at herself with all that singing – what a talented actress.'

Carmen Silvera was a warm, generous and highly amusing performer – and a great joke-teller to boot. 'She was always on the nail and very funny,' says Robin Carr, who remembers the novel way she secured a parking space at Television Centre's car park on recording day. 'She used to cry and would arrive in the studio with tears running down her face. Once, I asked what the problem was and she replied, "I'm all right, it's how I get in the car park." She'd burst into tears and the guys at the gate would let her in. She was the Mollie Sugden of the show, the mother, and everyone loved her. She and Gorden were very close.'

Carmen was popular among the cast and crew. 'She was a fabulous actress,' says Charles Garland, who recalls an occasion which highlighted the posturing and jockeying for position which occasionally happened among the cast.

After finishing a day's filming on location in Norfolk, the cast and crew retired to the unit hotel, The George, in the market town of Swaffham. Some of the team gathered in the bar, sitting at tables. 'Everyone seemed to smoke in those days,' says Charles. 'I used to be a restaurateur before coming into TV so some things I do without thinking because of my background. For example, I can't bear seeing a full ashtray so when Gorden Kaye's had three or four fag ends in it, I changed it because I couldn't stand the sight of it. Carmen noticed and within about 15 seconds turned to Roy Gould, saying: "Could you change my ash tray?" It was an example of the rivalry between them. There was a pecking order and Carmen thought she should have equal treatment.'

Roy remembers the occasion well and found it amusing. 'I was a stage manager in a former life so was familiar with this sort of behaviour and it didn't faze me. Actually, Gorden looked over at me after I'd given the ashtray to Carmen, shook his head and smiled. A little later, with a glint in his eye, he leant towards me and joked, "Roy, my ashtray is full," to which I replied, "Well go and ******* empty it then, and do Carmen's while you're at it!" Gorden thought this highly amusing but didn't empty either.'

The central German characters residing in Nouvion were played by Richard Marner, Sam Kelly, Guy Siner, Kim Hartman, Hilary Minster and, playing Gestapo, Richard Gibson and John Louis Mansi. All the characters were beautifully performed and for many the sitcom became the acme of their television careers. Most scenes for Sam Kelly – who played Captain Geering until leaving in Series 4, although he reprised his role later for a single episode – were with the late Richard Marner, who played Colonel Von Strohm. 'He could be difficult at times but had a heart of gold,' says Sam. 'When we were doing the stage show, my back went and I was in bed for four weeks. One day, a Fortnum and Mason van pulled up outside my house. A huge cake was delivered, a present from Richard. I was very touched by that.'

On one occasion, when Marner arrived at the rehearsal room he had almost lost his voice. During the morning session, the itinerary included the rehearsal of several scenes involving Colonel Von Strohm and Captain Geering chatting at a table in Café René. 'I was preparing to work on the book, therefore following the lines in the script, when Richard came up to me,' recalls Roy Gould. 'Almost whispering, he said, "I can't speak properly so you'll have to say my lines and I'll mouth them." I asked if he'd told Sam and he nodded. So we started the scene with Richard just opening his mouth like a fish while I spoke his lines. Sam stared at him, looked at me, turned back towards Richard and creased up. We had to do this all week so poor old Sam never heard the words come from Richard's mouth until the dress rehearsal. I'll never know how he got through the week.'

Frequently appearing in scenes with Kelly and Marner was Guy Siner. 'Sam is a wonderful actor, truly one of the best who has carved out an excellent career doing a wide variety of work – we were so lucky to have him. As for Richard, there's the famous quote of him saying, "Problem with the script is that it changes every week!" It used to be a bit frustrating at times when shooting, but you look at his performance now and it's wonderful. He was very good and that's what matters in the end – it's not so important how you got there.'

Hilary Minster, as General Von Klinkerhoffen, was regularly cast as German officers and was so believable in *'Allo 'Allo!*, never letting his guard down or cracking a smile.

Pigeon Post

Helga is taken to Herr Flick's private quarters for the first time.
HERR FLICK: These are my private quarters. I have had it made completely soundproofed.
HELGA: I can guess why.
HERR FLICK: Yes, the noise of the lorries was keeping me awake at night.

Robin Carr, who was head-hunted by London Weekend Television in the late-1980s and became executive producer in the station's comedy department, has nothing but fond memories of the cast. 'Guy Siner needed little direction: he knew what he was doing and was very sharp technically – a joy to work with, as was Kim Hartman,' says Robin, who recalls a conversation in David Croft's office one day which drifted on to the subject of spin-off projects. 'I always thought there should have been a spin-off of Helga and Herr Flick after the war. Kim and Richard were an astonishing double-act. David and Jeremy thought it was a good idea and started talking about where they'd be; one thing was sure: she'd be the domineering one now, not him.' But such conversations frequently took place amongst writers reviewing a successful series. 'Once, David wanted to do a late-night version of *Hi-De-Hi!*, seeing what happened behind the curtains. But it never happened.'

The long gap between the pilot episode being screened on December 30, 1982, and the first series kicking off in September 1984, meant it was necessary to remind viewers what the sitcom was all about. Therefore, the pilot was repeated on September 6, the day before the opening episode of Series 1. The first season consisted of seven episodes, after which the BBC's Broadcasting Research Department conducted an audience survey to assess what viewers felt about the sitcom's first outing on the screen. The department's Marion Greenwood presented her findings in a report, dated December 3, 1984.

The sitcom averaged audience figures of 7.9 million during the series, which would rise over 100 percent by the time the programme reached the zenith of its life. The report was a useful tool when BBC officials considered commissioning further series, especially when Greenwood reported that, 'Viewers extended a warm welcome to this new comedy series. Most of those reporting found it an entertaining and amusing series that quickly established itself.' Some respondees rated it the best comedy the BBC had transmitted for some time while a number 'praised the originality of the idea' and some added that it was a 'good parody of *Secret Army*'.

But Marion Greenwood's report was frank and highlighted the fact that the series was not universally popular, evidenced by the 19 percent of respondees who took the deliberate decision to stop watching. Responses from this group included that the series became 'banal and predictable' while others classed it 'very silly and irritating'. Only two percent, however, branded the sitcom 'in poor taste'.

A healthy percentage of viewers questioned were in favour of a new series, which they were rewarded with in 1985. In addition, the population of Nouvion increased by two with the arrival of Officer Crabtree, played by Arthur Bostrom, and Herr Flick's sidekick, Von Smallhausen, portrayed by the diminutive John Louis Mansi.

The arrival of the British Intelligence Agent – although, of course, he was anything but the world's brightest or perspicacious individual – added a new dimension to the series, while Von Smallhausen afforded the writers a useful character – almost a foil – who would enable much humour to be gained from the banter between the Gestapo officials.

Arthur Bostrom played his po-faced role superbly throughout, although it appears the late actor Edward Duke, who earned many plaudits for his one-man show, *Jeeves Takes Charge*, was initially considered for the part. It seems he became unavailable upon receiving an offer to take his show – which eventually occupied his career, on and off, for over 12 years – abroad. Ann Croft says: 'Edward, who was a friend of Penny's, was discussed, I believe, and something happened which meant he couldn't do it. But David's comment afterwards was how lucky we were that we got Arthur, it was a real stroke of luck for the programme; not that he was inferring that Edward Duke wasn't talented, but how we'd been lucky getting Arthur.'

CATCHPHRASES

"I'll disappear like a phantom."
(Michelle)

Officer Crabtree was David Croft's idea, and a 'brilliant one, too,' says Jeremy Lloyd. 'He spoke appalling French and we got lots of fun out of it. When we'd established the character, Arthur was able to say his lines with such a straight face that he was perfect casting.'

After debuting in the third instalment of Series 2, Arthur felt pleased and relieved. But he recalls a piece of advice from David Croft which helped him shape the character. 'David didn't give many notes but when he did you listened because he had so much experience. I was pleased with myself because the first episode had gone well. I probably played up the character and promoted him too much in rehearsal for my second episode, so David said, "Don't come in knowing you're going to be funny." That was the absolute key to the whole character. I don't think I needed to be told that again. It was a devastating verbal note to be given but absolutely right. That's what a good director does.'

As the sitcom moved into a third season, reviews in the national press remained mixed. A reviewer in the *Daily Mail* on October 29, 1985, noted that his earlier complaint about 'falsehoods and trivialisation of human suffering featured in the series' had provoked a 'formidable response' from readers. The reviewer was clearly unhappy about the show, stating that much anger must exist concerning a series which 'ignores the real suffering and mass village executions of the German occupation and prefers to project a picture which positively glows with good cheer.' Over at *The Guardian*, the critic, on September 8, 1984, felt the programme was overflowing with clichés and was 'entirely reprehensible', but admitted that it made him laugh 'more than anything else I saw this week'.

But while the critic at *The Sunday Telegraph* on September 9, 1984, thought 'the lack of any real danger so far is one of the problems', the *News of the World* that weekend classed *'Allo 'Allo!* as a 'comedy classic'.

But of all the reviews during the early years, it was one in *Broadcast* on July 12, 1985, which revealed a critic who had finally understood the premise of the series. He wrote: 'It in no way deserved the abuse that it got. It is very funny, it also pushes the world on a bit … trying to help us forget the obscenity of the Second World War and parodying all those monstrous films that continue to feed our appetite for violence.'

As Jeremy Lloyd states, 'The point is, it had a cathartic effect, basically.'

Good Staff Are Hard To Find

Captain Bertorelli is greeting the regulars in René's cafe with an embrace and a kiss. He then comes face to face with Lieutenant Gruber.

CAPTAIN BERTORELLI: Mamma Mia, who is this handsome officer who looka lika de film star?
COLONEL: (To Gruber) This is Captain Bertorelli.
GRUBER: (Holding out his arms to embrace) I heard about you from the General.
COLONEL: (To Bertorelli) This is Lieutenant Gruber.
CAPTAIN BERTORELLI: I heard about you from the General! (Offering only a handshake).

Although the cast remained largely intact throughout the nine series, there were occasional changes in personnel; several impacted on Series 4, a six-part season transmitted during November and December 1987. One performer who departed at the end of the previous series was Francesca Gonshaw. Keen to pursue new adventures; she achieved her goal almost immediately by joining the cast of *Howards' Way*, playing Amanda Parker in the BBC drama which focused on the yachting industry in the fictional town of Tarrant on England's south coast.

One colleague who tried persuading Francesca to reconsider her decision to quit was Vicki Michelle. 'I said at the time, "Do not leave." She was very young and had this gift of a part which other actresses would have given their eye teeth for. I think she had people telling her she should do Shakespeare or that she'd be typecast and ruin her career, instead of saying, "This is a gift of a role in a really successful series – stay with it." Of course, it was Francesca's choice but I tried talking her out of it because in her naïvety playing Maria, she came across as very funny.'

Writer Jeremy Lloyd, who had first met Francesca while holidaying in Spain, as detailed later in the book, was saddened to see the young actress leave the fold. 'Sue Hodge, who replaced Francesca as a new waitress, was very good but I'd have preferred it if Francesca had continued. Sue was an extremely good actress, but you want some crumpet in the show!' he says, smiling.

Café René's new waitress arrived in the third episode of Series 4 in the shape of Mimi Labonq, an aggressive individual who had shown her mettle by serving in the Resistance. Sue Hodge was an actress who had impressed David and Ann Croft in an open-air theatre production – despite having little to say. 'That was a rather strange piece of casting in a way but worked,' admits Ann. 'David and I had been to Regent's Park Open Air Theatre to see *A Midsummer Night's Dream* and there was this little actress playing one of the fairies; for whatever reason, as soon as she appeared the audience fell about laughing. She only had about three lines but got belly laughs on all of them. David turned to me and said: "My goodness, she's got a sense of comedy." He asked to see her and everything worked out well. Her butch, aggressive character made a change and brought a little fresh attitude to the show.'

Sue Hodge's have-a-go approach to her craft conjured up plenty of comedic opportunities. 'What you see is what you get with Sue Hodge,' says Robin Carr. 'She's a very funny lady and was game for anything. David really played on this.'

The same episode which brought Mimi Labonq to Nouvion also marked the arrival of Bertorelli, the Italian captain seconded to the local German unit as liaison officer, reporting to Colonel Von Strohm. Playing Bertorelli was writer, director and actor, Gavin Richards, who's arguably best known for playing Terry Raymond in *EastEnders*. Now residing in New Zealand, Richards' arrival increased the number of characters Lloyd and Croft could utilize within the German commandant's office after the departure of Captain Geering, played by Sam Kelly. ' Sam was great, always very funny and inventive. You'd always see him around laughing at other scenes – very much a team player,' says Robin Carr.

After the six-part fourth season it must have come as a shock to everyone when, in 1988, the fifth season contained 26 episodes, running at the shorter 25-

minute duration. The reason was simple: the American market. When interest was expressed by a leading network in the States, Series 5 was written to fit their requirements, including cutting episodes back to 25 minutes to allow for commercial breaks. Sadly, the prospective deal collapsed, although the series has subsequently been shown in the country, mainly on PBS (Public Broadcasting Stations).

Having attracted interest from across the pond, the show expanded and necessitated more elaborate sets; the need for more space saw the team swap Television Centre for Elstree Studios for the fifth season. 'We had railway stations, a village – everything. Each show cost at least £300,000 which in those days was a lot of money. We did it at Elstree because we needed bigger sets, but it seemed logical to write, rehearse and record the show there, too,' says Jeremy Lloyd.

Responsible for equipping David Croft and Jeremy Lloyd's office at the studios was Charles Garland, whose first port of call was a local branch of World of Leather, off the North Circular Road. 'They wanted a pale leather three-piece suite in their office so they could be comfortable, but I had a tremendous battle with the department about funding. Thankfully, we won the argument in the end and David and Jeremy enjoyed lounging on the chairs.'

Churning out 26 episodes created tremendous pressure for the writers who, for the first time, asked other scriptwriters – namely John Chapman and Ian Davidson as well as Ronald Wolfe and Ronald Chesney – to pen scripts, thereby alleviating some of the mounting pressure. It was an exhausting period. 'We'd be writing a show before stopping to see the previous script being rehearsed. After, we'd return to our office and continue writing – we were always one script ahead,' says Jeremy. 'It was incredibly hard work. Sometimes we wrote two shows a week. It was tiring and I could never drive home without pulling off the road for a quick nap; it was mind-draining.'

Nonetheless, Croft and Lloyd still found time to laugh as they holed themselves up in their office and kept the flow going. By 10am each day, the writers would be in the office beavering away, as Charles Garland recalls. 'They'd start by chatting before turning to writing, playing the parts with action as they prepared the scripts; we'd always hear roars of laughter. Then there would be a pause while David dictated what they'd just said into his recording machine. Eventually, they'd come out after a couple of hours, pass the machine to Bernadette Darnell, the production assistant, and she'd start typing the script while they headed for lunch. Usually, they had it bang on in terms of timing and we'd make it with few changes. But sometimes they'd go over and Jeremy would say, "We're writing for the waste paper basket, David." So they'd stop.'

Roy Gould witnessed Croft and Lloyd's writing partnership in action at Elstree, too. 'They had to do two episodes quickly and ended up writing them both in two days – it was remarkable. They sat in the room, worked it out and laughed a lot. Jeremy would say about 15 jokes to a page before David edited it back to about three prior to passing the script to the production assistant to type.'

It wasn't only the studio work which relocated to Elstree for this series. This mini factory was even used to film exterior scenes normally shot in Norfolk, which meant replicating the square of Nouvion in one of the stages at the studio, just behind the *EastEnders*' set. That was the challenge David Buckingham, set designer on four series and a Christmas Special, faced.

Buckingham was assigned to *'Allo 'Allo!* from Series 2 and found the prospect of working on a period sitcom exciting. 'Being set in wartime France was great for a designer because you don't normally get that range of work to do, even in a serious drama,' says David, who was responsible for sourcing a suitable painting when *The Cracked Vase With The Big Daisies*, a supposed Van Gogh creation, appeared in the storylines. 'In the 1930s, my father painted similar pictures, in the style of Van Gogh. So, after nearly 40 years or so of not picking up a brush, he painted the one used in the series – and it worked very well. '

The mock paintings seen in the various sets were the work of scenic artists at the BBC, painted to the specifications requested by David Croft. On screen, the paintings looked very effective and led to one woman, based in Bovey Tracey, Devon, writing to Croft about a portrait hanging behind Colonel Von Strohm, which she thought was a portrait of her great, great grandmother. Croft, though, replied on December 5, 1984, admitting the painting was 'pretty crude and I feel fairly sure that on close examination it would only bear a very superficial likeness to any reasonably well known work of art.'

Constructing Nouvion's town square in Lynford Hall Estate, near Thetford, Norfolk, had worked well. Now, thoughts turned to the daunting task of reconstructing it inside a studio. David Buckingham says: 'I remember one day in Norfolk, David and I were standing admiring how good the town square looked; then he turned to me, asking: "Could we reproduce this in a studio?"' A meeting was convened at Elstree to discuss the prospect. 'Duncan Brown's boss in Lighting was pushing very hard for it to be outside,' says Buckingham. 'David asked if we could do it inside and I said we could.' But that involved devising a method for cobbling the entire studio floor. 'We used a mesh and poured concrete on. Paul Cross, my fantastic assistant, and I then developed a system of using board dovetailed together without joins. This gave the TV cameras something to roll over because they would have struggled getting across the cobbles, making tracking shots difficult. I remember Gorden Kaye taking us to one side and saying, "Why don't you patent this, it might make you rich." At least it did the business.'

Gone With The Windmill

René has sworn a vow to be true to his wife but he hasn't told her in case he can't keep it up.

YVETTE: Oh, how about a quick cuddle in the back room?

RENÉ: Not tonight, Yvette.

YVETTE: But Madame Edith is poking in the kitchen the dying embers of the stove.

RENÉ: Well, speaking of dying embers, and I was not going to tell you this so soon, but this mad affair of ours is over.

YVETTE: Oh, René, say it is not so.

RENÉ: Well, it had to end some time, just as autumn follows summer and the leaves of the chestnut trees turn brown and shrivel and fall – not to mention the conkers.

YVETTE: René, is there someone else?

RENÉ: How could there be? Every spare moment I am with you, holding you and kissing you and running my fingers through your hair, feeling your warm breath on my cheek, holding your firm young body against my firm starched apron. Ohhh. Quick, the back room!

Switching from Television Centre to the unfamiliar surroundings of Elstree didn't stop the pranks occurring amongst the cast. One incident, however, nearly resulted in some actors getting in hot water for sneaking onto the *EastEnders'* set and pretending to be extras. 'We were filming in the adjoining studio and could walk through the make-up room in our studio to the *EastEnders'* set,' explains Richard Gibson. 'For the fun of it, Kim Hartman, John D. Collins – wearing his airman's moustache – and I found our way into the Queen Vic as extras. No one tumbled it for ages, even though the assistant floor manager kept trying to tell the floor manager that actors from *'Allo 'Allo!* were on the set; the floor manager kept saying not to distract him because they had a tight schedule. So we stayed until they had finished recording.

'The story was leaked to one of the tabloids and when the production company realized what had happened, they trimmed the scene before Sunday's omnibus.' There was a terrific outcry and the actors summoned before Julia Smith, co-creator and then producer of the soap. 'She asked what David Croft would think and we replied, "Actually, he's got a message for you: if ever you'd like any of your stars to be extras in *'Allo 'Allo!*, they're welcome any time,"' smiles Gibson.

'The *EastEnders'* situation was hilarious. There was a final shot – a close-up – where Mike Reid comes into the Queen Vic, but you catch sight of me taking a swig of a pint,' smiles John D. Collins. 'I don't think Julia Smith had seen *'Allo 'Allo!* and the pay-off from David Croft was wonderful. She tried getting us fired, I believe, and David refused, saying he couldn't possibly do that. He was as supportive as he could be, being a senior BBC producer. He couldn't condone it but secretly laughed because he loved practical jokes; he liked actors being a bit naughty – and Richard, Kim and I were; Kim was even more naughty than us!'

Although John D. Collins was a stalwart of Croft's, popping up in small parts within most of his shows, David always struggled to remember the names the writers has chosen for the airmen, played by Collins and Nicholas Frankau. 'Whenever he sent in scripts, he'd say on his Dictaphone things like "Cloisters" and "Fairborne". If I heard this while Bernadette Darnell was transcribing the recording, I'd shout across, "Fairfax and Carstairs!", says Roy Gould. 'Also, David could never remember which actor played which part. I'd tell him it was opposite to their surnames, so John D. Collins is Fairfax and Nick Frankau is Carstairs.'

Although Collins rarely played a substantial role on TV, he was among that valuable and dependable band of actors who would come in and deliver the required performance without fuss. 'David always believed in having people who understood the comedy and where it was in the script,' says Roy. 'He wasn't in for long discussions about the philosophy of comedy; it was a case of "it's on the page so can you play it or not?" The people David employed understood this and got on with it.'

The fifth series ran for nearly half a year before the curtain came down on February 25, 1989. But by the time the sixth season began, six months later, the cast had lost one of its original members: Jack Haig, alias Monsieur Leclerc. The death of Haig in July 1989 meant further casting was required; the role of

Leclerc had been important to the series and the writers were keen to retain, at least, his characteristics. Thankfully, Lloyd and Croft resisted the temptation to simply retain the character but replace the actor, an action which rarely works; instead, they decided to replace Roger Leclerc with his brother, Ernest, played by Derek Royle, who fitted in quickly, ensuring a smooth transition between the characters.

There was a 15-month hiatus between the broadcasting dates of Series 6 and 7, due in part to the cast transferring the highly-successful stage version of *'Allo 'Allo!* – which had broken numerous box office records around he UK – to Australia. But that show and the future of *'Allo 'Allo!* on television was placed in jeopardy by a tragic accident which left Gorden Kaye fighting for his life.

In late January 1990, a vicious storm blew in from the Atlantic leaving 39 people, including many children, dead in its wake. Others were seriously injured as winds demolished buildings, tore up trees and wreaked havoc. Gorden, who was making final arrangements before joining the rest of the cast on the trip down under, was driving when the hurricane-force winds ripped a hoarding from the ground. Within seconds, a piece of wood crashed through the windscreen and embedded itself in his forehead. Gorden was rushed to hospital and underwent emergency surgery. While the actor was fighting for his life, his agent tried desperately to contact David Croft to break the news that not only was Kaye seriously injured but wouldn't be travelling to Australia.

Roy Gould was in Croft's office, clearing up before flying off on holiday, when the phone rang. On hearing the shocking news, Roy was stunned and ensured Gorden's agent that he'd inform David Croft as soon as he could reach him; trouble was, Croft was halfway between London and Australia, where final preparations were being made for the arriving stage show. 'David tended to go the slow route, stopping off at various places along the way. I spent the rest of the day trying to find him but, thankfully, Peter Farago, who directed the stage show, located him in Singapore, under the name of "Mr. OBE"; I'd tried the hotel and asked the receptionist to check under David Croft, David Croft-Sharland and David Croft OBE but there was no record because they had registered him as Mr. OBE!'

Croft was equally aghast to hear the shocking news but quickly had to turn his thoughts to replacing Kaye in the stage show. Back in the UK, Gorden remained critically ill after undergoing a five-hour operation. 'I rushed to Hammersmith Hospital to see him and he obviously wasn't able to go anywhere – he couldn't remember who he was or anything about the programme,' admitted Jeremy Lloyd whilst being interviewed for the BBC's *Return Of 'Allo 'Allo!*. As for the sitcom's future, Jeremy had serious doubts whether it could continue, as he expressed during the interview. 'We thought it was over because you couldn't replace him – and wouldn't have replaced him. But he came back and did lots more.'

In fact, Gorden Kaye made a remarkable recovery; he was back on his feet earlier than anyone could have predicted. Eventually, with Kaye at the helm again, small screen adventures at Café René continued for another three series. But there would be a notable absentee: David Croft.

A hardened producer, director and writer, David Croft knew the TV industry inside-out. During his long and distinguished career, he had shepherded many sitcoms to their rightful place in the pantheon of British Comedy. But with such experience under his belt, he always knew when a programme had run its course. After six series of ' Allo 'Allo!, he thought the time was right to wave goodbye. Ann Croft recalls the time her late husband reached his decision. 'He always said that you can't get any more juice out of an orange. He didn't want the show to tail off in a tatty fashion. He thought we'd had enough Knockwurst sausages and "Fallen Madonnas With The Big Boobies" and couldn't go on and on. He very seldom said "no", but if ever he did that was it; it would have taken a great deal of skill to change his mind. He thought about such decisions very carefully, so when the BBC asked him whether they could do another series, his instinctive reaction was to say "no" because enough had been done. Then, Jeremy rang because he thought it was ridiculous turning down a series, especially as so many people were struggling getting a programme on. David gave it about a week before telling Jeremy that he had no objection to him writing more. He wished him the best of luck but didn't feel he could contribute further.'

Jeremy was grateful to receive David's blessing. 'I thought there was more mileage in it and proved that by writing over 20 further episodes. Yes, it was a wrench to lose David but I managed. Of course, I lost him not only with the writing but producing and directing, too. Thankfully, we had some great producers and directors for the remaining episodes. Mind you, the series was so established by then and the characters well established, it made life easier.'

A new writing partner was required to help Jeremy pen the scripts and Gareth Gwenlan, the then Head of Comedy, had the answer. 'Gareth said he'd received a couple of scripts from a writer called Paul Adam and they seemed promising,' recalls Jeremy. 'He wondered if I'd look at them and take him on as a new writer? I thought, "Oh, lord!" But he turned out to be very bright and quick.'

Paul Adam, now a novelist, was an up-and-coming writer desperate to break into the world of TV scriptwriting. 'Around 1988, I sent in a script as a potential sitcom pilot.' On the advice of Richard Waring, who had written, amongst others, *Marriage Lines* but was working as a script editor at the BBC, Adam undertook further work on his script. 'Sadly, it never actually got anywhere, but my idea was set in a rundown Northern swimming bath. It didn't work, probably because *The Brittas Empire*, set in a leisure centre, was happening – and that had a swimming pool. But Gareth liked my writing and we met, at which point he informed me that David Croft was pulling out of *'Allo 'Allo!* but Jeremy wanted to carry on. Gareth thought my style of humour might fit *'Allo 'Allo!* so commissioned me to write a trial script – thankfully, he liked it. Next, I met Jeremy. From his point of view, he knew he could work with David but could he work with someone entirely new? But he obviously agreed and we were commissioned to write Series 7. It was exciting for me: I'd been sending material in but hadn't got anywhere; I'd written books which no one wanted to publish, so as a new writer you're grateful for any opening.'

CATCHPHRASES

"The Resistance people – who I do not know."
(René)

When he started writing scripts with Lloyd, Paul Adam was living in Sheffield, before moving to Cambridge and, eventually, Nottingham, from where he wrote the final series. He'd regularly catch the train to London before heading across the capital to Jeremy's mews cottage in Knightsbridge, where they spent the morning writing. 'What Jeremy is brilliant at – and something he loves doing – is throwing ideas out. I loved the sessions we had because he's a very funny bloke, full of stories. He'd have a coffee and cigarette and we'd throw plot ideas around while I made notes.'

After a morning's toil, Lloyd and Adam retired to Drones in Pont Street, just up the road from Jeremy's London home, for lunch. 'Afterwards, I'd go home and spend the next couple of weeks writing the script, putting together what we'd come up with, writing the dialogue and structuring it. Then I'd send

Jeremy the finished script. He'd play around with it, editing and altering it as he saw fit.'

Paul was surprised to discover that Lloyd didn't even keep a typewriter in his house. 'He'd write everything by hand and then read it into a Dictaphone before taking it to a secretarial agency around the corner. But once we were happy with a script, I'd travel back down to London to start on the next.'

Stepping in when an experienced member of a writing team drops out, particularly when you're a relatively green scriptwriter, can be fraught with hazards but Paul Adam admits he soon struck up a comfortable working relationship with Lloyd. 'I don't know how he worked with David Croft but got the impression it was similar in the sense that David probably got the script typed and ready; I slipped almost into that role, but at a much more junior level. But I think it suited Jeremy that he could carry on coming out with these brilliant lines and plotting and then someone would take it away and put together the script.'

Overall, Paul Adam thoroughly enjoyed the experience of writing scripts with Jeremy Lloyd and didn't face any insurmountable problems. 'Because it was an established show I knew what had to be done. It was fun because you could almost do whatever you liked. It was a type of farce and outlandish so you could get away with things. You had to rein in to some extent to avoid going too far, to keep it reasonably credible and within the boundaries set for a series like that; but there was plenty of freedom.'

Change was the name of the game for Series 7 with three new people joining the team. Veteran actor Robin Parkinson arrived to replace Derek Royle – who sadly died between the sixth and seventh series – as Ernest Leclerc and Roger Kitter, who had begun his career as an impressionist, replaced Gavin Richards as the Italian captain, Bertorelli, after Richards moved on to pastures new, eventually leading him to New Zealand.

A major change, however, was finding a producer to take over the show from David Croft. A man of experience was required and Mike Stephens – who produced, among others, *Clarence*, *First Of The Summer Wine* and *Hi-De-Hi!* – fitted the bill. 'Before *'Allo 'Allo!*, I'd directed the last series of *Hi-De-Hi!*, which was the first time I started working in place of David, and that was because he'd been ill at the time. Also, I did *Grace And Favour*, the sequel to *Are You Being Served?*'

As Mike explains, when a series is getting old one wonders if there is any more life left in it, but he needn't have worried. 'As soon as I saw the scripts, I knew it would work. We might have tweaked it here and there, but tried to get as much out of it as possible.' He acknowledges that the show's success was due largely to the fact it had every essential ingredient in place. 'It had the complete pantomime cast, really, because David's work was very much like a pantomime on tele where you know the characters intimately: so well, in fact, that half the laughs come before the characters have even opened their mouths. It was well-crafted comedy with identifiable characters, good storylines and a strong cast.'

A Tour De France

Edith, the servants and Officer Crabtree are remembering René so Monsieur Alfonse can re-create him in a statue.

EDITH: Well, he was ...

YVETTE: Tall.

EDITH: Yes, tall.

MIMI: Thinning on top.

EDITH: Yes.

OFFICER CRABTREE: And rather plimp with a big bim.

EDITH: Yes, yes that was him. Tall, balding and fat.

MICHELLE: Whatever did you see in him?

EDITH: I am beginning to wonder.

Among the technical changes Mike Stephens introduced is one which shaped the show for the rest of its screen life. 'On previous series I'd worked on, I started taking the studio technical crew on location and shooting electronically, meaning it was video production rather than film, which it had been previously.'

Another development saw Mike shoot scenes using two cameras, which hadn't happened on the series before. 'It was better for the artists because you work faster and cover material quicker. You can take two shots at the same time, such as a long-shot and close-up. With film you might have shot one scene three or four times to get different angles, whereas you cut the time by half with this procedure.'

A further disadvantage of film compared to video was that film had to be processed, resulting in editing being impossible until Mike Stephens returned from location and could watch the rushes. On video, the editor attended the location shooting meaning scenes could be edited on the spot. 'Also, joins between the scenes shot in the studio and those on location didn't show because everything was taken in the same quality.' Before, when outdoor scenes were shot on film, there was always a huge clash in colour and texture when it came to mixing with the studio scenes on video. This problem was eliminated.

While Roger Martin was the videotape editor on Series 7, Chris Wadsworth rejoined the team for the final two seasons, working with John B. Hobbs, who took over from Stephens to produce Series 8 and 9.

Roger and Chris's job was, basically, to blend location shooting, studio shots and audience reaction. Chris states that *'Allo 'Allo!* was among the easier shows he edited, partly because in those days programme duration wasn't such an issue. 'You could present the network with a 31-minute show if there was good reason and it would be accommodated – that wouldn't happen today. Plus, *'Allo 'Allo!* was also well performed so the quality of the material meant it was a simple job for an editor.'

The introduction of video for location shooting meant Roger Martin and Chris Wadsworth would join the unit out in the field. 'By that time, equipment was becoming portable so I was carted off to Swaffham, Norfolk.' A room at the George Hotel became Chris Wadsworth's base. 'Inside the room, I'd set up an edit suite with a Sony 900 controller. I'd go across to the location for lunch – with John Hobbs constantly pulling my leg about only turning up when food was around – pick up tapes and take them back to the hotel room for editing. John would pop in to look at the rushes once outdoor shooting was complete for the day to see if I was roughly on course. It was a simple process.'

Having Chris Wadsworth on location in Norfolk, though, nearly caused a major problem for the television show. After all these years, he's happy to confess that he nearly lost several master tapes containing the outdoor shooting, 'We were back at Television Centre the next day, so to save the producer having to cart them down on a courier, I said, "No, I'll take them, they'll be fine." Famous last words.

'I came home with my baggage, some of the editing kit and several tapes. I unloaded the car, took everything inside, sat down and reintroduced myself to my house. Next morning, I was horrified on opening the front door to find that, tucked around the corner, I'd left the bag of tapes out all night – and these were original masters! I'm not normally unreliable but, goodness me, I just forgot it; it was one of those awful stomach-turning moments when you go ashen white. What if they'd been stolen? If ever there was a low point in my career, that was it. From that day, I have never wanted to handle tapes or anything which is of that unique quality.'

When it came to replacing Derek Royle, who had played Ernest Leclerc before his death, Mike Stephens turned to Robin Parkinson, although he acknowledges the difficulties involved in recruiting a new actor for an existing role. 'Robin had a small part in a series of mine and he was an extremely good actor.'

Finding someone to step into Bertorelli's shoes was made easier because Roger Kitter was already playing the character on stage during a summer season in Blackpool, 'He played the role beautifully on stage,' says Mike, who had to broach a rather delicate matter with the actor. 'At that time, Roger had a long ponytail. I didn't know how we were going to get around it. It's fine on stage because you've got a wig on but it's not the same as being on tele. I told him he'd have to cut it off but he point-blank refused. Before contracting him, I had to see Make-up and ask them if they could hide it. In the end, the make-up department sorted it out by giving him a bigger wig, concealing the ponytail. I thought Roger was very good. To some extent, he was mimicking Gavin Richards but had no option, really, because that was the character which had been created; you couldn't deviate from that.'

A change of personnel at the top, in the shape of Mike Stephens, didn't stop certain members of the cast engaging in pranks and tricks – and, again, Richard Gibson was usually in the thick of the action. One scene shot on location in Norfolk saw a telegraph pole – which was actually made of scaffolding poles covered in cardboard – collapsing with Herr Flick and Von Smallhausen clinging hold for dear life, although in reality the valuable visual effects team had inserted a hinge into the bottom of the pole which was gradually lowered.

Richard Gibson takes up the story. 'John Louis [Mansi] and I had stuntmen for when the telegraph pole fell down, but Kim and I told him that the stuntmen they'd got didn't look anything like us so we had to do the stunt. I said we should show a united front and complain to the management informing them that we weren't going to do it. So we went along to see the director, Mike Stephens. As we arrived, I said: "Mike, John is not happy at all about this." John Louis turned to me, saying: "I thought you weren't happy, either?" I said, "No, no, so long as it's all right with the director, it's all right with me." Of course, the director was in on the joke so poor John was standing there looking confused, thinking, "But I thought we were complaining together?" Mind you, he'd always get even.'

Visual effects, although a major part of the costings in any programme's budget, were used extensively in 'Allo 'Allo!. Colin Gorry and Stephen Lucas were just two of the visual effects designers who worked on the show; between them, they were responsible, with their teams, for a vast number of the effects used.

Colin, who's credited on two series but worked on many more episodes, remembers having to build a supposed rocket-propelled wheelchair for Rose Hill's character. 'We buried a track in the ground and fitted the wheelchair with a set of little wheels to fit the track. Then we fired it along by releasing a huge number of strong rubber bands which we'd cranked up on a winch – it acted like a giant catapult.

'We tested the chair with someone from my team, who was slight in build, but as it went very fast we thought a stunt person should sit in for the actual take. Unfortunately, the stunt person who turned up was absolutely massive; dressed up as the old lady, he was too big, really, so slowed the chair down. But it achieved what we wanted,' says Colin, who remembers everyone wanting to try it out afterwards. 'Some of the crew and cast queued up to try it out – it was like a showground ride. David got cross because he'd spent money on a stuntman and could possibly have used one of his crew.'

Saville Row To The Rescue

Edith is talking to Yvette behind the bar.

EDITH: It is time I am singing again. I need something to steady my nerves. You know, singing to a crowded room takes a special kind of courage.

YVETTE: It's lucky you are so brave.

(Edith pours herself a drink from a bottle on the counter)

RENÉ: What are you doing with that bottle?

EDITH: I am just going to whet my whistle.

RENÉ: You fool. This could blow your whistle through the top of your head.

EDITH: So what are you saying?

RENÉ: I am saying it is to blow up a train. I am saying it is nitroglycerin.

(Edith bangs the bottle down on the counter and they all take cover)

EDITH: I have given some to my mother and the chickens.

RENÉ: Oh no! This is disaster. Those are the only chickens we have.

EDITH: What about my mother?

The visual effects team was called upon for a host of reasons, like producing a flattened car to represent Herr Flick's staff car which was squashed by a steamroller. Stephen Lucas says: 'The demolished vehicle was, in fact, various parts from modern cars flattened for the purpose. A little smoke was added to enhance the affect.' Their efforts and imagination were greatly valued by David Croft, Mike Stephens and John B. Hobbs.

Although the sitcom ran for three further series after the departure of David Croft, no one should underestimate the effect caused by losing someone with such experience, proficiency and foresight. He was, inevitably, missed by the cast, although being professionals they were more than happy to continue, knowing that in Mike Stephens and, for Series 8 and 9, John B. Hobbs, the show was under astute stewardship. There was sadness, nonetheless. 'I was sad because he was part of our family,' says Vicki Michelle. 'But none of us wanted it to end because we loved the series; Jeremy and Paul Adam did a great job with the rest of it, but there was a big hole because David wasn't there. Of course, Mike Stephens and John B. Hobbs were lovely to work with, but not having David overseeing the entire project was sad.'

At least for those taking over the helm, the ship was left in good running order with everyone understanding their positions. Sue Hodge, although upset to see David Croft depart, retained her usual bubbly, positive outlook. 'Perhaps having new directors coming in brought something different and shook everybody up in a positive way. We still had Jeremy. We might have lost our captain but still had our dad. Jeremy was hilarious,' says Sue, smiling on remembering what he often said to her. 'Because he's so tall and I'm so short – four foot eleven – he used to joke, "Why did we employ you? I always go home at the end of the week with such backache after talking to you." He was always great fun and applauded our naughtiness!'

David Croft was a percipient writer and director; it could be argued that the scripts became more erratic after he left because amongst the many qualities he brought to the show was one of being the balancing act, keeping a control over Jeremy's fertile and extremely imaginative wit.

'There were no weak characters in the whole series. They were clearly defined, had their own voice, own identity and were absolutely on the nail,' says Charles Garland. 'Also, casting was spot-on. Some people say David and Jeremy wrote postcard humour and in some ways it was, but at other times it was tremendously subtle. When you look at the scripts David and Jeremy wrote, then subsequent ones, there was something missing. They didn't have the same magic and were kind of laughing at one's own joke. It wasn't quite as it had been and the family was falling apart, somewhat, with various cast changes.’

The change in the scriptwriting team was particularly noticeable to Roger Harris, set designer on the seventh series. When writing scripts, David Croft wore many hats, not just that of writer. Because he understood better than most how TV shows were made, down to every minute detail, he was always mindful of the practicalities of turning a script into a TV show. He considered not only the dialogue but how the cameras would shoot the scene, whether sets were too elaborate – all the mechanics behind transferring a show from page to screen. ‘David knew exactly how much you could have in a studio comfortably so his scripts were written with this in mind,’ says Roger. ‘You’d have the café set and a few other fairly permanent sets but he wouldn’t introduce lots of new ones because he understood the limitations of the studio.

‘When I worked on Series 7, the writers weren’t as knowledgeable and, sometimes, would write several new sets into one episode, resulting in us having to fly sets in and out and setting them inside one another so that the walls would fly up in the air to reveal another behind. It was the only way we could squeeze everything in. The writers weren’t as knowledgeable as David in the sheer organisation of a studio.’

When asked for her views on the three remaining series after David’s departure, Ann Croft says, ‘It’s probably understandable that I sound extremely prejudiced, but I think it went off a bit in the end – it lost its bite. There were some very funny scenes but they didn’t seem to have much logic. Artists changed, of course. Bertorelli, for example, started off with that wonderful actor Gavin Richards but ended up like a cartoon character, with Roger Kitter taking over for one series. Jeremy is a genuinely funny, talented man but he’s not so good when it comes to construction.’

The ten-episode Series 7 may have meant set designer Roger Harris had his work cut out designing and organising sets in the studio, but he was equally busy on location filming in Norfolk. One episode involved him and his team constructing a moat on Lynford Hall Estate. ‘We built the moat above ground but there was a drought that year and as soon as we filled it with water, it was populated with ducks and birds from the neighbourhood because they were struggling to find water; it made it very noisy for filming.’

The third episode’s storyline – which saw René and Edith, although the café owner had hoped it was Yvette, heading for London – necessitated half a plane being built. It was no easy task. ‘We had to get it into the back of a lorry and then build it on a disused runway in Norfolk. It was pouring with rain when we started to reassemble it, but it had been jammed so tight into the scenery lorry that we struggled getting it out. In the end, we had to cut it to get it out.'

Having been manhandled didn't help when trying to move the aircraft along the runway. 'It was pulled with ropes by the scenery guys,' says Roger Harris. 'But because the plane had got bent whilst being transported to the location, Mike Stephens wasn't sure if we were going to get the shot. But we went for it and it worked, although while it was being pulled along it started veering off and tilting to one side because you couldn't steer it. As it started approaching the Resistance girls, who were on the runway with their bikes, they dropped their cycles and ran away. Fortunately, we got our shot just before the undercarriage collapsed!'

For the final episode in the series, 'René Of The Gypsies', in which the British airmen are hiding in the sewers underneath the town square, Roger and his team were tasked with an unusual job. 'We were trying to manufacture poo which would float on water. In the end, we made it out of foam used to fill gaps in walls and painted it dark brown – they floated beautifully down the pretend sewer.'

The actors, John D. Collins and Nicholas Frankau, were in for a surprise, though, as they crawled along the make-believe sewer. 'What they didn't know is that we were going to throw water over them. Mike Stephens wanted to get a real reaction from them. There were vent holes in the sewers so when it came to the take, they crawled along, nice and comfortable, when suddenly this cold water poured all over them; they nearly swore because they weren't expecting it.'

Despite having his work cut out, Roger enjoyed working on the series. 'It was great for designers because although it was a comedy, it was like a historical drama in terms of trying to make everything look as authentic as possible.' Roger admits, however, that there was one thing amongst his episodes which wasn't in keeping with the period. 'There was an ice cream van in which Yvette sold squirty ice cream which wasn't invented until years later.'

One series was all Mike Stephens produced before moving on to new projects, including *Grace And Favour* and *The Brittas Empire*. He says: 'I tended to do about three series a year, which is as much as anyone can cope with.' For the last two series, numbers eight and nine, of *'Allo 'Allo!*, another experienced producer, John B. Hobbs, whose long list of credits includes *Three Up, Two Down*; *Terry And June*; *Brush Strokes* and *Bread*, took charge.

It was while producing *Bread* that Robin Nash, who had just become Head of Comedy, arranged for John to meet Gorden Kaye over dinner at the Halycon Hotel in London's Holland Park. Nash was checking to see how Hobbs and Kaye hit it off. 'I'm pleased to say, we got on very well. I knew why I was meeting Gorden. The BBC were keen to do another series and were trying to keep Gorden sweet, so gave him the courtesy of meeting me first instead of telling him I was going to be the next producer.'

When he first discussed taking over the show in Robin Nash's fourth floor office at Television Centre, John was delighted by the prospect, although just about to embark on a long-awaited holiday. 'Robin told me I couldn't go, so I reminded him that it was his suggestion in the first place. In the end, I cancelled my trip to Tunisia and took over *'Allo 'Allo!*.'

John had always enjoyed the show's style of humour. 'It was like a run of seaside postcards with a tremendous amount of innuendo, but very funny innuendo; there was nothing that really upset people. During my time on the show, I didn't receive many letters of complaint – a few from people who felt offended by *The Fallen Madonna With The Big Boobies*, regarding it as an insult to their religion, but that was about all. As for the war element, I just thought it was very amusing, and my father fought in the war, too.'

John had been friends with Jeremy Lloyd for some time and, fortunately, the writer was pleased with the new incumbent. 'I'd always been interested in Jeremy's stage plays and toured many of them, the last being *Business Affairs*, so I knew him well,' says John. Whenever the scripts for Series 8 and 9 landed on his desk, John was always pleased with the quality. 'You would have thought that David Croft had written them with Jeremy. Paul Adam seemed to have the same feel of what was required. They were always on time and full of such wonderful ideas. The episodes were expensive to make because there were lots of special effects, but were always beautifully written.'

The two series Hobbs produced contained several changes and developments. For starters, the opening episode of Series 8 began in a different fashion, inasmuch as two years had elapsed since we last visited Café René. There were cast changes, too, with three characters departing. Captain Bertorelli was dropped by the writers to reflect the fact that Italy had left the battle front. Meanwhile, the two British airmen finally managed to reach British shores. 'The problem with the airmen was that there wasn't much you could do with them,' admits Paul Adam. 'They were basically a couple of idiots being hidden all over the place and after so many episodes it was starting to wear a bit thin. It was getting difficult to structure plotting around them; Jeremy felt that over the course of the programme he'd done just about everything he could with them – plus, we couldn't think where else to hide them.'

For a time, it looked like Series 8 would be the last – and for Richard Gibson, it was. Richard describes later in the book why he decided to leave. Although John B. Hobbs tried his utmost to persuade him to stay, he was unsuccessful.

'Richard was very good because he had a wonderful dry sense of humour. I liked him immensely and was disappointed I couldn't persuade him to do the final series. It wouldn't have been a question of money because they all got the same, other than Gorden and Carmen.'

Gone With The Windmill

René is standing behind the bar when Officer Crabtree walks in.

OFFICER CRABTREE: I winder if by chance you have in your kifé anything for a haddock?

RENÉ: We have a rather nice tartar sauce you could put on it. Where is the haddock?

OFFICER CRABTREE: In my hod.

RENÉ: Oh, a headache!

CRABTREE: That is what I sod. I've git a bit of a hongover. I hit the bittle a bot last nit.

RENÉ: Here is my secret recipe. Try that.

CRABTREE: Ah! That hits the spit. I'm very grootful to you, Roné.

Before recasting the role of Herr Flick, John had to ensure it wasn't going to end at eight series. 'I was keen to keep it going because, like Jeremy, I thought there was another series in it. Everyone at the BBC was pleased to do it, even at the very top, because it still pulled in a good viewing figure; I didn't have to fight for another series like I had to for other shows.'

Throughout its life, the BBC controllers had appreciated and enjoyed *'Allo 'Allo!*. The BBC's archives reveal a memo from Michael Grade, then BBC1 Controller, who wrote to Lloyd and Croft on September 7, 1984, congratulating them on the programme. He wrote: 'Having been out of the country for three years I missed the first two transmissions ... and only caught up with it last night. It is without doubt one of the finest half-hour comedies I have seen for many, many years and I feel privileged that it is part of the portfolio of programmes I have inherited. I should love to add a note of criticism in order to balance the praise but, frankly, it was a faultless half-hour from every point of view.'

One of Hobbs' first tasks in securing a further series was to approach Gorden Kaye to ensure he was prepared to continue. John remembers the moment he decided to broach the subject with Kaye. 'We were up in Norfolk on location, reaching the end of the three-week filming for Series 8. The conversation was over a bacon buttie. We'd just finished a scene and the sun was shining. During the break, I approached him rather tentatively because he seemed to be telling everyone that this was going to be his last, but when I spoke to him he was very happy, so long as I continued to produce and direct,' says John, who remembers the special relationship Gorden enjoyed with Carmen Silvera. 'They used to go on holiday together and she was very fond of Gorden. Occasionally, they would fall out over silly things. But, next thing you knew, he'd arrive with a big bouquet of flowers for her to put matters right.'

John will never forget his first morning on location in Norfolk, which involved shooting scenes with Kim Hartman, as Helga. 'I spent the first hour having breakfast and didn't know it was Kim sat next to me. She wasn't in full costume and I spent an hour talking to her; it was only towards the end of the conversation when I asked what part she played that she told me Helga – I would never have known. Without the wig she looked totally different. If I'm honest, I thought she was one of the extras. But, seriously, she played her role very well.'

Anticipating the departure of Richard Gibson – although hoping he could still be persuaded to stay – the writers had to draw up a contingency plan. Therefore, a storyline was written to fit in with swapping actors. In the script, Herr Flick, realising the Germans are losing the war, needs to escape the country; to help, he ends up having plastic surgery and changes his appearance. 'If Richard had decided to make the series after all, we could have undone the bandages and it would be his face,' says Jeremy Lloyd. 'Alternatively, we'd undo the bandages and find out he'd had plastic surgery and looked quite different with another actor playing his part.'

By the time the green light had been given to proceed with the six-part Series 9, it was clear Gibson had called it a day. John B. Hobbs, therefore, turned his attention to finding someone to take over the role of Herr Flick, a character indelibly engraved into the national psyche as belonging to none other than Richard Gibson. One wonders if such a vivid character should have been retained; perhaps it would have been wise to replace him with, for example, a brother or cousin, similar to what happened when Roger Leclerc was replaced with Ernest Leclerc after Jack Haig's death. But John B. Hobbs had his reasons. 'He was such a wonderful character, it made for a lot of interest and comedy so I wouldn't have wanted him to disappear. If you'd replaced Herr Flick with another character, perhaps his twin brother, you would have had to start with certain storylines. Helga's relationship with Herr Flick, for example: if we suddenly had a different character, it would have made that thread of comedy difficult; and as it was definitely going to be the last series, you don't have time to alter those aspects.'

David Janson, who had already played the character on stage as well as portraying Hitler in an earlier television episode, quickly became the obvious choice. Knowing the actor's work, John made a point of not interviewing Janson. 'I was always taught not to call in actors and actresses for auditions if they were well known. As a producer, you should know their work. I much preferred talking to them on the phone, inviting them in for lunch and working in that way rather than asking actors to come across London for an audition. Having been an actor myself, it seems the correct way – unless, of course, it's a performer whose work you don't know.'

The curtain dropped on the ninth and final series with the episode, 'A Winkle In Time', being transmitted on December 14, 1992. The British had arrived to free the citizens of Nouvion. 'Everyone was sad and we had a big party,' recalls John B. Hobbs, who was presented with an engraved silver platter at the Topo D'Oro in London's Notting Hill Gate. 'It's beautiful and holds pride of place in my dining room.' He's convinced that some people almost believed that it might happen again. 'I'm sure most would have happily done another series. But by that time things were beginning to change and it was decided financially that they couldn't have gone again; it might have been different if I'd been able to find someone to champion the cause upstairs on the fifth floor, but couldn't. It was an expensive series due to the big cast, the props and visual effects, which are always expensive in this business.'

Having to reshoot scenes affected the balance sheet, too. Fortunately, this happened rarely, but Jeremy Lloyd remembers watching a scene on location during the eighth series where he insisted it was reshot. 'We had a big battle scene where actor Jack Hedley was head of a special German SS force trying to catch Hitler and Goering, who were René and Edith in disguise. It was filmed in Norfolk at night. Afterwards, I asked the director what it had cost and he said about £80,000. I told him he'd need to shoot it again. When he asked why, I replied, "Because the actors had got carried away and some had fallen down as if they'd been shot dead. No one is killed in 'Allo 'Allo!. A brick might hit someone's helmet and bounce off, but that was as dangerous as it got. So we had to reshoot the whole scene.'

When it came to the final episode, the storyline involved a leap into the future, affording viewers the chance to see a post-war Nouvion at peace, an aged

René in a wheelchair and his old friends and foes revisiting the sleepy town; it was a clear indication from the scriptwriters that there was no turning back. This was undeniably the end. 'I had to finish at some point because we were beginning to repeat ourselves slightly,' admits Jeremy.

Being in the recording studio to record *'Allo 'Allo!* for the very last time was an emotional occasion for everyone. 'It was sad but, if we're honest, we knew it had to finish,' says Kim Hartman. 'Richard had already left so I was certainly thinking that the ninth would be the end for me, too. But it was decided for us and I think we were ready to bring it to the end – after all, it had run much longer than the war itself.'

Kim had been involved in the scene depicting post-war Nouvion. 'That was strange because it was the only time I went into the make-up room afterwards and looked better when they had actually taken it all off – it was normally the other way round! To make me look more creased in my skin, they used latex.'

Some performers leave a steady job behind with trepidation, but not Kim. 'I went off to do a tour of *Double Double* which I enjoyed enormously, so I was positive about the future; mind you, I had a strange feeling inside knowing it was actually the end.'

Sue Hodge can remember vividly the moments after recording the closing episode. 'I was standing beside Vicki. Everyone was waving to each other and I remember turning to her, saying, "They're actually waving goodbye for the last time." It was emotional and I remember thinking that we'll never have this again. Usually everybody went back to their dressing rooms and there would be a din, like school's out. But this time there was an air of coldness and silence, almost as if someone had died – it was strange. Leaving the studio was like shutting the door on something for the last time. There were tears streaming down my face – and not just mine – because it was the end of an era.'

It wasn't quite the end everyone thought it would be – at least not for Gorden Kaye and Carmen Silvera. Two years later, in August 1994, John B. Hobbs dreamt up the idea of a "Best Of" programme. 'At that time, BBC Enterprises were keen to make a video so I came up with this idea in which we looked back over the series, with the link-ups being René and Edith celebrating their anniversary.'

John B. Hobbs was determined to film the link-ups in France so headed to Normandy to source a suitable location. After finding a picturesque village, everything seemed to be going swimmingly – that is until he arrived on the first of the two days of scheduled filming. 'One thing I hadn't checked was the date. Believe it or not, the date I'd chosen to do it – and we'd just arrived – was

Bastille Day. Processions, car rallies – everything was planned. Eventually, I had to go to the mayor and get his permission to divert the traffic. The authorities were wonderful and moved all the vehicles away from the main square so I could shoot *'Allo 'Allo!* – now that says something.'

The ever-popular story of *'Allo 'Allo!* didn't stop there, either. To the delight of the sitcom's millions of fans, a special treat was dished up in the shape of *The Return of 'Allo 'Allo!*, a one-off programme in 2007 to coincide with the show's 25th anniversary. Viewers returned to the setting of Café René to find René Artois still still the proprietor but also writing his memoirs at the same time. Some familiar faces popped in to say 'hello', including Hubert Gruber, Michelle Dubois and Mimi Labonq, while documentary inserts helped tell the story of the show.

The programme, written by Jeremy Lloyd and made by Objective North for the Beeb, was recorded in front of a live audience at BBC Manchester. Demand for tickets was overwhelming with over 2,000 applications received for only 300 seats. The popularity of the programme surprised many, but at long last the wartime sitcom was recognized when *The Return Of 'Allo 'Allo!* was later given the accolade of Royal Television Society Best Network Entertainment Programme for 2007; the award was presented to Jeremy Lloyd at the city's Midland Hotel, an occasion he classes as a 'proud moment of my career'.

One of the programme's producers, Robert Katz, remembers meeting Jeremy Lloyd to discuss the 2007 show. 'He was keen from the beginning and had ideas for the script, so it was written at his dining room table. We were going to write an entire episode but in the end decided to mix it with a documentary.'

Unfortunately, the deadline given by the BBC meant an extremely tight timetable for the actors, particularly Gorden Kaye, who – as expected – had the lion's share of dialogue. It wasn't an entirely happy experience for him, as he explains. 'There was little rehearsal time for the programme, which was recorded in front of a live audience where the first three rows seemed to be full of men with bald heads and white aprons trying to look like René – it was a little off-putting.

'But rehearsal would be, at the very most, a little over half an hour for the whole episode – or so it seemed. As it worked out, René was writing his memoirs and it looked like he was doing that in the café; but that was, in fact, the script.'

Martin Dennis, who directed the café segment of the programme, sympathizes with Gorden regarding the rehearsal period. 'By the time we could get everyone in the same place at the same time we effectively had about four hours' rehearsal, whereas normally if you're doing an audience sitcom you'd have four days and then a whole day in front of the cameras. So time was really short. Even the camera rehearsal which we had with the actors, limited as it was, was full of publicity photographs being taken and lots of other things at the same time. So, yes, we had a very, very short rehearsal time which is why Gorden didn't have time to learn the dialogue. As it was a memoir-based idea, we suggested that he kept the script with him, just in case he needed it; thankfully, it worked out well in the end, although we were busking it a little on the night, I must admit.'

Robert Katz, who produced the show, realizes it was hard for Gorden and accepts there wasn't much time to rehearse. 'But that's the nature of these things; we didn't have a lot of money and it's not like the old days when you could have a week or so and make it in a civilized way. Although the BBC were behind it they didn't throw a massive amount of money our way.' There wasn't much time between commissioning and delivery date, either. 'Gorden had the script about a week beforehand, I think,' says Robert, who – despite the aforementioned factors – thinks the show worked well. 'What you couldn't do was recreate the times that *'Allo 'Allo!* was based in – you couldn't go backwards. But what you could do was bring a bit of closure to it, which is what we tried doing in the script. It gave fans another chance to see some of the characters they liked.

'Short of writing a whole episode and then filming it, which was possible but beyond the means of the BBC because it would have been too expensive, our approach was probably the best way. We recorded about half an episode in three hours, then added in the clips to complete the show.'

Despite numerous attempts to persuade Richard Gibson to return as Herr Flick, even explaining that a new scenario was being written by Jeremy Lloyd, the actor decided to decline the opportunity. Another notable absentee was Kim Hartman, who was busy in a theatre production and couldn't be released. Nonetheless, the continued popularity of *'Allo 'Allo!* meant that the show recorded an audience over 3.5 million, BBC2's most popular show that weekend. The magic of the wartime-influenced sitcom hadn't waned and, 30 years since it first graced our screens, it still hasn't.

THE CAST AND CREW

RENÉ, EDITH AND THE CAFÉ REGULARS

René Artois, the proprietor of Café René in the centre of Nouvion, was a self-proclaimed coward coerced into helping the French Resistance in their myriad attempts to repatriate the British airmen; he found himself pulled in every direction, though, because the Germans blackmailed him into hiding precious items stolen from the Château which they intended selling after the war to make their fortunes.

Also known by his code name, Night Hawk, René had a cousin in Bordeaux and was married to Edith, a bossy old harridan, for over 25 years. Edith thought highly of herself: believing she could carry a tune, rather than hire a singer at the café, she tried entertaining the clientele herself, resulting in everyone rushing for the door or reaching for lumps of cheese to block their ears. Despite her stern demeanour, Edith was immeasurably gullible when René spewed out countless feeble excuses whenever caught embracing one of his waitresses, with whom he was having affairs behind his wife's back.

Living under the same roof as René and Edith were Edith's elderly mother, Madame Fanny La Fan, and her aged beau, Roger Leclerc, a forger and safecracker by trade, who arrived in Nouvion tasked with preparing papers and identity passes for the British airmen; to the Germans, though, he was supposedly René's cousin who helped at the café. The former jailbird turned out to be Madame Fanny's ex-lover and hung around until he could stand Edith's cooking no longer; while visiting his twin brother, Ernest – who was in prison serving a long sentence for driving a getaway car without due care and attention – he swapped places after deciding prison food looked more appetising. Although bed-ridden, the gin-loving, eightysomething Madame Fanny finally married Ernest, son of a Paris bus conductor, who was a bookmaker by trade.

A café regular – and supporter of the Resistance – was Monsieur Alfonse, who'd worked as a newspaper reporter in his early years. Not only was he smitten by Edith, he was intent on walking her down the aisle but never, alas, realized his dream. Considering himself a man of substance, his business interests included being Nouvion's undertaker, running a butcher's shop, being a hairdresser, photographer and vineyard owner.

GORDEN KAYE
(René Artois – 85 episodes)

When Gorden Kaye first received the script for the *'Allo 'Allo!* pilot he thought its subject was a drag artist. 'My agent rang after spending 40 minutes on the phone with David Croft discussing the programme and told me the script was in the post. I received it the following morning and mistakenly thought David wanted me to play the part of Renee; I thought he was some kind of drag artist. Then I realized it was René and opened the script; even on page one, I read the altercations between René and Edith and was laughing before reaching the bottom of the page. I knew this was going to be a good 'un.'

The cast gelled from the beginning and the working relationship between Gorden and Carmen Silvera, who played Edith, couldn't have been stronger. 'Carmen was a joy to work with. She was delightful and we became great friends; we went abroad together a couple of times to Switzerland.'

Gorden enjoyed working for David Croft. 'He was always approachable, very special and there won't be another like him. The crew would say, "If David is happy with you, you're doing all right." A couple of times, he said, "Have you got a couple of minutes? You're pushing too heavily on that knowing it's leading to a decent laugh, which it is, but don't stretch it, just do it. That's why you're René Artois and no one else is. OK?"'

As well as holding many happy memories of the TV series, Gorden also enjoyed taking the *'Allo 'Allo!* stage show around the UK before playing in front of packed houses in London's West End. There is one particular moment he'll never forget.

'I was caught out by Eamonn Andrews, presenter of *This Is Your Life*, at the Prince of Wales Theatre while performing the stage show.' Although the show was officially starting at the theatre on the Wednesday, they performed the play in the lead up to the opening night. At the end of one show, the cast did their customary bow and waited for the curtain to drop. 'But it didn't. I thought, "Come on, if it's going to be like this on Wednesday for the opening night, it'll be daylight by the time we get out." Then there was a roar from the audience and I looked to the left and saw Eamonn Andrews walking on wearing a pilot's flying jacket and a hood with goggles on top; he was carrying the red book. I thought it must be Jack Haig's *This Is Your Life*.' Gorden was shocked to discover he was the subject of the programme.

Gorden was instrumental in creating one of TV's most popular comedy characters. But tragedy struck three months after the sixth TV series had been screened, and on the eve of the tremendously popular stage show heading Down Under, when Gorden suffered serious head injuries in a car accident.

On January 25, 1990, 39 people, including several children, were killed by a devastating storm that swept across the UK leaving destruction in its wake. Gorden was driving when hurricane-force winds gusting in from the south-west resulted in a hoarding being thrown into the air. 'A piece of wood flew through the windscreen and embedded itself in the centre of my forehead,' recalls Gorden. 'I was rushed to hospital and couldn't go to Australia with the gang for the stage show. But I've been subsequently, the last time with Sue Hodge, Guy Siner and myself backed up by a dozen Aussie actors, who were very nervous; we performed at the Twelfth Night Theatre, Brisbane, for five weeks. I'd also been there in a Ray Cooney play working with a very good actor, shorter than I am, called Max Gillies.'

It was Gillies who took over the role of René when the stage show travelled to Australia in 1990. Gorden recalls an occasion when producer David Croft visited him in hospital. One of the topics of conversation was the play's progress. 'I was recovering by this time. I asked how it was going and David replied, "Really good. It's the best we could ever have hoped for." I replied, "Oh, thank you, David, that's very cheering." I asked who was playing René, and when he told me Max Gillies, I said, "He's not tall enough." But David said, "He's doing a great job and it's improved the show because the rest of the gang had got used to your rhythm; he has a very different rhythm so they're having to listen. In their heads, they could almost finish the line when you did it because they knew your pace, Gorden, but Max Gillies is doing it his way, and it still gets many if not more laughs.'

The Australian actor may have helped save the day on the other side of the world but the sitcom's fans were delighted to have Gorden back when, thankfully, he surprised many by making a speedy recovery. While being interviewed for BBC's *Comedy Connections* programme, he said, 'I was back in less than six months of the accident, which could have been thought to be too soon. But because I loved the show so much, whether it be the stage or television version, I was determined to honour my contract.'

When Gorden returned to make the seventh TV series, transmitted during the first three months of 1991, there was a notable absentee: David Croft, who felt he had taken the series as far as possible. Although everyone was sad not to have him around, service resumed as normal. 'It wasn't difficult,' says Gorden. 'We missed him but Mike Stephens and John Hobbs knew exactly what to do. It wasn't a case of "We'll do it our way", it was "We'll do it David's way". They were aware what was required.'

Gorden was born in Huddersfield, Yorkshire, and attended the local technical college in the early-1960s. But before the decade was out, he'd moved into the acting profession and made his TV debut. Early screen credits included playing a railway guard in an episode of Peter Ling and Hazel Adair's *Champion House*, a clerk in *Inside George Webley* and Bernard Butler, Elsie Tanner's nephew, in *Coronation Street*.

He was regularly in demand during the 1970s and a long list of credits include *Villains*, *Emmerdale*, *The Gordon Peters Show*, *The Flaxton Boys*, *Till Death Us Do Part*, *The Growing Pains Of PC Penrose*, *Sykes*, *Shoestring* and *All Creatures Great And Small*. On the big screen, he appeared in the 1977 Terry Gilliam-directed film, *Jabberwocky*, starring Michael Palin; he was later cast in Gilliam's *Brazil*.

Gorden first worked for David Croft playing a soldier in a 1977 episode of *It Ain't Half Hot, Mum* before appearing as Nick Manson in Lloyd and Croft's ill-fated sci-fi sitcom, *Come Back, Mrs Noah*, and popping up three times in *Are You Being Served?*.

Croft wanted to find a vehicle for Gorden and planned having him front the sitcom, *Oh, Happy Band!*, which he'd written with Jeremy Lloyd. Although free for the pilot, an industrial dispute delayed a show Gorden was making for ITV, deeming him unavailable for Croft's series. With no alternative but to recast, Croft offered the lead role to Harry Worth. Gorden, though, has no regrets. 'Harry Worth was exactly the right person to play the part. It needed somebody well-known and talented. Such people don't come in bucket loads.'

Gorden retired from acting in March 2009, soon after touring with Sue

Hodge in the two-hander, *Elsie and Norm's Macbeth*, an hilarious rewrite of Shakespeare's popular classic; it was a production he'd performed previously with actress Madge Hindle.

Now living in Yorkshire, he'll forever be remembered for his accomplished performances as René. 'We were blessed with wonderful scripts in *'Allo 'Allo!* and had a lot of fun.'

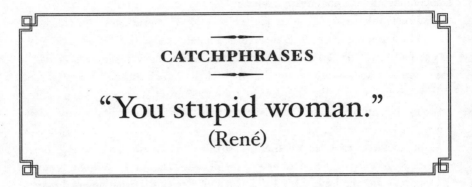

CATCHPHRASES

"You stupid woman."
(René)

CARMEN SILVERA
(Edith Artois – 85 episodes)

Born in Toronto, Canada, in 1922, Carmen Silvera moved to England with her parents but was evacuated to Montreal during the Second World War. She narrowly escaped death when the ship she intended sailing in was full, forcing her to take a later crossing, only for the original ship to sink with the loss of many lives.

Upon settling in England, she trained in ballet from the age of three and before long harboured dreams of becoming a dancer. When evacuated back to Canada, she was afforded the opportunity to attend lessons with the Ballets Russe, a travelling Russian ballet company; later, she appeared in three productions with the company.

After the cessation of hostilities, Carmen returned to England but switched her attention from dancing to acting. Upon training at LAMDA (The London Academy of Music and Dramatic Art), she began her career in repertory theatre. Her TV debut came in *Z Cars* before landing the prominent role of Camilla Hope in BBC's 1960s soap, *Compact*, created by Hazel Adair and Peter Ling. Among her many TV credits were appearances in *New Scotland Yard*, *Doctor Who*, *Within These Walls* and *The Gentle Touch*. She was also seen in *The Generation Game*, *What's My Line?* and a touching episode of *Dad's Army* experiencing a brief encounter with the straight-laced Captain Mainwaring.

On stage, Carmen appeared in numerous West End productions, including *Waters Of The Moon* with Ingrid Bergman, *Hobson's Choice* with Penelope Keith and *School For Wives*.

Carmen was living at Denville Hall, the actors' retirement home, when she celebrated her 80th birthday in June 2002; she died two months later of lung cancer, having been diagnosed earlier that year and opting not to undergo chemo or radiotherapy.

CATCHPHRASES

"René, what are you doing holding that servant girl in your arms?"

(Edith)

ROSE HILL
(Madame Fanny La Fan – 78 episodes)

After winning a scholarship to train at the Guildhall School of Music and Drama, Rose Hill, who was born in London in 1914, started her professional career in 1939 as an opera singer.

She debuted at Glyndebourne before joining the Sadler's Wells Opera Company. For the Glyndebourne Festival Opera she sang Barbarina in *Le Nozze Di Figaro* and, in 1948, Lucy in the world première of Benjamin Britten's adaptation of *The Beggar's Opera*.

During the 1950s, her career took a different route when she began appearing on stage and screen in acting roles, starting with the 1958 B-movie, *The Bank Raiders*, before other films, such as *Wildcats Of St. Trinian's, Footsteps, Heavens Above!* and the big screen version of Thames Television's popular sitcom, *For The Love Of Ada*, in which she played a mourner. On the small screen, her credits included *Dixon Of Dock Green, Thingumybob, Take A Sapphire, Waterloo Sunset, Dad's Army* and, latterly, *A Touch Of Frost* and *The Bill.*

She continued acting into her eighties and spent her final years at Denville Hall, the actors' retirement home, until her death in 2003.

JACK HAIG
(Monsieur Roger Leclerc – 51 episodes)

London-born Jack Haig grew up in a family of entertainers. His parents, Bertha Baker and Charles Coppin, were primarily music hall performers who formed a double-act, Haig and Esco.

Jack kicked off his professional career as a comedian in revues, touring shows and pantos up and down the country before entering the TV industry in the 1950s, playing Wacky Jacky, the popular children's character, for Tyne Tees Television, a role he used later on *Crackerjack.* Among his many small screen roles is gardener Archie Gibbs in *Crossroads.* But he also appeared in such shows as *Hugh And I, All Gas And Gaiters* and *The Gnomes Of Dulwich* during the 1960s, *Here Come The Double Deckers!, Keep It In The Family* and *Dad's Army* in the 1970s and *Are You Being Served?, Sorry!* and *All Creatures Great And Small* in the 1980s.

His film work was restricted to small roles in pictures like *Oliver!, Superman* and *The Adventures Of A Taxi Driver,* while on stage his many credits included Sir January in *Canterbury Tales* in the West End.

Jack, who was married to revue artist Sybil Dunn, died in 1989, aged 76.

CATCHPHRASES

"It is I, Leclerc."
(Monsieur Leclerc)

DEREK ROYLE
(Ernest Leclerc – 8 episodes, Series 6)

Derek Royle was born in London in 1928 and began his showbiz career as an acrobat, performing in the group, The Adonis Three, before deciding to study at RADA.

He was spotted on stage and screen from the mid-1960s until his death in 1990. On stage, his acrobatic skills were useful when appearing in Brian Rix's *Whitehall Farces* as absent-minded characters prone to falling down stairs only to stand up and dust themselves off.

His film credits included a supporting role in the Beatles' *Magical Mystery Tour* in 1967 but the lion's share of jobs were in comedies, such as *Don't Just Lie There, Say Something!*. On television, he turned up as Doctor Hogg, alongside Wendy Richard and Pat Coombs, in the children's comedy series, *Hogg's Back*, and an instalment of *Fawlty Towers*, playing an unwell guest who dies during the night in the hilarious episode, 'The Kipper and the Corpse'. Among his last screen appearances were roles in *The Setbacks*, *Chance In A Million*, *Young Charlie Chaplin* and *The Bill*.

Derek died of cancer in 1990, aged 61.

ROBIN PARKINSON
(Ernest Leclerc – 22 episodes, Series 7-9)

Robin left school and worked for his father, a commercial artist, before attending drama school. He entered the business in 1958, appearing in a TV series while finishing his drama studies. Regular TV and film work soon came his way. He made his big screen debut in the 1963 movie, *Billy Liar*, as a jeweller's assistant. Other film credits include *Twisted Nerve*, *Catch Me A Spy* and *The Family Way*.

He's made numerous TV appearances, including 20 episodes of the 1970s series, *The Many Wives Of Patrick*, an episode of *Dad's Army*, *The Dick Emery Show*, *Girls About Town* and an instalment of *Outside Edge*.

KENNETH CONNOR
(Monsieur Alfonse – 61 episodes)

A mainstay of the *Carry On* films, Kenneth Connor, son of a naval officer, was born in London in 1916 and made his stage debut aged two. By the time he reached eleven, he was already performing various acts with his brother in revue shows.

Deciding that he wanted to concentrate on becoming an actor, he attended the Central School of Speech and Drama. Upon graduating, his first professional job was as Boy Davis at His Majesty's Theatre, London, in 1936. He went on to act in numerous repertory theatres, later becoming a member of the Bristol Old Vic Company; although the outbreak of war in 1939, during which he served with the army's Middlesex Regiment as a gunner, put a temporary halt to his career, he was for part of the duration attached to George Black's company, Stars In Battledress, touring the Mediterranean.

After demob he returned to acting in a West End play at the Strand Theatre and, before long, a role in the television soap, *The Huggetts;* but he made his name for the array of character voices he created on radio shows such as *Just William* and *Ray's A Laugh* with Ted Ray, the start of a long and lasting association with the comedian. His success in *Ray's A Laugh* saw Ted Ray engage him as his top supporting player in the television series, *The Ted Ray Show.*

Kenneth appeared in the 1955 comedy, *The Ladykillers,* before playing Horace Strong, a hypochondriac, in *Carry On Sergeant*, the first of many *Carry On* roles. Other film credits started as early as 1939 with *Poison Pen,* along with *The Black Rider, Davy, Make Mine A Million, Watch Your Stern, Nearly A Nasty Accident, Dentist On The Job, What A Carve Up* and *Rhubarb.*

On television, he appeared in, among others, *A Show Called Fred, Blackadder The Third, You Rang, M'Lord?, Rentaghost* and provided the voices for the popular children's show, *Torchy The Battery Boy.* But he's probably best known on TV as Monsieur Alfonse and Uncle Sammy Morris in the holiday camp sitcom, *Hi-de-Hi!*

Having starred in over 50 films he was awarded an MBE in 1991 for services to showbusiness. He died of cancer two years later, aged 75.

THE WAITRESSES

René and Edith employed a loyal band of waitresses at their café, all of whom had the hots for René and embarked on secret affairs with the plump café owner. Unfortunately, the claustrophobic environment in which they worked and the lingering presence of Madame Edith restricted their dalliances to brief moments of lust in insalubrious settings like the cellar and broom cupboard.

When not on duty at the caff, the girls could be found fraternising on the streets of Nouvion or entertaining German officers upstairs with a little help from wet sticks of celery, flying helmets and egg whisks. But their services didn't come free: silk stockings, cigarettes, supplies for the café or, in Yvette's case, money for her sick mother were always part of the deal.

Yvette, perhaps the most loyal of all, was 19 when we first met her at Café René working alongside the naïve brunette, Maria; when the petite, seemingly innocent Maria left the staff after disguising herself as a Red Cross parcel and subsequently posted back to Switzerland while attempting to break out of a POW camp, the tough-talking, aggressive blonde, Mimi, an 18-year-old who was a gang leader in the Paris-based French Resistance, took her place with gusto.

VICKI MICHELLE
(Yvette Carte-Blanche – 85 episodes)

According to Vicki Michelle, who appeared as coquettish waitress Yvette in every episode of *'Allo 'Allo!*, many people – usually men – are under the illusion that the waitresses spent much screen time parading in stockings and suspenders. 'If you actually watch the series, we're not in them that much. It's like those who say how they loved my little short skirt. My outfit was actually a cream or white shirt, pinnie and satin knee-length skirt. Admittedly, we were occasionally seen in more revealing outfits, but not that often,' she confirms, smiling.

The sexy character's popularity, however, is not in doubt and resulted in Vicki receiving a constant stream of fan letters. 'I got a couple of dodgy ones but most were lovely. Some people wanted to take me out for a meal while others asked if I'd marry them. I even had soldiers request suspender belts; I've been known to send out a couple but only to soldiers because I thought it would be good for morale – it's all harmless fun.' With the sitcom still repeated around the world, letters keep arriving. 'It's not surprising, I suppose, considering *'Allo 'Allo!* sold to over 80 countries. It's only relatively recently been bought by German and Russian channels, and, apparently, it's on all the time in India, so someone told me the other day.'

Desperate Doings In The Graveyard

Madame Fanny has come down to the café from her bed, announcing that Monsieur Ernest Leclerc has asked her to marry him. Shortly after, Monsieur Leclerc enters.

LECLERC: Fanny, I have something for you. I have a ring for you. See, look how it sparkles in the light.

FANNY: Oh, Ernest. It is a whopper. But how could you afford such a ring?

LECLERC: You forget the trade I was in when we met.

EDITH: (To René) Was he a jeweller?

RENÉ: He was a burglar.

LECLERC: Fanny, come with me to the town square and I will tell the world of our love.

RENÉ: Yes, off you go, your wheelchair and crutches are just outside.

LECLERC: René, do not worry, you are not losing a mother-in-law, you are gaining a father-in-law.

RENÉ: Oh, my God.

EDITH: Mamma, when will the happy event take place?

FANNY: As soon as possible after we are married. What a stupid question.

Vicki first worked with *'Allo 'Allo!*'s original producer/director and co-writer David Croft in the 1978 sci-fi sitcom, *Come Back, Mrs Noah*, starring Mollie Sugden, Ian Lavender and Donald Hewlett. Another Lloyd-Croft collaboration, there was also an appearance by Gorden Kaye, playing a TV presenter, and Vicki's sister, Ann – who was pivotal in getting Vicki the part of a robotic French Maid. 'Ann and I went for the same part – that of Scarth Dare – and David couldn't make up his mind; he eventually chose Ann. In the series, there was a French maid robot. Ann suggested to David that I'd be good for it and, fortunately, he agreed.'

Later, when David and Jeremy were planning *'Allo 'Allo!* and needed French waitresses to work in Café René, they turned to Vicki. 'I remember my agent asking what my French accent was like. I told her fabulous – you made out you could do everything in those days – and I was invited to read for not just Yvette but Michelle of the Resistance, too.' After the audition, nearly nine months passed without a word from Croft's office. 'It was such a long time I assumed I'd been unsuccessful.'

She needn't have worried, though, because when David Croft finally secured a commission from the BBC hierarchy to make a pilot, Vicki was offered the role of Yvette and a script duly despatched. 'When I first read it, I laughed out loud and knew it was good material. The pilot is a brilliant episode, very intense, serious and real,' says Vicki, who noticed everyone settled into their roles swiftly. 'The sitcom evolved during the opening series. You're working with actors for the first time and it can take a while to build up a relationship – but, fortunately, it happened pretty quickly. I grew in to my role and she became me, in many respects. As soon as I put the clothes on, I was Yvette.'

As the sitcom progressed, catchphrases emerged for many of the characters, but not Yvette. Vicki was desperate to have her own. 'Even Arthur Bostrom came in speaking cod French and ended up with his wonderful, "Good moaning!" I didn't have one and kept asking David, who'd repeatedly say, "No, darling, we've got enough." I tried wearing him down but it didn't work,' smiles Vicki, who took matters into her own hands with the help of Robin Carr, who directed five episodes in Series 3. 'My dialogue often contained the line, "Ooh, René" so I started turning it into, "Oooooh, René". Gradually, it got longer and David didn't seem to mind, although he'd smirk so perhaps realized what I was doing. In one of the episodes Robin directed he asked me to duck down behind the bar when René came in to the café. I grasped the opportunity so that all you could hear was "Ooooooooh … " from behind the bar before I popped up; but it was important I sustained the growl for a long time. When it came to the recording, I got such a big laugh that I carried on saying it that way for the rest of the series. So I finally got my own catchphrase.'

In October 1989, with *'Allo 'Allo!* riding high in the ratings, Vicki gave birth to her daughter, Louise. For a while, the pregnancy had been a worrying time because she feared – unnecessarily, as she later discovered – for her job. 'I'd always wanted to get pregnant but, yes, was scared of losing my job. When you're pregnant your hormones are racing around and you don't always think straight. I thought that if I told David I'd have to leave the series, so was very worried.

'I had to consider my options: did I get rid of something that I'd always wanted or risk losing my job? When you think about it in the cold light of day, you say, "Of course I'm going to have my baby."' But it took months before Vicki plucked up enough courage to inform David Croft. 'By that time, I was four months', but David's response was, "Oh, darling, that's fantastic – how many months are you?" I told him three, even though it was four, and he was so pleased, assuring me that I wouldn't lose the role; he said they'd work around me and if the bump started showing, they'd write it in. So all that worry I'd put myself through for four months was totally unnecessary – and I should have realized because David was a true family man.'

As the weeks passed, Croft ensured that any scenes involving Yvette were shot in such a way as to conceal her growing bump. 'If you looked at me from the front, I was quite slim, so that's how they tended to line up the shots involving Yvette. But if you saw me from the side, I was like Alfred Hitchcock!' Vicki recalls an occasion when a member of the studio audience at a recording noticed her expanding girth. In the audience that night was Vicki's husband, Graham. 'A couple of women behind him said, "Ooh, Vicki Michelle has put on a bit of weight." He turned around and replied, "Actually, she's seven months' pregnant." I was seven or nearly eight by the time we finished that series.'

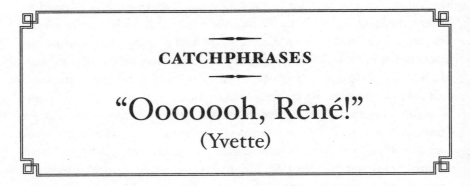

CATCHPHRASES

"Ooooooh, René!"
(Yvette)

Unfortunately, Vicki suffered a couple of scares during the pregnancy which made headline news in the press. 'We were working really hard and it was quite stressful,' admits Vicki, who recalls scenes involving lifting coffins. 'People warned me about lifting anything heavy, but I thought I'd be fine and didn't want the rest of the cast making exceptions or excuses because of my pregnancy.'

During a doctor's appointment, some warning signs were detected and Vicki was hospitalized for bed rest. When it looked like she'd miss a recording, her sister, Ann, was placed on standby to replace Vicki in the episode. 'Fortunately, I was released the day before the recording.'

Before making her name in the genre of comedy, Vicki was regularly cast in straight roles, appearing in, among others, *Softly, Softly, The Professionals, Minder* and *Play For Today*. But it's *'Allo 'Allo!* which brought her into the public eye and she's grateful to have been part of its success. 'It's repeated regularly and people still come up and tell me how much the show makes them laugh – it's a lovely feeling knowing you've helped make people happy.'

When the final series came to a close in 1992, it was inevitably a sad occasion for the cast, many of whom had become good friends. 'We knew each other well so it was like a big family splitting up. They were wonderful times,' says Vicki.

After leaving Café René behind, Vicki feared that having played a popular character for so long would make it difficult finding new work, but she went straight into theatre. 'Also, I set up a business, Trading Faces, in 1991, providing, among other things, after-dinner speakers and celebrities for personal appearances. Just in case I found myself typecast, I felt I needed another string to my bow to help pay the mortgage; I run it with two of my three sisters – Ann and Suzi – and it's working well.'

Fortunately, acting opportunities have never dried up and Vicki – who made her professional stage debut alongside Dudley Moore in *Play It Again Sam* – has worked virtually non-stop in the theatre. Her many roles include Jacqueline in *Don't Dress For Dinner*, Mina in *Dracula* and several Ray Cooney plays, including the role of Linda Harper in *Wife Begins At Forty*; on TV she's been seen in *Emmerdale*, *Doctors* and the TV film, *All In The Game*, as Emma, the screen wife of Ray Winstone.

But it doesn't take long to choose her favourite role: Yvette, and she'll never forget the practical jokes that were played from time to time. Once, the waitress was caught by Edith in a passionate clinch with René. 'The excuse used was that Yvette had fainted from lack of food, so I was supposed to eat potato peelings meant for the chickens. During rehearsal they were made from rice paper but when it came to the recording, they'd been swapped for the real thing. So I ended up with a mouthful of grit and raw peelings!'

She recalls another jolly jape, this time while touring in the stage show. 'Gorden put my foot in a bucket of water while I was standing behind the bar; I had no alternative but to squelch around for the rest of the scene. They were such happy years and my lasting memories of working on the show will always be filled with fun and laughter.'

The Execution

The British airmen are in bed together.

CARSTAIRS: Drum war isn't it, Fairfax?

FAIRFAX: I was just thinking, if the Gerries find us dressed in civvies it'll take quite a lot of explaining.

CARSTAIRS: If they found us in bed with each other it would take even more explaining.

FAIRFAX: Carstairs?

CARSTAIRS: Umm?

FAIRFAX: Are you a grammar school boy?

CARSTAIRS: How do you know?

FAIRFAX: You're wearing your socks in bed.

FRANCESCA GONSHAW
(Maria Recamier – 21 episodes)

While holidaying in Marbella, on Spain's southern coast, Jeremy Lloyd spotted an attractive young actress who would be offered a role that would launch her career. The actress was Francesca Gonshaw, who spent summers at her parents' house in Spain.

'During the evening, I'd run around like crazy going to nightclubs while during the day would recover with friends at the Marbella Beach Club, which is where Jeremy used to stay and I got to know him. I think Jeremy has always had an eye for pretty women and had a lovely name for me: the pocket-sized Venus because I'm so tiny.'

Francesca had just secured an agent but was spending three months in Spain. 'Jeremy said he was going back to England to begin a new TV series, whereas I was just starting out, really, and didn't know much about the industry.'

Not long after Jeremy returned to London, Francesca's agent rang telling her to come back to England because the BBC wanted to see her about a comedy pilot. 'I was young and having great fun so didn't really want to,' admits Francesca. 'I didn't even know who David Croft was at that point, but my agent wouldn't leave me alone so in the end thought it best to return.'

Francesca, like most aspiring performers, had subscribed to PCR (Production Casting Report) which provided information of upcoming television projects. Spotting that Croft was launching a new series, *'Allo 'Allo!*, she posted off a short letter (which is retained in the BBC's archives), attached a photo and offered her services if a suitable part came up in the show.

She recalls arriving at TV Centre for her audition. 'I was very young, suntanned with the shortish ra-ra skirt and was shocked when I walked in and saw Jeremy there. I didn't really know what I was doing but got the job, although I think they originally wanted Mary Stavin for the part.'

When it came to developing the character of Maria, Francesca acknowledges Croft and Lloyd's astuteness. 'Back then, I had a problem with my Rs and they noticed the way I pronounced René, for example; picking up on this, the character became "Spitting Maria" with Jeremy and David writing as many words as possible beginning with the letter "R", which is very mean. But I was very innocent and naïve and they played on that.'

Scenes showing René wiping spit off his face whenever Maria spoke within close proximity of the café owner were always well received by the audience – as were those showing Maria grabbing a stool. 'She needed the stool to reach René's lips when kissing him – those scenes were really unfair, too,' smiles Francesca. 'It wasn't a very glamorous part, really: Spitting Maria on her stool.'

Yet she'll never forget the laughs. 'From the minute we arrived for breakfast, Jeremy was there making jokes; we were like a bunch of kids. It was a happy production and everyone was great fun.'

Francesca learnt much about her craft while appearing in the wartime sitcom. 'Vicki Michelle was really motherly towards me. She'd offer advice, saying things like, "Every time you embrace René, you're not looking at the camera – you have to be aware of the camera." She was very sweet,' says Francesca, who admits being kicked out of drama school. 'I went to St Paul's Girls' School where we were taught to have opinions, but I think people at drama school thought I was too outspoken and arrogant, especially when it came to Shakespeare. But I never really lost that. I can't really remember why I was thrown out but my outspokenness must have been part of the problem.'

Francesca feels, however, that leaving drama school was fortuitous because before long her career had begun in earnest with the role of Maria. But after three series, she decided it was time to wave goodbye to Café René. 'It was nothing to do with money because at that age it was irrelevant. I was very young, just starting out and hadn't done anything else, really. The others had worked in repertory theatre and other TV shows – I hadn't. Being a young ambitious actress, I had dreams of playing Shakespeare and Ibsen; I wanted to try other things.' By now, the popular sitcom had been adapted for the stage by Lloyd and Croft and was imminently embarking on what would become a record-breaking tour; Francesca didn't want to be part of it. 'No, I didn't want to travel with the show because I'm not someone who likes touring.'

By the time she left *'Allo 'Allo!* she'd already bagged her next TV role. 'I did a workshop at the Actors' Centre in London and was offered the role of Amanda Parker in *Howards' Way* – before I'd even left *'Allo 'Allo!*.

'I was very fortunate because things happened pretty quickly. Soon after appearing in the *'Allo 'Allo!* pilot I got offered the role of Arsinoe in the mini-series, *The Cleopatras*. I was on a roll after that and very lucky,' says Francesca, who also appeared in, among others, *Biggles*, *Crossroads* and *The Russ Abbot Show*.

Francesca doesn't regret leaving the wartime sitcom and questions whether playing such a memorable character so early in her career might have had a negative impact. 'Appearing in the series was a fantastic experience but it was very hard leaving Maria behind. She was a very liked, well-known character. There is huge snobbishness in the industry in England, which is a shame, and I think it held me back. I wasn't seen as a genuine contender for more serious roles in films, which was unfair because I think I had the ability.'

Soon after leaving *'Allo 'Allo!* Francesca attended art school and subsequently switched careers. 'I was making a film with Joanna Lumley and Sarah Miles and we were all in a car when I told them about how much I loved painting. They were pushing me to go to art school and so virtually overnight, I altered direction. I took my portfolio of drawings to The Byam Shaw School of Art and was offered a place.'

After studying fine art for a year, Francesca needed to earn a living and joined the staff of Miramax Films, an American entertainment firm which built a reputation for distributing independent and foreign films before being snapped up, in 1993, by Walt Disney. During her time in New York, she helped launch the firm's publishing arm with company co-founder Harvey Weinstein, working as Senior Vice President of Creative Affairs. 'But I always kept painting and drawing.'

She's since turned art into a full-time career and runs her own London studio. Although she'd quit acting by her mid-twenties, she's often asked if she'll ever return to the stage and screen. 'It's incredibly difficult. I can't face the idea of attending auditions and being rejected. The only thing I do now is paint, mainly big figurative oils which take forever.'

Looking back on her days as Maria, Francesca – who hates watching herself on screen – remembers being deluged with fan mail. Also, she recalls the day she visited the Chelsea and Westminster Hospital to see a specialist. 'When I left I was handed an envelope and thought, "Gosh, that was quick with the bill." I opened it and it was from a surgeon who'd been with a patient when I arrived. Apparently, he'd loved the show and had this thing about me. The note was so sweet. Some time later, we went to a big dinner but he had this preconception of me. People often thought I was like Maria, forgetting that I played a character. I'm not that stupid, naïve little innocent and sometimes people are disappointed because they like that; a similar thing happened with *Howards' Way*.'

Overall, Francesca – who in 1992 collaborated and starred in Peter Gabriel's Grammy award-winning music video, 'Digging the Dirt' – enjoyed her time on *'Allo 'Allo!*. 'They were wonderful people to work with and it was a funny programme. It was a great platform.'

The Nicked Airmen

The British airmen have been captured whilst trying to escape in a submarine.

CARSTAIRS: I'll tell you what, Fairfax, we could cut our rubber suits up into strips, tie them together into a sort of elastic band, secure them to the pillar and jump out the window.

FAIRFAX: But we wouldn't have any clothes on.

CARSTAIRS: Good point.

FAIRFAX: And if we went running around the countryside without uniforms we could be shot as spies.

CARSTAIRS: I've got St Michael on my Y-fronts.

FAIRFAX: The Nazis are not interested in religion.

SUE HODGE
(Mimi Labonq – 62 episodes)

The cheeky, diminutive blonde waitress Mimi Labonq joined the staff of Café René in the fourth series and couldn't have been more different than her predecessor, Maria Recamier. They may have been similar in height, but Mimi was far more aggressive with her in-your-face, have-a-go approach to life.

'She's just like me, really,' jokes Sue Hodge, who played the character in 62 episodes. A real toughie who didn't shirk her responsibilities, Mimi found herself in some tricky predicaments, like the time she hung upside-down from the café door as a Patagonian fruit bat! 'David said it would be a wonderful shot if I could do it. Scaffolding was erected, and when David suggested having crew members hold my legs, I refused, claiming not only were my abdominal muscles really strong, but I'd be able to hook my feet around one of the scaffolding bars and simply uncurl. So that's what I did and David was very pleased.'

He was more concerned, though, when a stunt in a cornfield outside the Norfolk market town of Swaffham didn't go to plan. Sue recalls the afternoon she played the flying nun. 'I don't have any fear, which is just as well because I always agreed to do daft things like attach myself to a crane as a flying nun.'

A stunt-double had been engaged to carry out the lion's share of the sequence with Sue being filmed for the opening of the scene which involved being around four feet in the air. 'I was flapping my arms and kicking my legs for what seemed like a long time. Thinking they must have filmed long enough, I stopped but David started waving his arms in a circular gesture for me to continue. The crane driver thought it was his cue to drive off, so he raised the crane and began driving down the lane. I was hanging off the end, ever so high, flying across the cornfield. I could see the rest of the cast disappearing into the background but before they did everyone started to panic. David rushed across the lane, shouting, "Frightfully sorry, Hodge, are you OK?" What a day that was.'

After impressing David Croft while reading for the part at his home in London's Regent's Park, Sue Hodge was offered what would become her biggest TV role. When it came to finding the right style for Mimi early on in her screen life, the make-up designer dreamt up the idea of the golden wig.

'The designer thought it would be fun because I was going to play a soliciting tart and the image of the wig – which reminded me of a poodle stuck on my head – would fit that part of the character,' explains Sue. 'As I walked out of make-up wearing it, David Croft said, "Oh, gosh, I wasn't sure if it was Betty Grable or

Betty Boop." He loved it and thought the wig – which never moved and seemed like it was banged on with nails – worked well. He said that if it was OK with me, he was going to keep it because it made me different from the rest of the girls, who were dark with long, cascading hair.' Sue didn't have any objections. 'It was fine with me. In fact, my own hair was shoulder-length and blonde so almost the same as the wig, other than having it in the French style which looked like bread rolls were stuck on the side of my head.'

As Sue clocked up more episodes, she settled into the character. 'Mimi grew into a comfortable, natural character whereas she'd been a bit aggressive at the beginning. But she was incredibly volatile, although always the kind of person you'd want around if the chips were down.'

Such tenacity is a trait Sue has shown throughout her career. Having always wanted to tread the boards, she trained at the Bird College, Sidcup, Kent. 'You learn most from getting out there in front of an audience, something I did from a young age. I made my professional debut in panto in *Jack And The Beanstalk* at 15 and before reaching 18 had appeared on TV in various programmes, including *The Dick Emery Show*. Dick was like a father to me. He'd give advice and try to help make my performance better.'

Sue played child parts in Emery's sketches. In one, she was dressed as a bridesmaid. 'I was just starting to develop boobs but because my character was much younger, an elastic bandage was wrapped around me. I had no shape left. So, from a young age, I discovered what you have to do for your art!'

She plied her trade on stage and screen, but her big break was landing the part of Mimi. David Croft saw Sue playing Peaseblossom, a fairy servant in *A Midsummer Night's Dream*. 'Five months later, my agent phoned me in Colchester, where I was appearing in a play. She asked me to return to London to see David Croft. But being the opening night of the play, I wanted to attend the after-show party and asked if he could see me another time? My agent was furious and insisted I return. I was so disappointed, but can you imagine asking someone like David Croft to reschedule?'

Luckily, Sue took her agent's advice and returned to meet David and Jeremy Lloyd. 'After offering me the role of Mimi, David told me the months I needed to be available. I asked if I could just check my diary, which made him laugh. But I left with a bundle of scripts and within a couple of months had joined the cast – an event which changed my life. Obviously, I had no idea the series would become such a major part of my career.'

Being recognized for appearing in one of the UK's most popular sitcoms happened almost instantaneously. 'The day after my first episode was screened,

I went to my local cheese shop and was mobbed,' says Sue. 'Initially, I found it hard to cope because I'd never experienced anything like it. People passing shouted "Mimi!" while others wanted to stop and chat. It took a while before I felt comfortable dealing with the attention.'

When Series 9, the final season, drew to a close, Sue, although ready to move on, was incredibly sad. 'I couldn't imagine getting up the following week and not travelling to the studio or seeing my friends; it was a weird feeling. It had been a special time in my life; it had felt like being part of the biggest and longest-running party ever. There were other wonderful jobs and will be in the future, but I don't think they'll ever be as special as *'Allo 'Allo!* – it was a magical time and I thank the lord I was part of it.'

Sue keeps in touch with most of the cast and occasionally attends memorabilia shows around Europe with members of the team. Sue and her husband, Keith, run their own production company, Maxon UK, and have taken cast members to various fairs around the world.

'*'Allo 'Allo!* is a sitcom which could be revived,' suggests Sue, whose other credits include roles in stage shows such as *Don't Dress For Dinner* at the Apollo Theatre in Shaftesbury Avenue and Duchess Theatre in Drury Lane as well as *Arms And The Man* for the New Shakespeare Company which took her to Spain, Germany, Italy and the Middle East. 'The cast would be up for it. We could focus on the café post-war. I'm sure it would be welcomed back. When we recorded *The Return Of 'Allo 'Allo!* for BBC2 in 2007, it attracted the channel's biggest audience.'

Playing Mimi led to Sue's own stage show, *Mimi And The Boy*, which she has toured with her husband. 'It's a mixture of comedy, music and the story of *'Allo 'Allo!*. We've been taking it around the country, abroad and on cruise ships since 2004. We've also performed at charity events, raising money for worthwhile causes.'

Sue does panto each year and makes the occasional screen appearance. 'I'm still out there hunting for something as good as *'Allo 'Allo!* but don't think anything will better it. But if that's the case, I'll still die a very happy person for having been part of such a classic sitcom.'

The Camera In The Potato

General Von Klinkerhoffen has been stood up by Helga so is looking for another woman to take her place at his table. Edith offers her services.

EDITH: Good evening, General. *(Lifting her skirt as she raises her leg onto the chair next to him)* I understand you fancy a little sophisticated company to while away a leisurely hour? A man like you should always have at his side a beautiful woman.

GENERAL: I agree, but sometimes the roulette wheel of life throws up the odd zero.

EDITH: Of course, I do not sit with ordinary soldiers – although they crave my company.

GENERAL: Hmm. When it is wartime, men a long way from home get very desperate.

EDITH: Are you very desperate, General?

GENERAL: Not yet. You, over here. (Beckons to René) It's very old and flat.

RENÉ: Really, it's one of our best vintages.

GENERAL: Not the wine, the woman.

THE GERMANS

The Germans controlling Nouvion were headed up by ruthless General Von Klinkerhoffen, who resided at the Château. At junior staff college he was deemed a hot-head because whenever a fancy dress ball was arranged, he'd dress as Attila the Hun. Possessing a fiery temperament, he thought nothing of ordering the shooting of French 'peasants' if locals showed any defiance or stood in the way of his plans.

Reporting to Von Klinkerhoffen was the ineffective Colonel Von Strohm, the town's commandant, who was married to Rosa, although he hadn't spoken to her for at least three years. Not the kind of man to stand beside you when the going got tough, the acquisitive German from the Black Forest was more interested in looking after number one and discovering what pleasures the girls at the café could provide with the help of wet sticks of celery, egg whisks and flying goggles!

If there was anyone at German HQ with an inkling of guilt or remorse for the pain and suffering the war was causing, particularly to the residents of Nouvion and a certain café proprietor in particular, it was Lieutenant Gruber. He tried his best at playing the German soldier but wasn't cut out for a rough-and-ready military life – especially on the Russian Front, where he served before his arrival in Nouvion.

An Enigma Variation

Edith comes into the café with a rather fancy new hat.

EDITH: Oh René, look. Is it not beautiful? I could not resist it. It was the best one in the window of Madame Lenare's.

RENÉ: How much did it cost?

EDITH: What does it matter now that we are rich. René, I have been thinking why do we not buy a new car?

RENÉ: What use do we have for a car? Anyway, we have an old one rotting in the shed.

EDITH: But it does not go and I know you have been thinking of changing it.

RENÉ: What makes you say this?

EDITH: I heard you saying to Yvette only last week, 'I cannot wait to get rid of the old banger.'

The gay Lieutenant, who lived in quarters at the Château and had a maid called Veronique, was expelled from art school before working in an art gallery and, later, becoming a window-dresser. The loves of his life were his little tank, Hubert – driven by the unseen Clarence – and René, who he took a shining to from day one. Captain Geering, who was always a beat behind everyone else – rather like Corporal Jones in *Dad's Army* – was the Colonel's rather easy-going former assistant who had once had his jackboots confiscated because he refused to kick a peasant.

When Hans disappeared to England, Private Helga Geerhart – who'd always announce visitors to the Colonel's office at the top of her voice – grasped the opportunity for a little more limelight. The blonde bombshell of the German army was a vampish temptress who'd do whatever it took to get a slice of the action or a share of the proceeds from selling the *Fallen Madonna With The Big Boobies*.

Daughter of a poor Bavarian strudel chopper, she lived above a bakery and with her shapely figure – which she relished showing off by stripping to increasingly elaborate underwear – soon became pin-up of the Tank Corp. She was much more than the Colonel's secretary and often in the thick of the action, although much of her time was spent with Herr Flick, with whom she had an 'enigmatic' relationship.

GUY SINER
(Lieutenant Hubert Gruber – 85 episodes)

'It was one of those extraordinary days in an actor's life,' says American-born Guy Siner when reflecting on the day he was offered the role of effeminate Lieutenant Gruber.

'Not only was I appearing in a London play but in the middle of a TV show, too. I can't remember the titles but was snowed under with work.' To top off a busy day, he'd just recorded a voice-over with Richard Briers. 'Later on, my agent called and said David Croft, with whom I'd never worked before, wanted me to go along and discuss a pilot programme – which turned out to be *'Allo 'Allo!*.'

After receiving a script, Guy sat down to read it and within seconds was enjoying the humour emanating from every page. 'But I did feel a certain amount of trepidation, wondering if it was going to work. I remember sitting in the foyer at Television Centre with the script. My eyebrows were somewhat close to my hairline, which I had back then, because I was thinking seriously about how it would work. Of course, if anyone could make it succeed, David Croft could, but the idea of humour based around Germans and the Gestapo made one question if it was in the best possible taste – but I needn't have worried.

'In some respects, *'Allo 'Allo!* was a send-up of *Secret Army*. On the first day of rehearsals, I told co-writer Jeremy Lloyd that I thought it broad-minded of the BBC to allow him and David to send-up one of their sacred programmes. He joked, "For god's sake, don't tell them, they haven't noticed yet!"

'But we weren't making fun of the war, we were sending up the genre of telling the war through films. Sadly, I don't think *'Allo 'Allo!* could be made now because of the ghastly politically correct attitudes which pervade our country, where we dare not offend anyone. The only letters I received regarding my character being German were appreciative. I speak German so didn't have any complaints about my accent.'

For his interview, Guy was ushered upstairs by Susie Belbin, then Croft's production manager. 'I read to David and he pretty much offered me the part of Gruber there and then. I walked out of the room with the job.'

One of the main topics of discussion before rehearsals started was the character's sexuality and how that should be portrayed, as Guy recalls. 'It was written as a gay character and I had a conversation with David and Jeremy at the beginning. I remember saying, "This is a very delicate character so do you mind if I play it very straight and genuine – or do you want a Mr Humphries from *Are You Being Served*? If you do, I'm not the right person."' Much to Guy's relief, Croft and Lloyd wanted Gruber played exactly how he'd envisaged it. 'They wanted him to be truthful, gentle and delicate. I remember David saying, "There will be occasions when you swing your handbag, but we don't want that to be a feature of the man."'

A scene from the pilot, which remains one of Guy's favourites from the entire series, made viewers aware of Gruber's strong feelings towards René. 'The "Matches" scene was based entirely on the fact that he was gay. "Are you one of them?" he's asked before replying with the fantastic punchline, "Well, it was very lonely on the Russian Front"; he misunderstood René's secret code word and thought he was asking him out.'

The adroit piece of writing is regarded among many *'Allo 'Allo!* aficionados as one of the best scenes in the entire sitcom and certainly induced uproarious laughter among the studio audience. 'They couldn't stop when we recorded the scene. In fact, David had to halt the recording because the audience wouldn't quieten down. It was a wonderful piece of writing and from that moment I knew we had a potential success.'

It wasn't long before Guy started receiving feedback from viewers. 'I got many letters from gay people congratulating me on the way I played Gruber. I was pleasantly surprised because I expected letters from people who enjoyed dressing in leather asking for bits of underwear and such like, but fortunately I never had any of that. People thanked me for not making fools of them. If you think back, gay characters were often the objects of ridicule – over-the-top humour. There was a time when you had to have loose wrists and be a screaming queen to get laughs as a gay character on TV; Gruber didn't do any of that, he just happened to fancy René. He was sweetly in love with him and there are some great scenes spotlighting his subtle advances and René's reactions.'

Guy will never forget a particular conversation concerning the way he'd portrayed the German lieutenant. 'One of my closest friends said to me, "I've never told you this, but I'm so grateful for your character, Gruber, because it gave me permission to admit to myself how I felt and that it was all right." He's gay and being quite young at the time, it moved him that here was a character basically saying it was OK. It moved me to tears when he told me, realising how much it meant to him. I'm sure there were lots of people who felt that way. For the first time, really, a gay character in a comedy series had been allowed to be gay without being a figure of ridicule.'

When he joined the cast, Guy didn't know any other cast member. It wasn't until Hilary Minster arrived on the scene as General Von Klinkerhoffen that he was reunited with an actor with whom he'd worked. 'I'd appeared in an episode of *Secret Army* with Hilary. It transpired that we'd both played Germans in that,' says Guy, who had fun not only making *'Allo 'Allo!* but driving around in his little tank. 'It's really an armoured car and I got the chance to drive it, although most of the time the owner was behind the wheel. It was easy to steer, just like driving a car. The only awkward thing was that you had limited vision. But it was a wonderful old vehicle and although it had a new body, the chassis survived the Battle of the Bulge.'

Remarkably, fan mail is still received for the vehicle. 'Hubert's little tank became better known than me,' laughs Guy. 'One chap wrote explaining he was having trouble with his neighbour parking a car outside his driveway and wondered whether I'd bring my little tank and move it?'

Thankfully, no mishaps occurred whilst using the armoured car in the series. 'I'm quite a decent driver and was very careful, aware that it was a museum piece,' explains Guy, who does recall an array of humorous moments while making the series, including a scene in 'A Fishy Send Off', the penultimate episode of Series 9, where Gruber and the Colonel wear false suicide teeth. 'That was wonderful and is endlessly played on Youtube. It was hysterical because it took so long to shoot; there was take after take because we couldn't get through it. Firstly, no one could understand a thing Richard Marner was saying. Then, we'd do a take and there would be a terrible rustling noise. David Croft would shout, "Cut!" and it turned out to be the script supervisor laughing so much that the script in her hand was shaking which the sound man was picking up. Next, we'd have camera shake because the cameraman was in hysterics; it was so hard getting through the scene.'

In reality, there are too many memorable moments to single out favourites, although the popular matches scene in the pilot takes some beating. But breathing down the neck of that is one involving Guy acting with a true comedy great:

the interrogation of Monsieur Alfonse. 'The reason I've picked it is because of Kenneth Connor. I remember thinking while shooting it that there I was standing on a stage at the BBC playing a two-hander with one of the greatest comedy actors we've ever had – a man I grew up watching in the *Carry On* films. It was a wonderful feeling.

'Since *'Allo 'Allo!*, I've lived in Hollywood for ten years and worked with some big stars but it was just a wonderful moment in my career. I miss Kenneth: he was a wonderful man and a consummate comedian.' But no sooner have you thought of one amusing scene than another hilarious situation springs to mind, such as the episode in which Lieutenant Gruber, Colonel Von Strohm and others sit around the table at the back of Café René with paper bags over their heads. 'Oh, that was hysterical and so beautifully timed. It was an absurd little joke but worked perfectly – but that was David Croft's genius.'

In the opening episodes of the first series, Croft and Lloyd watched proceedings intently before gradually writing scenes which exploited the actors' strengths. 'They didn't know me from Adam in the beginning, they'd just seen something they liked. But by the time we were halfway through the first series, David and Jeremy were writing dialogue for me – as for the entire cast. Comedy is difficult by definition, but the character wasn't particularly tough to play. Very quickly, I assimilated myself into him and he became part of me. As soon as I put the uniform on, I was Gruber.'

When the sitcom eventually reached its climax with the Allied troops arriving in Nouvion, there was inevitable sadness but a realisation that it couldn't go on forever. 'I'm sure it had run its course – after all, we'd lasted nearly twice as long as the war itself! If I'd been asked to do more I would probably have agreed. But by the same token, one felt that the time had really come and it was nice to move on to other things.'

Although it's nearly 20 years since the end of Series 9, Guy is still asked about Gruber and the show almost on a daily basis. 'The letters still pour in, and because it was good family viewing I get fan mail from kids who weren't born when we finished the series, let alone started it, and say they've become fans after discovering the programme on their own or after being shown it by their parents. *'Allo 'Allo!* was the show that made my face known in the world of TV. I've been stopped in the street from New York to Sydney, even once whilst I was wearing a suit and sunglasses. It has worldwide appeal.

'We were so lucky that it caught the public mood and that it's continued; one would think it would date, but it hasn't. I hate seeing myself on TV because I always think I could have improved my performance. But I love watching my friends, so occasionally put on an episode.'

Born in America, Guy was five when his English-born mother brought him to Britain to receive an education in the UK. After schooling, he trained at the Webber-Douglas Academy before working in the theatre and making early TV appearances in shows like *Z Cars*, *Doctor Who* and, ironically, an episode of the drama, *Secret Army*.

After *'Allo 'Allo!* had ended its run, upon finishing a six-week cabaret based on the work of Noël Coward at Raffles Hotel, Singapore, in 1994 Guy moved to America. Wanting to make films and try something new, he stayed in Los Angeles for eight years, appearing in 16 films, including *Lost Highway*, *Playing God* and *Pirates Of The Caribbean*, and numerous TV shows, such as *Seinfeld*, *Knots Landing*, *Diagnosis Murder* and *Martial Law*.

Guy returned to England in 2003 to be near his mother. 'I felt I couldn't justify being 5,000 miles away with her reaching her 80s. I am still working as an actor in films, TV and theatre, both at home and abroad, but am now mostly involved with writing and producing my own movie projects.'

Although Guy remains very busy, he'll always be proud of *'Allo 'Allo!*. 'Gruber is definitely my favourite screen character. I always say that he's a much nicer man than I am. He was a lovely person and I miss him deeply, even after all these years.'

The Airmen De-nicked

Yvette comes downstairs into the café dressed as a school child.

RENÉ: Yvette, you are supposed to be serving. Why are you wearing the uniform of Nouvion Grammar School?

YVETTE: Shhh! There is a gown, a mortar board and a cane.

RENÉ: Oh, I cannot go upstairs with you now we are open.

YVETTE: No, these clothes are so we can run away together and find happiness.

RENÉ: We cannot leave the area without a pass.

YVETTE: We can say that you are my headmaster and that we are on a nature ramble.

RENÉ: No, I cannot let you take the risk, Yvette, but hang on to the outfit!

KIM HARTMAN
(Private Helga Geerhart – 85 episodes)

It was a fortuitous phone call which introduced actress Kim Hartman to the character who would dominate not only her TV career but her life ever since. After completing a voiceover in London's White City, just around the corner from BBC Television Centre, Kim headed for the nearest phone box. 'I phoned David Croft and asked if we could meet for coffee. He replied, "I haven't got time for coffee, darling, but why don't you come in and read for a part?" And that was it, my involvement with Helga had begun.'

Kim first met David Croft at Coventry's Belgrade Theatre prior to studying drama at London's Webber-Douglas Academy. 'To become a member of Equity, you had to work for 40 weeks on a provisional level. So I got a job at the Belgrade Theatre as a student ASM (assistant stage manager), earning about £1.50 a week. I was halfway through the 40-week period, during which I'd painted scenery, made tea, ironed costumes – everything.'

Croft was at the Belgrade Theatre directing a musical version of H. G. Wells' novel, *Ann Veronica*, for which he'd penned the lyrics; an ambitious Kim decided to grasp the opportunity. 'I pursued David relentlessly the entire time, pleading with him to make me an ASM when the production moved to the West End. Of course, he couldn't because Equity wouldn't allow it but we kept in touch.'

The discussion in David Croft's office at Television Centre that Thursday afternoon turned to the subject of accents, with the writer/producer enquiring about Kim's German accent. 'I told him it was brilliant, which was a little white lie because it was terrible; in fact, I began the series speaking like I was Swedish, apparently. After a few days rehearsing for the pilot, David approached me and said, quietly, "You need to re-think your accent." My heart nearly stopped, thinking he'd recast me.'

In the pilot, Helga featured briefly. 'I was delighted just to be involved, but with only a couple of small scenes for me, I didn't know if the character would make it into the series.' But Kim needn't have worried. 'I was concerned because she didn't really say much, other than "Yes, Herr Flick" a few times, so I tried to make my performance as interesting as possible, ensuring each of the "Yes, Herr Flick" replies was different.'

Suitably impressed with her performance, albeit brief in terms of screen time, Croft retained Helga; during the nine series that followed she became a pivotal character, famous for her sexy and, at times, outrageous underwear and willingness to flaunt her beauty when necessary.

Kim recalls the fun she had choosing Helga's costumes. 'I loved that aspect of the character,' she enthuses. 'The stocking and suspenders developed as the show progressed. It reached the point where before starting a new season, I'd receive a call from the costume designer. She'd say, "I've been through the scripts and we've got six scenes where you'll be wearing corsets. Shall we have a leopard-skin version – or a diamante?" We'd meet and end up crying with laughter thinking of the most outrageous outfits possible.'

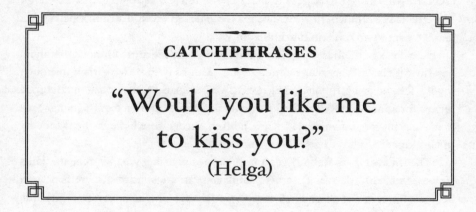

CATCHPHRASES

"Would you like me
to kiss you?"
(Helga)

One of Kim's suggestions incorporated diamanté and fishnet arms. 'The costume designer would always create something more outrageous than I'd imagined. My favourite outfit had a leopard-skin panel down the front, fishnet arms and fringing hanging beneath the arms.'

An outfit Kim squeezed in to which she won't forget in a hurry happened in a scene where she stripped for General Von Klinkerhoffen at the Château; it was certainly a tight fit. 'I got into it after lots of heaving and it brought me down to a 17-inch waist.' By the time the episode was later recorded, Kim had been squashed inside the outfit much of the day. 'On the Sunday, I bent over to tie my shoe and slipped a disc; I've always wondered if it was the result of squeezing myself into a 17-inch waist; at the time, though, vanity prevailed and I had fun trying to get into the corset to make my waist that small. They were very structured, big and stiff which is probably why I didn't mind wearing the contraptions – I never felt undressed in them.'

One of Helga's trademarks was her long blonde mane, usually plaited but occasionally free-flowing, especially when she adopted her seductress mode to wheedle information out of her victim. Kim wore a wig throughout the show and is grateful for that. 'My hair was blonde but short. I never looked anything like Helga out of costume which meant I didn't suffer typecasting.'

Kim thought that opting for a wig would make her life easier, and it was exactly the opposite because the make-up department wanted to dress it, in terms of putting it into the correct style for the character, once it was on her head. This meant they could incorporate bits of Kim's natural hair from around the hairline to help conceal the join. 'So I was always the one called at 6am for make-up when everyone else strolled in at 7.30!,' she says, smiling, before explaining about Helga's lips. 'I tried getting them as big, red and square as possible – a bit like Rita Hayworth would wear. The make-up designer and I would have a good laugh trying to make them big and jammy.'

Helga was particularly popular with members of the armed forces, prisoners and little girls. 'It's a strange combination,' laughs Kim. 'Two girls wrote such lovely letters, we kept in touch. One lived in Australia and we exchanged letters for about 20 years. When I was working over there a few years ago, we met. Another fan, now married with children, meets me whenever I'm working in Nottingham.

The character of Helga lives on in the form of regular TV repeats, talks Helga is asked to deliver on cruise ships and fan conventions; there is even a dedicated Helga and Herr Flick website. Although she acknowledges that the German private is an important and valued part of her life, Kim is glad that minus the wig and make-up, she's rarely recognized as Helga. 'Occasionally I attend charity dos in character. As soon as people spot me in uniform, they'll shout, "Oh, it's Helga!" They make quite a fuss. It's lovely in short bursts and I enjoy it enormously, but if I was being recognized like that all the time it would be wearing.'

The relationship between Helga and Herr Flick of the Gestapo was a source of much hilarity in the show. Although she appeared to be genuinely smitten by Otto Flick, you sometimes suspected Helga of scheming in an attempt to look after number one – particularly when it came to getting her cut of any monies from the sale of the Fallen Madonna. 'I think Helga regarded Herr Flick as a bit scary and dangerous, although she must have been attracted to him. But she was keen on grabbing a bit of action, ensuring that she'd feathered her nest by the end of the war.'

Working with Richard Gibson, alias Otto Flick, was a scream, says Kim. Many times she struggled to contain her laughter while filming scenes. 'It was a nightmare because he was so funny. He had this amazing semi-outraged intensity all the time as Herr Flick which frequently made me want to cry with laughter.

When he was being serious and acting the part, I found it difficult continuing the scene. Once, the camera focused on Richard with just a quarter of my face visible. He was saying something terribly seriously but from my profile you could see my cheekbones rising because I'm grinning like mad at what he's doing: sometimes, I had to stick my fingernails into the palm of my hands to stop myself laughing.'

When Richard Gibson decided to leave before the ninth and final series, a valuable dynamic within the show's fabric was lost. Kim Hartman agrees. 'I got on well with David Janson but there was such a special chemistry between Richard and me that was obviously going to be missed. We were a good double-act and have remained close friends.'

Puddings Can Go Off

René and Yvette are locked in an embrace when Officer Crabtree walks in.

OFFICER CRABTREE: Good Moaning! Oh, I see you were having a curse and a kiddle. I will turn a blonde eye.

RENÉ: What is it that you want?

OFFICER CRABTREE: I have for you two expleeding Christmas poddings.

RENÉ: I suppose they are down your trousers as usual?

OFFICER CRABTREE: Do not be ridoculous. (He reveals two puddings tied around his shoulders under his coat) Mind the hilly, it is very prockily and do not drop them or they will go off bong.

Appearing in such a high profile show gave Kim's career an enormous boost. 'Helga got me known and soon I was being offered many excellent and varied parts, which are still coming in to the present day, particularly in theatre. Highlights include playing Jacqueline in *Don't Dress For Dinner*, which took me to New Zealand as well as the West End for a year, and Josie in *Steaming* which, again, took me to New Zealand.'

On TV, Kim has appeared in, among others, *The Brittas Empire*, *Casualty* and the comedy, *15 Storeys High*; she also played Mrs Rawlinson, an eccentric science teacher, in *Grange Hill* for three years. Since the 1980s, Kim has also run Quinton Arts, a theatre production company, with her husband, John.

Reflecting on her time in *'Allo 'Allo!*, Kim rates Helga as her favourite small screen character by a mile. 'If when I attended the casting I'd known that it would become such an enormous part of my life, I'd never have got the job because I'd have been too nervous,' she says, smiling. 'I loved playing Helga.'

SAM KELLY
(Captain Hans Geering – 23 episodes, plus one voice-over)

Sam Kelly was surprised when offered the role of Captain Geering and didn't have to think twice about accepting. 'I'd never worked with David Croft or Jeremy Lloyd before. The offer came through my agent and, fortunately, I didn't have to see anyone.

'Gorden was the only person I knew in the cast, having worked with him in theatre at Sheffield, and I believe he suggested me to David Croft.' And he's glad Gorden did. 'As soon as I read the first script, I knew it was going to be well received; it was a hysterical piece of writing.'

One of the great pleasures playing the German captain, says Sam, was working with David. 'He was a terrific comedy director. If he didn't like something, he'd simply say, "No!". But if he did like it he wouldn't say anything, just laugh. So if he laughed at you, you knew it was right.'

A question Sam is asked more often than most – even now, years later – is what he actually said instead of 'Heil Hitler' every time Captain Geering saluted? 'It was my idea to be late, like Clive Dunn was on parade in *Dad's Army*. Not that I thought about Clive, it just happened, really.' Geering was slow on the uptake and couldn't be bothered saying all of Hitler's name so just uttered the second syllable, 'tler'. 'When I first did it, David Croft didn't stop me so I carried on. It became part of his character and cost me a fortune in stamps writing to people telling them what it meant.'

People have puzzled over the utterance for years. 'Barry Took, while presenting *Points Of View*, said that it was German for ditto, which he must have made up. After that, some people even denied that what I told them was correct. Most people thought I said "club", which is what it sounded like. The people who knew were few and far between. Whenever I was stopped in the street, this was the question they were burning to ask.'

When he first donned the Captain's uniform, Sam was uncertain about what voice to adopt. 'During the first week of rehearsal, I didn't quite know what I was going to do with the character and then Gorden Kaye suggested using a back-of-the-throat voice; I'm forever grateful to him for offering that piece of advice because it worked.'

Playing the doltish German led to a steady flow of fan letters. 'They were mainly from young boys intrigued by the stupidity of a character who behaved like a child half the time.'

Captain Geering found himself in some awkward situations but one scene Sam remembers most vividly involved a cuckoo clock striking four o'clock while shoved down the front of his trousers. The cuckoo had to emerge four times so the visual effects team supplied Sam with a piece of equipment. 'I had a small plunger in my pocket which I had to press. Sadly, the first time it didn't work properly, but the audience laughed nonetheless. Manfully, I carried on with the surprised expression I'd have had if everything worked as planned. We then re-shot the scene and all was fine. This time, the audience weren't expecting the movement inside the trousers and fell about laughing even more.'

Uproarious laughter wasn't uncommon in the TV studio on recording night, says Sam. 'One episode, we had to stop a woman laughing. She was relentless throughout the recording and eventually had to be stopped because David knew he wouldn't have been able to edit the show with her screaming constantly.'

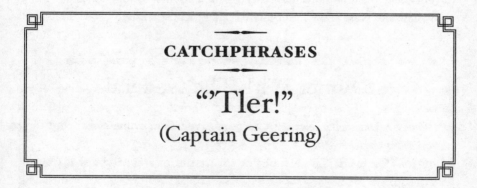

CATCHPHRASES

"'Tler!"
(Captain Geering)

Looking back over the myriad characters he's brought to life on screen, Sam ranks Geering high up the pecking order in terms of enjoyment. 'It's close to being my favourite, but I'll never forget appearing in *Bleak House* for the BBC in 1985. It was around nine 50-minute episodes with Diana Rigg and Denholm Elliott. I played Mr Snagsby, a nice part, and that is probably joint with Hans in favourite TV roles.'

Sam trained at LAMDA after working for three years in the civil service in Liverpool. He graduated from drama school in 1967 and was soon spotted speaking one line as a newspaper reporter in an episode of *Emergency – Ward 10*.

Four years of rep work around the UK followed, including spells at Liverpool, Sheffield and Lincoln. 'I became an actor because I wanted to be in the theatre, so for me TV work subsidizes the stage assignments. Then every now and again you get a little gem on TV which makes you realize what fun it can be.'

On the small screen, Sam's credits include a series of *The Dave Allen Show*, *The Dick Emery Show*, playing Bob Challis in *Coronation Street*, Norman in two series of *Now And Then*, Sam in three series of *On The Up*, Warren in *Porridge* and appearances in *Heartbeat*, *My Family*, *Outnumbered* and a major part in the sitcom, *Barbara*. Sam, who's also appeared in a handful of films, including two *Carry On*s and the *Porridge* movie, remains a busy actor.

Sam hung up his German uniform early in Series 4 of *'Allo 'Allo!*, although his voice was heard in an episode – explaining his disappearance from Nouvion – and he popped up once more in an instalment from Season 7, by which time Geering was working for British Intelligence. For Sam, leaving the cast behind wasn't an easy choice but he was keen to move on. 'When I first started, I only intended doing three series. Nothing changed my decision to leave because I wanted to try other things. People ask if I regret leaving and I don't; the only regret is that when the show was repeated endlessly not so long ago, hardly any of my episodes were shown, so I missed out on repeat fees.'

Dinner With The General

René is taking shelter from the RAF bombs and tries signalling them to stop with his torch.

OFFICER CRABTREE: Put out that lit or you will be shat on the spit.

RENÉ: Officer Crabtree, can you not explain to your English friends that we are on their side? If I am killed it will be the end of the Resistance in this part of France – well certainly in this doorway.

OFFICER CRABTREE: You should be grateful that the RAF bummers are still farting for freedom.

Sam enjoyed reprising the role for the solitary episode, 'Up The Crick Without A Piddle', in Series 7, although the audience reaction surprised him. 'When it came to recording the scenes in the studio, I expected people to remember who Geering was and give a big round of applause, but there was absolutely no reaction; they'd forgotten the character, I guess.'

But nothing will diminish the memories Sam holds of fun and laughter while making the sitcom. 'It was a wonderful part of my career and I'll never forget it.'

RICHARD MARNER
(Colonel Kurt Von Strohm – 85 episodes)

During the first three series, scenes involving Colonel Von Strohm usually featured Captain Geering, played by Sam Kelly, who recalls appearing with the Russian-born actor.

'He was a little bit on the grand side, but he'd had a long career and didn't want to be overlooked or ignored – he wanted to be prominent. Once he got to know me and trusted me in the part, we had a good laugh,' says Sam, who remembers Marner's predilection for horse racing. 'He was so keen on the sport that he bought a house near Newmarket race course so that he could go out early in the morning and watch the horses train.'

Born in Petrovgrad in 1921, as Alexander Molchanoff, he moved to England as a small child when his parents fled the troubles following the Russian Revolution. He completed his education at Monmouth School, after which he worked as assistant to the Russian tenor, Vladimir Rosing, at London's Royal Opera House in Covent Garden.

A brief spell in the RAF came to an end when he was invalided out, at which point he changed his name to Richard Marner and pursued an acting career. His first taste of the stage arrived on joining the casts of touring productions financed by the Arts Council.

Richard's early career focused on the stage, including a plaudit-winning performance as Dracula, before he started appearing on screen. Often cast in military roles, film credits began with 1950's *Highly Dangerous* followed by, among others, *Appointment With Venus*, *The African Queen* (alongside Humphrey Bogart and Katharine Hepburn), *The Spy Who Came In From The Cold*, *Reach For The Sky*, *Ice Cold In Alex*, the James Bond film, *You Only Live Twice*, and *The Sum Of All Fears*. On TV, he turned up in shows such as *Danger Man*, *Suspense*, *Crane*, *The Saint*, and *MacKenzie*.

Richard's daughter, Helen Molchanoff, says Richard adored *'Allo 'Allo!* and was thrilled to be a part of the sitcom. When it came to learning lines each week, Helen and her mother helped Richard. 'We often knew them before he did,' laughs Helen, who's so pleased her father finally got his big break before the end of his life. 'Usually, people have the break in their youth but he had the joy of making a real name for himself in latter life which meant he could enjoy it. He always wanted to be a comedian so it was fantastic that finally after years of playing serious roles, like KGB men and Gestapo officers, he could bring some humour to his work.'

Richard died in March 2004, aged 82.

HILARY MINSTER
(General Erich Von Klinkerhoffen – 60 episodes)

Born in London in 1944, Hilary's busy stage and screen career included many TV character roles, including appearances in *Crossroads*; *Tinker, Tailor, Soldier, Spy; Man About The House; The Duchess Of Duke Street; Poldark* and several episodes of *Secret Army*. He also appeared twice in *Doctor Who* and had a major role, as Yagon, in an episode of *The Tomorrow People* in 1978. On the big screen, he worked on such films as *Battle Of Britain, Cry Freedom* and *The Girl In A Swing*.

In the early 1980s, Hilary was presenter and producer of Central Television's current affairs programme, *Here And Now*.

He died in November 1999, aged 55.

THE GESTAPO

The much-despised Gestapo was the official secret police of Nazi Germany. Formed in 1934, the Gestapo was under the administration of SS leader Heinrich Himmler when war broke out in 1939. Often feared and seldom trusted, there was an air of uneasiness among the rank and file of the German army whenever the black-uniformed Gestapo arrived on the scene.

The same edginess could be detected around the streets of Nouvion, inside Café René and among the offices of German HQ whenever Herr Flick, donning his obligatory black leather coat – his peculiar sidekick, Herr Smallhausen, in tow – appeared on the scene.

Always ready to inform people that his godfather was none other than Himmler, Flick – an orphan raised by nuns – had power bestowed by other people; he wasn't in his position on merit, he was there because of his godfather. Although not the brightest star in the universe, the Gestapo officer's stark image meant people felt compelled to obey him.

Herr Flick claimed to be shy but his cold, impassive manner and inability to crack a smile did him few favours; he had little going for him, as did his assistant, Von Smallhausen, an eccentric member of the Gestapo whose only claim to fame was being a champion cross-country runner in days gone by.

RICHARD GIBSON
(Herr Otto Flick – 78 episodes, Series 1-8)

It was telling jokes with a German accent at a wedding party which brought Richard Gibson to the attention of David Croft. The producer's daughter, Jane, had tied the knot and invited friends and family to enjoy a garden party in the grounds of her parents' Norfolk home; Richard, who'd just appeared in the TV series, *The Children Of The New Forest*, with her sister, Rebecca Croft, was on the guest list and was lying on the grass enjoying the sun.

'People were telling all sorts of jokes, including utterly tasteless ones about prisoner-of-war camps; they involved German voices and I ended up doing the voice of a camp commandant,' recalls Richard, who happened to notice David and his wife conferring. 'Obviously he was planning the pilot of *'Allo 'Allo!* and thought, "Richard Gibson can do a German accent, that could be interesting."'

Croft was, indeed, interested in recruiting Richard to the pilot's cast and put a call in to the actor – unfortunately, he wasn't in when the phone rang. 'But David left a message saying, "I hope you don't mind, but I've taken the liberty of sending you a script because I think you might be suitable for one of the characters in my new pilot. Have a read and if you're interested, call me back."'

Two days later, the script flew through Richard's letterbox. Eager to read it, he tore open the envelope and settled down to see what David had in mind. 'I started reading and long before reaching the bit where Herr Flick came in, I'd forgotten momentarily that I was reading it with a view to being in it – I was so caught up in this original and very funny script.'

After reading for David and Jeremy at TV Centre, weeks past without contact from the production team; Richard assumed that either he'd been unsuccessful or the pilot had been abandoned. 'A couple of weeks later, I rang my agent asking if she'd heard anything about the project.' To Richard's astonishment, she confirmed that the role was his and that he was starting the following Monday.

'The whole process had been so low key that I hadn't realized he'd already offered me the job!'

When deciding how to transfer Herr Flick from page to screen, Richard knew how he wanted the character to look – even if no one else shared his views. 'I had in mind lots of prosthetics: false limbs, clockwork hands, glass eyes,' laughs Richard, influenced by Ronald Lacey's portrayal of bizarre, bespectacled Gestapo agent Major Toht in the 1981 film, *Raiders Of The Lost Ark.* 'I had to be reined in, though, and ended up being allowed one dodgy leg – but at least I was able to choose which one!' Opting for a false leg, however, made a rod for his own back. 'It meant having to continually use a walking stick and keeping my leg stiff, pretending it was false; but at least it made him instantly recognisable.'

Herr Flick's attire included a trademark leather coat, equally sombre-looking suit and black leather gloves. 'I never took the gloves off, which was a little touch I did for fun and it stayed with the character; having the gloves on made him look sinister.'

Among other trademarks were the character's intensity and seriousness; Richard says it was apparent from the beginning that playing the character in a deadpan manner was the way forward. But there was another reason behind this decision. 'Until I played Herr Flick I'd never done comedy before,' admits Richard, who'd always been cast in dramas. 'I didn't know how to do gags and was rather cautious about attempting them. So I tended to play it straight for that reason.'

He does, however, prefer comedy played in a straight, believable manner, and in presenting Herr Flick in this fashion created one of the sitcom's most popular and memorable characters. 'Otto thinks he's wonderful, witty, clever and the master of disguise – and he's not, he's hopeless at everything.'

There is no hesitation in confirming that Herr Flick is his favourite screen character. 'Yes, no question. He was a gift and you only get one of those characters in a lifetime.' Many of Flick's scenes were played out with Helga, to whom he was attracted. Underneath his cold, unsmiling demeanour lay a fixation for the attractive blonde private who would regularly be ordered to undress in front of him to satisfy his desires for a glimpse of Helga's stockings and suspenders. Occasionally, Herr Flick donned such undergarments. Richard laughs as he recalls the scenes. 'They were a send-up of all those films like *Cabaret* and those reflecting the decadence of Berlin in the 1930s.'

The screen relationship between the two popular characters would become a well-mined strand of comedy in the show, and their popularity remains as evident today. 'People ask us to appear as a double-act, which is great fun, and we even have our own joint fan club,' says Richard, who recently returned from an engagement on a cruise ship bound for South America. 'Kim [Hartman] and I talked about our time playing Helga and Herr Flick. We performed sketches and chatted – it was good fun.'

As professional actors, every cast member took their role seriously but there was always time to let off steam, to indulge in a little naughtiness and Richard, along with Kim Hartman and John D. Collins, were often the instigators of any pranks. 'Kim and I were always a bit hyperactive and often setting each other off. Also, we'd wind up John Louis Mansi,' smiles Richard. 'He was sweet but very anxious. Picking up on this, we'd often tell him to change in to a particular costume so that he'd appear on set in the wrong outfit. He was occasionally nervous about his lines and would always have a script near him; we'd substitute it for another so that when he came to look at it, it would be the wrong one. It was all good fun.'

Recognition follows success so as the sitcom's popularity escalated, the actors started being noticed in public. Fortunately for Richard, this didn't happen often. 'No, I wasn't recognized very much. Kim and I were able to take off our characters, hang them on a coat hanger and walk away. It was nice having the choice of being anonymous. People like Gorden and Arthur are so recognisable that they had a completely different experience; they were always massively famous but we weren't.'

All good things come to an end and despite enjoying his time on 'Allo 'Allo! immensely, Richard Gibson decided to leave the show after eight series in 1992, resulting in David Janson playing Herr Flick for the final season. It was a decision Richard had been contemplating some time. 'By this stage, David Croft wasn't writing the scripts anymore. Also, it was reaching the point where it seemed that the last two or three series were going to be the last. So when it became clear there was going to be a ninth season, I decided to call it a day because I wanted to move on.'

He admits, however, that had he known Series 9 would definitely be the end, he'd probably have pulled on the black leather coat and gloves one final time. 'I thought it was going to keep going on and on, especially when previous series were supposedly marking the end.'

Stepping into the shoes of another actor, especially when the character is well established and extremely popular, is no easy task. That was the challenge facing David Janson. 'If I'd been Jeremy Lloyd, I'd have given David a new character. If the programme was continuing beyond Series 9 perhaps they would have.' This would have afforded Janson a free rein to develop the role the way he wanted. 'Taking over Herr Flick, even though the character had undergone plastic surgery, meant David was obliged to make people think it was the same person; it's not easy when there have been so many episodes before.'

After waving goodbye to Otto, Richard could have faced the typecasting which can dog performers after leaving behind a popular character from a long-running series. He says: 'Being in something as popular as *'Allo 'Allo!* gave people reservations for a while but not to a great extent, thank goodness.'

Richard began acting as a teenager in 1970, playing Marcus in the Joseph Losey-directed film, *The Go-Between*. 'I was picked from school, which was fantastic, and followed that with a TV series, *Tom Brown's Schooldays*, so I had a flying start.'

After finishing his education, Richard enrolled at the Central School of Speech and Drama. Upon graduating, he was soon busy on TV, appearing in, among others, *Hadleigh*, *Poldark*, *The Children Of Yhe New Forest*, *Park Ranger, Penmarric* and *Wainwright's Law*. Much of his career, however, has been spent on stage, a medium he enjoys. 'In the last few years I've done more theatre than television.'

When not acting, Richard often works as a journalist on national papers. 'I've always had an interest in writing so studied it at night school. When my eldest son, Billy, was a baby, my wife, Kate, and I decided we'd each have one night a week for going out and doing something that we really wanted to do. I fancied attending a journalism class at night school because it's the career I would have followed if I hadn't become an actor.'

After paying a £12.50 fee, he completed the 12-week training course at Westminster College in the 1990s, followed by an additional course in subbing. 'IPC Magazines had a one-week work experience course which I did and that led to freelance work. I loved it and it gave me the opportunity to be around when the children were small. It's something I've continued and have worked for lots of newspapers, especially the *Guardian*.

But Herr Flick remains an important part of Gibson's working life, even though it's 20 years since he appeared in his final TV episode. 'I still receive letters. The sitcom is shown in a lot of countries; it's incredibly popular in Sweden, Denmark and Holland. It's always being repeated somewhere.'

DAVID JANSON
(Herr Otto Flick – 6 episodes, Series 9 plus 1 as Hitler)

Actor David Janson was no stranger to *'Allo 'Allo!* when asked to take on the role of Herr Flick for the final season because he'd just played a Hitler lookalike in the previous series. 'I had fun doing that. Then the stage tour went out into the provinces and Richard didn't want to do it, so I was asked if I was interested in playing Flick.'

Despite being extremely keen, David called Richard before making his decision. 'I had a chat with him. He'd done the stage show before and was ready to move on, so I jumped at the chance.'

David – who appeared with Gorden Kaye in Thames TV's 1980's series *Don't Rock The Boat* – was equally thrilled to accept the role in the final TV series, although he admits to being extremely nervous when filming the episodes. 'Richard was brilliant as Otto Flick so, yes, I was nervous about taking it on because they were big shoes to fill. It was an iconic part and well loved. On stage it was fine because you're moving around the provinces and there is a limited audience each night, but on TV it's different – there was a lot more gravitas attached to it.'

But David's job was made easier by the warm reception received from fellow cast members. 'Everyone had been doing it for ages and having so much fun; it was nice to slot in and feel totally at home. It was one of my most enjoyable TV jobs.'

One episode he remembers vividly is 'A Fishy Send Off', which saw him wearing a heavy pair of shoes: Herr Flick had a secret compartment made in the soles to conceal the remainder of his ten million francs while preparing to leg it to Argentina to escape the clutches of the Allied Forces. 'In rehearsals, we just went along with the idea of how it would work in terms of the mechanisms. But for the recording, there was a rivet in the floor and the shoes, which had a recess on the sole, attached to it. I had to ensure the shoes were locked in place so that I could lean forward – then Helga had to push me back. Kim Hartman was lovely to work with.'

Reflecting on his time, albeit short, as Herr Flick, David – whose long list of TV credits include appearances in *The Newcomers*, *Doomwatch*, *The Brothers*, *Get Some In!*, *Brush Strokes* and *Keeping Up Appearances* – says: 'It was one of those fortuitous moments when you go in for one episode and end up doing the tour and final series – I was immensely grateful.'

JOHN LOUIS MANSI
(Herr Engelbert Von Smallhausen – 63 episodes)

The diminutive actor John Louis Mansi, who died in August 2010, achieved screen prominence as Von Smallhausen, the junior Gestapo officer, who is constantly badgered and mistreated by his emotionless boss, Herr Flick.

Until joining the sitcom in the second series, Mansi's screen career had largely consisted of peripheral figures, often waiters, criminals and clerks, in a host of productions, including *Citizen James*, *Gideon's Way*, *Orlando*, *Department S*, *Tottering Towns*, *The Fenn Street Gang* and *Robin's Nest*. During his screen career, however, he had the opportunity to work with a host of top names, such as Spike Milligan, Michael Bentine, Dick Emery and Frankie Howerd.

But it's his portrayal of the eccentric, bungling Gestapo officer in *'Allo 'Allo!* for which he remains best remembered, always at Herr Flick's side and wearing not only the same style attire but having the same gammy leg. He was the perfect foil for the friendless Herr Flick and Mansi, who played the character through to the end of the series, retired soon after putting away his uniform.

Born in London, son of an Italian father and Irish mother, he served in the Merchant Navy and RAF during the war before studying at the Central School of Speech and Drama. He made his screen debut in Ealing Studio's 1952 film, *The Secret People*, starring Audrey Hepburn. With Italian blood in his veins and a mop of bushy dark hair, he was often cast in such roles as an Italian in 1952's *Hammer The Toff* and a traffic-control official experiencing the mayhem of the Mini chase in 1969's *The Italian Job*. During his career, he was to play several other foreigners in shows like the air stewardess-based sitcom, *From A Bird's Eye View*.

After leaving the cast of *'Allo 'Allo!*, John Louis Mansi enjoyed a quiet retirement in East Sussex until his death aged 83.

THE RESISTANCE

Michelle Dubois, leader of the local French Resistance, was a mainstay of the wartime sitcom and renowned for her 'Listen very carefully, I shall say this only once' catchphrase and trademark mac and beret. Dedicated to the cause, Michelle – codenamed "Blue Tit" – was prolific when dreaming up increasingly far-fetched schemes to repatriate the British airmen, most of which were destined for failure from the beginning. When not conducting Resistance business, she worked as a sub-postmistress in the next village, alongside the bakery, but upon donning her mac and beret was a hard-working, serious individual ably assisted by an equally selfless bunch of Resistance girls, most notably Henriette, her trusty assistant.

Much more dangerous were the Communist Resistance, cut-throat fighters who fought for the cause, too, but in a more brutal manner. Although a couple of girls appeared in early episodes credited as leaders, the Communists' first true chief was Denise Laroque, an old sweetheart of René's from his days back in Nantes, but when the leadership eventually came up for grabs, the husky-voiced beauty, Louise, stepped into the breach to run the band of lusty warriors.

THE FRENCH RESISTANCE

KIRSTEN COOKE
(Michelle Dubois – 82 episodes)

The sitcom spawned several catchphrases but none so memorable as, 'Listen very carefully, I shall say this only once', which was first uttered in the pilot episode by Kirsten Cooke, who played Michelle, the region's French Resistance leader. 'I said it three times during one scene. If it hadn't worked it would have been discarded, so I'm really glad I pulled it off. Even now it is what everyone wants to hear me say. Once, two children knocked on my door and asked, "Can you say it, please?" So, of course, I did.'

Strangely, many people think that because Kirsten played Michelle with a French accent, she's fluent in the language. 'I speak a little but it's hardly my second language, much to some people's surprise.'

Kirsten, who still receives fan letters, was touring in a play when David Croft invited her to read for a part in *'Allo 'Allo!*. She rushed to the BBC rehearsal rooms for the audition with Croft before dashing off to rejoin the theatre company at their next venue.

'Apparently, the reading was a formality because I phoned my agent two weeks later and she said, "Oh, yes, the role is yours." I was so pleased because it was general knowledge in the business that David had the Midas touch.'

A soon as Kirsten started reading the scenes she'd been sent prior to the audition, it became apparent how to play Michelle. 'It was clear she was a very serious person dedicated to the cause. I knew where to go with the character and must have got something right at the audition, otherwise I would not have been given the role. Successful comedy always needs a straight man or woman; I could see that was what Michelle was destined to be, and maintaining that stance created many comedic situations. I can't remember ever feeling it necessary to smile as Michelle. All her complicated plans were destined to fail, outrageous disguises disguised nothing and yet she persisted, all of which contributed to the comedy.'

Red Nick's Colonel

The Colonel and Captain Geering are tied to a post in a barn, having been caught by the Communist Resistance.

COLONEL: Hans, look at it how you will, this is a very serious situation.

CAPTAIN: Do you think they are really going to shoot us?

COLONEL: They are French. The French are very unreliable, especially after lunch.

CAPTAIN: Colonel, why are you wriggling about?

COLONEL: You will be pleased to hear I've managed to get my lighter out of my back pocket.

CAPTAIN: I thought you were trying to give up smoking?

COLONEL: I am going to burn through the ropes, untie your wrists, then you can untie me.

CAPTAIN: Oh good. I saw this in a film with Conrad Veidt.

COLONEL: Keep your voice down and stand back.

CAPTAIN: I am ready. What is the delay?

COLONEL: I'm pulling up my wick to get a big flame.

CAPTAIN: Even Conrad Veidt didn't think of that.

COLONEL: Here we go.

CAPTAIN: Ahhhhh!

COLONEL: Quiet, dummy.

CAPTAIN: You are lighting the hairs on my wrist.

COLONEL: Don't be a baby.

CAPTAIN: I'm not a baby! Ahhhh!

COLONEL: Well done, Hans, I felt the rope go.

CAPTAIN: That was the strap of my wrist watch.

COLONEL: There's someone coming. Try not to smoulder.

Throughout the series, Michelle was rarely seen without her trademark mac. 'It was very warm, so ideal when out filming on location.' Kirsten wasn't, however, so enamoured of the beret. 'It didn't do me any favours and flattened my fringe, not a great look!' Despite the beret, Kirsten enjoyed playing the role. 'It's great to get a character from scratch and not something several other actresses have already played. To make something entirely your own is a rare treat.'

One of Kirsten's abiding memories of working on *'Allo 'Allo!* is the convivial atmosphere surrounding the programme and, in particular, 'being up very early in the morning and driving along country roads in Norfolk, where all the location shots were filmed.'

She adds: 'It was good, too, that most of the cast started out on the same level, there were no huge "stars" as such, not until people like Kenneth Conner joined us. He, of course, had a marvellous CV and was delightful to work with – a genuinely funny man.'

Kirsten knew she wanted to act since she was five or six. 'My grandmother took me to a pantomime and, on another occasion, to see a production of *The Mikado*, in Brighton. I thought the actors where having a much better time than we were and decided I'd like to be up there on the stage rather than sitting in the audience. So that was that!'

She became the first family member to don greasepaint when, aged 18, she won a place at London's Webber-Douglas Academy. After graduating and completing two summer seasons in repertory theatre, Kirsten joined the company of *A Bedful Of Foreigners* at London's Apollo Theatre, working as an assistant stage manager and understudy. Within a fortnight, she had the opportunity to step into a lead role when one of the cast fell ill. 'Terry Scott and June Whitfield, the stars of the show, were very supportive,' says Kirsten. 'June gave me some very useful advice and I'd often watch her from the wings – she has perfect comedy timing.'

Having secured a good agent from that experience, Kirsten's career began to snowball and she became busy in both theatre – her first love – and TV. 'I enjoy the stage because you have the opportunity to constantly develop your role. Every show and audience is different. But TV reaches a wider audience and the medium is just as interesting.'

Her first small screen role was, coincidentally, playing a French student in *Happy Ever After*, again with Terry Scott and June Whitfield. Other TV work included *For Maddie With Love*, *Rings On Their Fingers*, *Dave Allen At Large* and *The Dawson Watch*.

Kirsten spent ten golden years working on *'Allo 'Allo!* but wasn't surprised when time was finally called at Café René. 'We were ready for it,' she says. 'It had been a fantastic experience and regular work, a luxury for any actor. But I think most of us were looking forward to getting involved with other projects.'

Nevertheless, she still felt great sadness when recording studio scenes for the closing episode, 'A Winkle In Time'. 'I felt oddly emotional. I can remember sitting in my dressing room thinking, "This is the last time I'll be at the BBC, putting this costume on and being Michelle of the Resistance." It had gone on for so long and become part of my life.'

In the acting profession, typecasting lurks in the shadows, threatening to impose itself on a performer's future prospects. But Kirsten is very matter-of-fact when talking about the subject. 'If you've had lots of exposure as one character, it's sometimes difficult for people to see you in another light. But it's up to the actor to convince otherwise. For me, appearing in the show helped my career. The success of something like *'Allo 'Allo!* – including a very popular stage version – provides a sense of recognition. People know who you are and that can only help.'

CATCHPHRASES

"Listen very carefully, I shall say this only once."
(Michelle)

After *'Allo 'Allo!* Kirsten made a TV series, *Down To Earth*, with Richard Briers, appeared in *The Upper Hand* and played Maddy the Baddy in children's programme, *Chucklevision*, which Kirsten remembers as 'brilliant fun'. She adds: 'But I haven't done much TV or theatre since; I had a young family and decided to put them first, and I'm glad I did.'

But Kirsten has appeared in *The Return Of 'Allo 'Allo!* and toured with several theatre productions, most recently as Miss Matty in the stage version of *Cranford*. 'But I shall always feel a special attachment to Michelle,' she says. 'I thought it was funny that in *The Return* ... she was still running about in her mac being very serious, obviously never quite able to shake off her wartime job.

'In recent years, although I haven't been so busy, I'm easily occupied. I read a lot, and write and perform my own poetry. I love walking and being outside and spend as much time as possible at the house my husband and I have on the wild west coast of Ireland. It is right by the sea and a little piece of heaven on earth.'

PHOEBE SCHOLFIELD
(Henriette – credited on 15 episodes, including two as Communist Resistance)

At the beginning of each series, Phoebe Scholfield would arrive armed with not only the essentials needed for filming but a dirty joke to tell the rest of the team. 'I'd bring one with me every time and would make it survive the entire period,' says Phoebe, smiling. 'John D. Collins coined the phrase "Filthy Phoebe" because I talked posh but had this dirty sense of humour.'

When she first heard that a sitcom was being made titled *'Allo 'Allo!*, Phoebe imagined it was a police-based comedy. 'There used to be something called PCR – Production Casting Report – which actors subscribed to. I was doing bits and pieces on telly and spotted in the report a project called *'Allo 'Allo!*. I have to admit my complete ignorance because I had no idea who David Croft was but thought I'd write a letter to him anyway. Thinking it was about the police, I wrote saying: "I'd really be interested in auditioning for the forthcoming project. I should add that I look very good in uniform and am good with alsatians."'

Phoebe was sent two scenes and duly invited for an interview and had David Croft and Jeremy Lloyd in stitches. 'My French accent was pretty good because I studied the language, so that was OK. However, I admitted to not knowing anything about the project but realized that having to say the lines with a French accent probably meant it was nothing to do with the police. They roared with laughter at that. The atmosphere was very friendly and the interview seemed to go too well – I didn't think I'd got the job.'

But she did and was soon seen as Henriette, Michelle's trusty assistant. 'I was 25 and working on this amazing series, trying to suss out where I fitted in because I was one of those people who had the odd line here and there; I was one of the young, pretty girls who added glamour to the show,' says Phoebe, who worked as a member of the Communist Resistance for two episodes, too.

Phoebe was seen in four series before leaving to join a touring stage production as juvenile lead; in hindsight, she wonders if she made the right choice. 'I should probably have stayed because during the two years I wasn't available, I might have done more on *'Allo 'Allo!*. But I'm grateful for the chances given to me on the show. I had a fantastic time and everyone was so supportive.'

Phoebe studied drama at university intending to teach the subject, but believing she needed experience of the profession first, she turned to acting after graduating. She played small roles in various TV productions, including *Hold The Back Page*, *The Bill*, *Love Hurts*, *In Sickness And In Health* and *Chiller;* she also played a maid in *Jenny's War*, a film for the small screen starring Dyan Cannon and Elke Sommer.

Soon after leaving *'Allo 'Allo!*, Phoebe's career began moving in a different direction. 'I met Jay, my husband, who was sort of Mr Voice-over, and I started doing commercials, which seemed more lucrative. I was the Asda mum for two years, patting my bum, the voice of Debenhams, narrated various TV programmes and recorded the 'Mind the Gap' message for London Underground.

Then her husband, Jay Benedict, introduced her to ADR (Automated Dialogue Replacement), the post-production process of recording and replacing voices on films and TV programmes. 'I had two children with Jay and this fitted in better with my life, so we set up Sync or Swim. I loved my days acting and had a very good career for ten years, making good money, but I thought this was a more family-friendly job. Normally, we work on at least 50 projects a year; recent assignments include *Quartet*, Dustin Hoffman's new movie, *Prisoners' Wives*, *Downton Abbey* and many more.'

THE COMMUNIST RESISTANCE

MOIRA FOOT
(Denise Laroque – credited on 9 episodes)

When asked to audition for the part of Denise, Moira had just returned from a Nimmo Tour of the Far East. 'I'd come from Papua New Guinea back to East Acton, which was a bit of a change, but it was great fun working for David Croft and Jeremy Lloyd again.'

She'd previously appeared as Glenda in the short-lived sitcom, *Oh, Happy Band!*, and Miss Thorpe, one of the glamorous secretaries in episodes of *Are*

You Being Served?, back in 1975. 'The costume was different to the secretary's because for the first time I was covered up!'

Initially, Moira was hired for three episodes but went on to make nine. 'It was great fun, especially working with Vicki Michelle, with whom I'd gone to drama school.'

Unfortunately, Moira was forced to leave the show when her mother became seriously ill. 'She went in to a diabetic coma and I was told she wasn't going to survive the night but, believe it or not, she lived another 17 years. But I had to take a step back from showbusiness so *'Allo 'Allo!* was my "goodbye, goodbye" in a way.'

After leaving school, Moira enrolled at Aida Foster Stage School before making her TV debut in Ronnie Barker's *Hark At Barker* series. Roles in, among others, *Doctor At Large*, *On the Buses*, *Bachelor Father*, *Billy Liar*, *Quiller* and *The Benny Hill Show* followed.

Playing Denise was her last TV role. After acting she launched a production company, Astral Productions, but now runs her own animal sanctuary in Sussex.

CAROLE ASHBY
(Louise – credited on 15 episodes)

Former model Carole Ashby was spotted by David Croft at a wedding. 'One of my good friends was Becky Croft, David's daughter, who I used to model with years ago. She was getting married to Simon Cadell, the actor who appeared in *Hi-De-Hi!*, and at the wedding, David asked who the blonde girl was – that was me.'

A few weeks later, when David was casting for more parts in *'Allo 'Allo!*, Carole was invited for an audition. 'So I got my part in the sitcom by chance after being seen at his daughter's wedding.'

Appearing in 15 episodes of the sitcom as the tough, no-nonsense sexy leader of the region's Communist Resistance changed Carole's life. 'Not only did I appear in about three series but I met Jeremy Lloyd. I was with him for a few years and we got engaged.' Eventually they split but remain good friends. 'We laughed so much and he certainly sharpened my wit. He's probably the brightest man I know. We had plenty of laughs, it was great fun.'

Despite being nervous on joining the cast, the rest of the team were so welcoming that it didn't take long for Carole's nerves to settle. Once confident in the role of feisty Louise, Jeremy remarked that the part was perfect for her.

'I loved playing the character and Jeremy said she was just right for me: one of these wild girls who capture men and take them to their underground bunker!'

Carole knew that Louise had been written in for a series but was uncertain about her future thereafter. Fortunately, her services were required longer. 'The Communist Resistance added a new element to the show and helped keep it ticking along. Appearing in *'Allo 'Allo!* is one of the highlights of my acting career; I enjoyed appearing in *Bergerac*, *Minder* and shows like that, while my Bond films were glamorous, exciting and involved lots of travelling. But one thing I discovered from Louise was that I enjoyed playing comedy and was probably better at it than anything else.'

Carole began her working life as a model but harboured dreams of acting. She branched out and began singing in clubs and bars in the north of England before eventually realising her dream. Early credits saw her become a hostess on *Sale Of The Century* and *The Saints Went Marching Out*. As well as *'Allo 'Allo!*, Carole – who trained at the Beverly Hills Playhouse – was seen in, among others, *Life Without George*, *Inspector Morse* and a string of films, including *Chariots Of Fire* and the James Bond movies, *Octopussy* and *A View To A Kill*.

Eventually, Carole changed direction when an opportunity to work in interior design arose, a career she's still pursuing. 'I'd had a run in modelling and acting lasting over 20 years, so I'd been lucky. It had been a good time but the business changed so it was time to move on. As well as interior design, I've returned to my roots and sing with a band, White Label, but I'll always look back on my days as Louise with great fondness.'

ANN MICHELLE
(Communist Girl – credited on Series 9, Episode 2, 'Tour De France')

Sister of Vicki, Ann made her acting debut playing a schoolgirl in the 1969 film, *Prime Of Miss Jean Brodie*, starring Maggie Smith; her TV break came a year later in *Dixon Of Dock Green*.

Although films have dominated her screen career, including three movies made in Hollywood, she's also clocked up many small screen credits, including *The Professionals*, *The Two Ronnies*, *The Liver Birds*, *Widows 2* and *Casualty*.

Like many other cast members, Ann – who, as well as acting and writing, is a director of Trading Faces – had worked with Lloyd and Croft before, playing Scarth Dare in their sci-fi sitcom, *Come Back, Mrs Noah*.

The café interior is prepared for recording the pilot episode.
(© Shelagh Lawson)

Construction of the set for the pilot episode.
(© Shelagh Lawson)

Right: Shelagh Lawson, set designer on the pilot
episode, puts the finishing touches to the café
exterior. (© Shelagh Lawson)

Vicki Michelle as Yvette, one of the show's ever-presents.
(© Getty Images)

Rain stops play on location for Kenneth Connor, Arthur Bostrom and Carmen Silvera.
(© Arthur Bostrum)

Above: Preparing to film a scene outside Café Rene, which was actually in Norfolk. (© Robin Carr)

Left: Richard Gibson (Herr Flick) and John Louis Mansi (Smallhausen) were caught on a telegraph pole, which was mounted in a scaffolding rig. (© Stephen Lucas)

Above: Arthur Bostrom on location with Richard Gibson. (© Arthur Bostrum)

Right: Production assistant Bernadette Darnell and the pantomime cow relaxing for a moment in the Norfolk woods. (© B. Darnell)

It's been a long day filming exterior scenes for Guy Siner.
(© Robin Carr)

Left: The relationship between Herr Flick
(Richard Gibson) and Helga (Kim Hartman)
became a hugely important and popular element
of the sitcom.
(© Richard Gibson)

Above: Co-writer and producer David Croft
takes a break with production assistant
Bernadette Darnell.
(© B. Darnell)

Right: Herr Flick's staff car is squashed by the
steam roller, although in reality the roller never
touched the mock up vehicle.
(© Stephen Lucas)

Above: The motorised wheelchair – constructed
by visual effects designer Stephen Lucas – was
powered by a lawnmower engine and was all
part of another mad plan to try and repatriate the
British airmen.
(© Stephen Lucas)

Left: Colonel Von Strohm (Richard Marner)
dons a tree costume to avoid being spotted.
(© Stephen Lucas)

Kim Hartman prepares to play Helga during the successful 1986 stage show.
(© Richard Gibson)

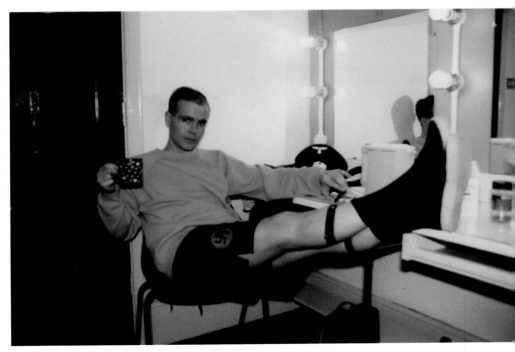

Richard Gibson (Herr Flick) relaxes in his dressing room during the 1986 stage tour.
(© Richard Gibson)

Gruber's 'little tank' became a popular aspect of the sitcom.
(© Stephen Lucas)

Richard Marner, Sam Kelly and Guy Siner relax in their dressing room during the successful 1986
stage show.
(© Richard Gibson)

Above: Jack Haig in the dressing room during the successful 1986 stage tour.
(© Richard Gibson)

Guy Siner and Richard Gibson unwind during the run of the successful 1986 stage show.
(© Richard Gibson)

Gorden Kaye and Camen Silvera relax during the run of the successful 1986 stage show. (© Richard Gibson)

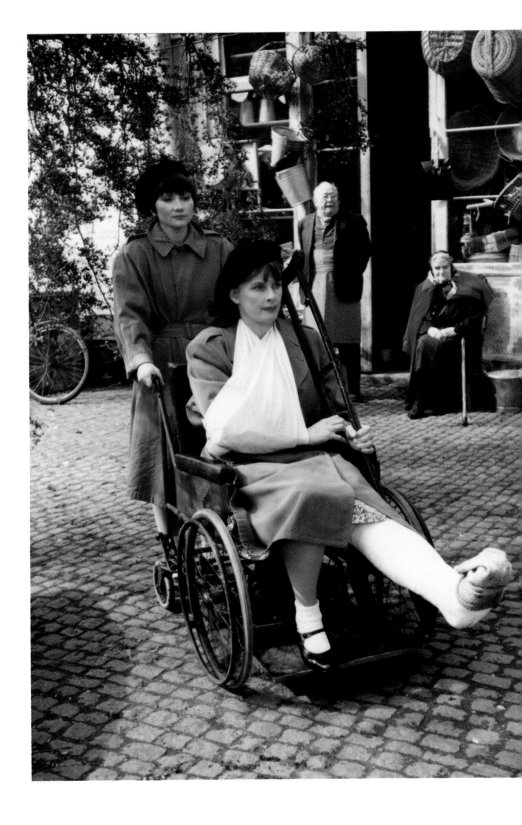

bove: Vicki Michelle, Sue Hodge and Kim Hartman
. Glasgow in October 1987.
② Mirrorpix)

eft: Michelle (Kirsten Cooke) is pushed along by
er loyal assistant, the props all part of another mad
heme to try and repatriate the British airmen.
② Stephen Lucas)

The Fallen Madonna With The Big Boobies
– but is it the real one?
(© Rexfeatures)

Ann, who also writes screenplays with her other sister, Suzie, was asked several times to appear in *'Allo 'Allo!*. 'Unfortunately, I was always busy on other projects. But when the chance to be in the last series came along, I thought it would be nice to get in before it finished. Luckily, the timing was right and I enjoyed being in such a wonderful series. Everyone was easy to work with.'

ESTELLE MATTHEWS
(Resistance Girl and Valerie Vendome)

Before Estelle appeared as a Resistance girl, she was seen as Valerie Vendome in 'Good Staff Are Hard To Find', the third episode of season four, applying for the waitress's job at Café René. During her interview, Vendome showed off her rather unusual party piece.

'David Croft had this plan for me to do an acrobatic back flip and somersault extravaganza, but when it came to laying out the dimensions for the stage there wasn't enough room for any heavy acrobatics; so we experimented and tried various things,' explains Estelle, who remembers her audition vividly.

'David was looking for people with good dance, movement and acrobatic skills, which is why my agent put me forward. They were looking for something different so when asked to show them what I could do, I walked up and down in front of the audition panel on my hands, about 30 steps one way, 30 steps back. I didn't go there with a polished routine, I just wanted to do something quirky.' Estelle got the job.

The actual recorded scene in the café sees Estelle forming a crab position, which came about by mistake. 'While warming up, I ended up in a crab and started walking along. David noticed and said, "Do that again, I love it." Next, he came up with a line, there and then, of "Very handy for cleaning under the carpets."'

Appearances as a member of the Resistance followed and, eventually, David Croft told Estelle he'd love to use her in a different show sometime. By then, she was already planning a career change. 'I moved into a different line of business: training as a journalist and becoming a reporter. People wondered why I turned down such a possibility but that's just how it worked out.'

Estelle earnt her Equity card as a member of Hot Flesh, a cabaret act which worked with a boa constrictor and fire. Soon after, small TV parts were offered, beginning with the job of magician's assistant on a Paul Daniels' show. Appearing as Mademoiselle Vendome happened soon after.

After switching careers a year after being part of the Resistance, Estelle was employed on *TV-am* as a showbiz reporter; later, she worked at Sky TV, ITN and BBC. Now, she also runs her own company, Elm Media, but misses her acting days. 'They were great fun.'

OTHER RESISTANCE GIRLS

Jacqueline Ashman, who played an assistant of Resistance Leader Michelle, also appeared in a 1987 episode of *Casualty* and played a housewife in the TV series, *Harry Enfield And Chums*, while **Rikki Howard**, appeared as Elaine 'Easy' Cerise, who'd been an assistant to a famous osteopath before joining the Resistance. Rikki now works as a trained counsellor. In her acting days she was seen in several episodes of *Hi-De-Hi!*, *The Two Ronnies*, *The Benny Hill Show* and a TV commercial for Cadbury's Creme Eggs. **Jackie D. Broad** appeared as both French and Communist Resistance girls in *'Allo 'Allo!*, but also appeared in, among others, an episode of *You Rang, M'Lord?* and *The Bill* in the 1990s and later the TV series *The Doctors*. Whilst **Denise Kelly** appeared as a hostess on several episodes of *The Price Is Right* amongst other jobs, **Lisa Anselmi** – whose appearances in the sitcom included playing a Communist Leader in the opening episode of Series 3 – started off as a model and dancer in Paris. Her first TV appearance was as an extra in *Hi-De-Hi!*, before playing the secretary, her first speaking role, in *Are You Being Served?* She is credited for one episode of *'Allo 'Allo!* but also had an uncredited appearance in the pilot. Other screen credits include *The Kenny Everett Television Show, Dempsey And Makepeace* and *Just Good Friends*. Lisa now lives in the USA and is a scriptwriter. **Gabrielle Dellal,** sister of film-maker Jasmine Dellal, was also seen in two episodes of *Robin of Sherwood* along with *Dempsey And Makepeace* in the 1980s. She has more recently turned to directing and writing. **Susan Kyd's** credits, meanwhile, include appearing in 'The Secret Of Bay 5B', an episode of *Inspector Morse*, *Lovejoy,* several episodes of *Married For Life*, *Casualty* and *Doctors*. She was also seen in the TV movie *Victoria And Albert*. In *'Allo 'Allo!* her appearances included playing a Communist Resistance Leader in Series 1, episode 6, while **Annabel Lambe's** other appearances include playing a reporter in *The Brittas Empire*. **Pia Henderson** – whose uncle was in the real French Resistance – did extensive repertory work as well as time with the *Royal Shakespeare Company*. She appeared in several episodes of the TV series *Capital City* and *The Bill* before quitting acting in the mid-1990s. More recently she has been Head of Performing

Arts at Ardingly College Junior School and is now a voice and communications skills coach. **Elizabeth Ash**, who appeared in three episodes of *'Allo 'Allo!*, was also seen in *Grange Hill*, playing Carol at the travel agency, two episodes of *Boon* and *Peak Practice*. **Cheryl Fergison** is best known for her long-running role in *EastEnders* as Heather Trott. Many people will also remember her dance routine to Vanilla Ice's *Ice Ice Baby* for Sport Relief. Other TV credits include *Bad Girls*, *Casualty*, *Dr Who* and *Little Britain*. **Christine Moore** has appeared in two episodes of *Heartbeat*, *The Bill*, *Brookside*, *The Royal*, *Holby City* and *Coronation Street* playing Gloria Hadden, whereas **Debbie Thomson** was seen in *Birds Of A Feather* and *The Bill*. Other Resistance Girls credited in the series are **Linda Styan**, **Sarah Hauenstein**, **Amanda Gibson-Lees** and **Sherry Louise Plant**.

Six Big Boobies

The Colonel no longer wanta to turn a blind eye to the activities being carried out in René's café and gives him an ultimatum.

RENÉ: Do not worry, Colonel, the British airmen have gone, for good.

COLONEL: Excellent. Then if you will tell me the names of the Resistance leaders, I will see that you are protected.

RENÉ: Protected, against who?

COLONEL: Me.

RENÉ: But Colonel, I do not know their names. They are mostly girls, they wear mackintoshes and little short white socks and berets like any other French girls; and they only reveal themselves at night.

CAPTAIN: Like any other French girls!

COLONEL: I wish I could get my hands on them.

CAPTAIN: We both do.

COLONEL: If you do not cooperate, René, I will have you shot.

RENÉ: Oh Colonel, you wouldn't?

CAPTAIN: He would, he did it before.

THE BRITISH INTELLIGENCE AGENTS

Although the vowel-mangling Officer Crabtree appeared in over 70 episodes, we learnt little about his background. But from his general demeanour, the undercover British agent who masqueraded as a gendarme seemed way out of his depth, bumbling along from one crisis to the next whilst trying to get by with his ludicrous cod French accent. He was joined for three episodes by Agent Grace, whose attempts at the French lingo were equally inept.

ARTHUR BOSTROM
(Officer Crabtree – 74 episodes)

Arthur will never forget the phone call in March 1985 which changed his life forever. It was Friday lunchtime and the Rugby-born actor was awaiting final details of an upcoming trip to Madrid. 'I'd just been offered a well-paid IBM conference in the Spanish capital; the company wanted to employ actors and, for me, it was welcome news because I needed the money.'

Picking up the receiver, David Croft's then production assistant, Bernadette Darnell, introduced herself before checking on Arthur's availability. Although he'd already been booked by IBM, Arthur didn't want to miss the chance of working for Croft so informed Darnell that he'd speak to his agent. 'I called her and she said, "'Allo 'Allo! is more important so if you're offered a job I'll get you out of the conference."'

Arthur left the matter in his agent's hands and before long heard that an appointment with David Croft was scheduled for 4pm that afternoon. With little time to spare, he grabbed a bite to eat and screamed up to the BBC to read for the part of Crabtree – although it wasn't a typical audition. The script Arthur was handed was typed phonetically – not that it fazed him. 'I think I just understood what David was looking for and guess that's why I got the part. Everyone always assumes it must have been hard learning my character's lines, but I didn't really find it that difficult. Perhaps that's why it suited me!'

Confirmation of the offer arrived quickly. By the time he returned to his London flat, a message was waiting on the answerphone advising he'd got the role of Officer Crabtree. Arthur was excited but knew there was another potential obstacle to overcome. 'I was booked to appear in the TV series,

Return To Treasure Island, in three months' time. I'd already accepted and was due to fly to Spain the day after completing filming for *'Allo 'Allo!*. We had to let David Croft know about these constraints.'

Fortunately, Croft wasn't concerned: after all, he'd got his man after a rapid piece of casting forced upon him when the actor originally considered for the part, the late Edward Duke, wasn't available to take up the role, if it were offered. 'It was all so quick. Although I didn't know it was a recast at first, I wondered considering the suddenness of everything. But I didn't know for sure until one of the cast mentioned it; by then I had the job so it didn't matter, other than it feeling odd for a while knowing I was performing a part meant for somebody else. However, by the time I'd become a permanent member of the team, Jeremy and David were writing for me.'

Even today, Arthur admits he's never delved too deeply into the matter. 'Sadly, Edward is dead now. My understanding, although I'm not entirely sure, is that it was written for him and then he had a change of plan; one story I've heard is that he received an offer to take his one-man show, *Jeeves Takes Charge*, to America, but I'm not sure.'

One advantage Arthur had when reading for David Croft was that he'd already watched the sitcom and appreciated its style of humour. 'I wanted to be involved because the pilot was brilliant.' Arthur was so enamoured of the programme that he had already penned a letter to David, offering his services. 'I'm glad he didn't give me a small part in the first series because look what I would have missed out on?'

Officer Crabtree was a character devised by Croft, but Arthur played a key role in shaping the intelligence agent during his audition. 'Crabtree reminded me of Edward Heath, the prime minister, who was a great Francophile but spoke the language with no accent at all. Hearing him talk used to crack me up: the words were correct but there was no attempt at a French accent. How British is that? My suggestion during the interview was to base the character's delivery on Edward Heath's and David really liked the idea.'

As is the norm, fine-tuning took place during the screen character's early life. 'Initially, he sounded like one of the British airmen but simply talking in his unique jumbled way. After the first take of the opening scene, David said I needed more of an overlay of a French accent, but we never forgot that, ultimately, he was a rather upper-class Englishman,' explains Arthur, who first worked for David Croft in an episode of holiday camp sitcom, *Hi-De-Hi!*.

In the Series 4 episode, 'The Society Entertainer', he played The Hulk, who had a brief fling with chalet maid Peggy, played by Su Pollard. 'What sort of a fling we can only imagine, but I don't think it mounted to much because he was as thick as two short planks,' smiles Arthur. 'It was only four lines but got some laughs.'

At the time, the fleeting scene may have seemed inconsequential, but his appearance, albeit brief, brought him to the attention of Croft. 'In common with many people who became regulars in David's series, he'd try people out in a small part; if he liked you, he remembered you – and that's what happened to me.' Not that Arthur was aware of this until Jeffrey Holland, alias Spike Dixon in *Hi-De-Hi!*, sidled up to him at the end of the scene offering words of encouragement. 'He said, "The boss – meaning David Croft – really liked it. Most of us in the series have got here because we did a bit for David before, so I hope it happens for you." It's one of the kindest things another actor has said because it encouraged me. Three years later, when I got the part of Crabtree and happened to see Jeffrey, he said, "Told you!".'

Bringing the character to life on screen was a challenge Arthur relished; initially, he took his lead from Kirsten Cooke's portrayal of Michelle, leader of the region's French Resistance. 'The trick was to be dead serious while putting the stresses on the same points you would have done if speaking normally. It definitely helped already knowing the style of the show. Kirsten was brilliant with the serious, deadpan nature of her delivery; I always admired what she did. For me, she was the benchmark because my character was often with her during the planning stages of missions.'

David Croft once commented that typing Crabtree's dialogue phonetically in the scripts threw the word processor's spell-check function into confusion. But Arthur was never left scratching his head: in fact, he became so used to the style of speaking that even today he can still make it up as he goes along. 'Crabtree suited me because I like odd characters. The irony is that the next part I played – Don Felipe, a Spanish aristocrat in *Return To Treasure Island* – spoke with a Spanish accent and a pronounced lisp. So I paid arguably two of the most bizarre characters of my career back-to-back; 1985 was a very interesting year!'

As the programme progressed, subtle changes occurred to most of the characters, including Officer Crabtree. 'It was only little things like thinking he was becoming more confident in his French, although his grasp of the language never really improved. It was his innocence which made it so funny: being such an idiot, it never occurred to him that what he was saying was wrong; also, he forgot sometimes why he was over there, thinking he was a real policeman.'

One memorable element was the emergence of Crabtree's catchphrase, 'Good moaning!'. As with most catchphrases they happen by chance with the scriptwriters latching on to what is often little more than a throwaway line because of the studio audience's reaction during recording. 'I said it in one episode and everyone came in to rehearsals next day saying it, which David and Jeremy noticed,' recalls Arthur. 'So I ended up saying it every episode as my opening line – it just took off. It rapidly became a catchphrase and I'm still reminded of it today with people shouting it out in the street. Once you're on telly your privacy goes out the window and it's strange being recognized, but I never had problems coping, perhaps because everyone loved Crabtree.'

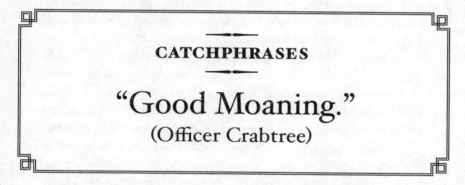

CATCHPHRASES

"Good Moaning."
(Officer Crabtree)

Reflecting on the sitcom's phenomenal success and perennial appeal, Arthur points to the atmosphere among cast and crew as a key element. He admits there was occasional friction, which is expected among a team working together for so long. 'That's typical of any working environment, but by and large it was a fun atmosphere.'

Anther contributing factor in the show's popularity was everyone pulling together. 'We were a close unit and totally focussed on what we wanted to achieve. Everyone in the show was perfectly cast, too, which is down to David Croft. You could never imagine someone else playing, say, René. Jeremy and David created great characters and the scripts were consistently funny.'

The performers worked for each other and always had the show's best interests at heart. 'As a company, we were very generous to one another. You'd see a script, spot a line someone was going to say and couldn't wait to hear them because you knew it would be funny; you appreciated the quality of the performers around you.'

This quality is not only appreciated by fans in Britain – it's popular around the world, especially mainland Europe. 'I receive emails from everywhere,' says

'LONDON CALLING'

Throughout the course of the sitcom several 'voices' were employed as 'London Calling', the men back in Blighty who were in regular communication with not only the two British airmen but the Resistance, too. Of those whose voices we heard, **Paul Cooper**'s was the most frequently used. His involvement in *'Allo 'Allo!* consisted of being the unseen man from London in Series 3, ep 2-6; Series 4, ep 5; Series 5, ep 2, 9, 10, 23; Series 7, ep 7; Series 8, ep 1-2 and Series 9, ep 4 and 6; he also notched up two other credits, appearing as a tailor and, later, soldier in the POW camp.

'Some time before taking on the role of "London Calling", I was Herr Flick's tailor in "The Nicked Knockwurst", which is how I got in to the series,' recalls Paul. 'David Croft wanted me back in again but that storyline finished so it wasn't possible in that role. Later on, he asked me to appear in "Prisoners Of War" as a prisoner dressing up in order to escape. I ended up being disguised as Hitler and a dog, which was hilarious.'

Subsequently, the chance to take on the role of 'London Calling' came along. 'David asked if I was interested. Although it was really a voice-over, David and Jeremy wanted to make it more of an acting role – to be part of the team.'

If Croft and Lloyd's perception of the role had remained simply a voice-over, it would have entailed Paul arriving purely on recording day. But as they wanted to raise the role's profile, it necessitated his involvement from day one. 'They wanted me to come in and rehearse the whole week so they could time it property and make it really work – even though I never had more than a few lines; that was brilliant because it meant I got to observe all this wonderful comedy going on.'

Paul's introduction to the sitcom was due in part to a friend, who told him about the role of Herr Flick's tailor. 'I'd known Robin Carr, who was a member of the production team, since working together on a play in the West End; he was stage manager at the time. He told me about the part of the tailor coming up and thought I was right for it. So I auditioned and was offered the job; after that, it feels like I stayed with the show forever.'

Although other actors had been hired as 'London Calling', Paul is pleased he was asked to take up the reins when the writers decided to develop it into a character voice. 'I was in the right place at the right time. The part grew, really, and was great fun.'

When recording the attic scenes where radio contact is made with London, Paul wasn't tucked away from all the action in the bowels of Television Centre. 'I was literally around the back of the attic set. I had a microphone and monitor so could see what was going on and would simply sit and wait for the right moment.' Rather than read his lines from the script, Paul decided to learn them – although his air time was brief. 'It was the best way because I wanted to make 100 percent sure that it didn't sound like it was being read.'

Paul launched his acting career at Chesterfield Rep in 1970. A year later, he started working in various theatres before small and big screen appearances came his way, including roles in *Britannia Hospital, Dempsey And Makepeace, Minder, Only Fools And Horses, Never The Twain, Grace And Favour* and *The Bill*. Most recently, he's been working in theatre at The Mill at Sonning.

Other voices heard on the crackly radio relaying messages from London belonged to: **Philip Kendall** (Series 1, ep 7; Series 2, ep 6-7) worked for David Croft in *Are You Being Served?* and *Hi-De-Hi!*, playing a customer and police sergeant respectively. Other TV credits include *The Gentle Touch* and *Blackadder*. **James Gow** (Series 2, ep 2) also donned a police uniform for Croft, but as a constable in *Hi-De-Hi!*. Peter Bradshaw (Series 4, ep 2) has appeared in *Northern Exposure* and the TV movie *Under Siege*, while **Owen Brenman** (Series 5, ep 13 – also heard as 'Kingfisher' in Series 5, ep 15 and 'French radio voice' in episode 16) has built up a long list of credits, including *No Place Like Home, Jeeves And Wooster* and various roles in Alexei Sayle's *Stuff*. He's had a regular role as Doctor Carter in *Doctors* but for many is remembered for his fine performance as Nick Swainey, Victor Meldrum's oddball neighbour in *One Foot In The Grave*. Writer David Renwick subsequently cast him in his comedy-drama, *Love Soup*.

Arthur. 'A few years ago, I even visited Norway with Vicki Michelle to open a café. The owner was a big fan and asked us to open the establishment in character.'

When deciding on favourite scenes, it's almost an impossible task for Arthur because there were so many. However, when pushed, he says: 'There is the famous one where I enter the café and say I was "pissing by the door" rather than "passing". The reaction was enormous; no one had said anything like that on British television, even though it wasn't what I was supposed to have said,' laughs Arthur, before mentioning an episode in the lengthy Series 5. 'I had my own set, a small police station, in a scene where René wanted to stay in one of the cells. Rather than let him as one of the Resistance, I said he couldn't unless he'd "committed a cream" and then delivered this ludicrous over-the-counter discussion about what kind of "cream" he'd committed – I even produced a list of "creams". It was a wonderful piece of writing.'

Playing a distinctive character in a popular, long-running series can often have a negative impact on an actor's on-going career; typecasting can be the bane of a thespian's life. With Crabtree being such an extreme character, Arthur realized it could affect the rest of his working life, particularly on the small screen. 'Yes, it's definitely affected my TV career but I was prepared for it; and as I've got older, it's become less of a problem. But, overall, I wouldn't have missed playing Crabtree for anything – it was the most amazing job. To be in such a successful series and help create a wonderful character is a once in a lifetime offer and I'm pleased to have been given the opportunity.'

Although one never knows if Arthur lost potential TV jobs because of his association with the British intelligence agent, it's clear opportunities have arisen because of it – and continue to. 'I was in a play three years ago at Manchester's Royal Exchange and it turned out that the director watched 'Allo 'Allo! with her gran every Saturday night; apparently, whenever I came on, she'd nudge her grandmother. It's remarkable that we ended up working together.'

Arthur began acting at Durham University, where he studied geography. Originally intending to pursue a career with the forestry commission, he changed direction and attended drama school in London after graduation.

Work in various repertory theatres followed before small TV parts came along, including an instalment of *BBC2 Playhouse*, *The Crystal Cube* and *Just Good Friends*. Since 'Allo 'Allo!, Arthur has spent plenty of time in the theatre, his first love. 'I've remained busy in the medium, touring in, among others, *The Merry Widow*, *Anyone For Breakfast* and *Twelfth Night* for Kate O'Mara's British Actors' Theatre Company.'

TV credits include two appearances on *Big Brother's Big Mouth*, presented by James Corden – who co-wrote sitcom *Gavin And Stacey* – and Mathew Horne, who plays Gavin, both fans of Crabtree; and in 2006, Arthur played Crabtree's brother in a Dutch production, *Sinterklaas*, made for charity fundraising. His most recent television appearance was Martin Parnaby in an episode of *Doctors*.

'I'm writing more nowadays,' says Arthur, who's enjoyed a recent sabbatical from acting to pen a novel. 'I'm also writing a sitcom with a friend, Jennie Campbell. I can't say much about it but it's something I've wanted to do for ages. I'm hoping to sell that, too.'

Arthur is also a trained life coach, helping people from all walks of life fulfil their potential and achieve their goals. 'This developed from my work in recent years as a volunteer for the Samaritans. Perhaps I'll switch to it full-time one day.'

Whatever the future holds, Arthur will forever be grateful he landed the role of Crabtree. 'I'm proud of *'Allo! 'Allo!* and think it stands up well today whenever repeated. Its continued success has allowed me to concentrate on things I want to do, like writing and travelling, rather than panicking about how to pay the bills. I'm enormously grateful for being given the opportunity in the first place and to the British public for still wanting to see it. Kids who weren't even born when it was originally shown have become fans.'

SARAH SHERBORNE
(Agent Grace – 3 episodes)

Giving her phone number to Martin Dennis at a party proved to be a wise move for Sarah Sherborne because it resulted in her playing Agent Grace in three episodes.

Martin, who directed six instalments of the sixth series, had studied drama with Sarah at Birmingham University. 'I'd done some comedy just before Agent Grace and got chatting to Martin at the do. I didn't think anything more about it until, later, he phoned asking what I was doing that afternoon and would I pop along to the BBC for an audition?'

Sarah explains that Agent Grace – nicknamed Urgent Grace – was introduced to help further develop Arthur's character. 'They wanted a tall actress who was not only funny but able to do the accent. Luckily, I could; and being 5 foot 9 compared to Arthur's 6 foot 4, I fitted the bill.'

Arriving at David Croft's office at Television Centre, Sarah was asked to read for the part. Just like Officer Crabtree's lines, Agent Grace's were typed phonetically – not that it caused Sarah any problems, either. 'You always ask if you can have a moment to look through the script, which I did, but it was pretty clear how I should deliver the lines; that's part of being an actress.'

After finishing the reading, Sarah, who lived in nearby Hammersmith, started to hand the script back. 'But David didn't take it. He said, "You'll be needing that." I remember walking home thinking it had been a good day's work.'

The character first appeared in the episode, 'The Crooked Fences', and when Sarah joined up with the team to begin location work, she wondered how Arthur Bostrom would react. 'I thought he might not like it but he was happy and very welcoming.' In fact, she learnt much from him. 'I like those verbal jokes. Arthur was very good at them and gave me sound advice: you pronounce the words as if they're everyday speech and utterly believe that you speak like that – he helped enormously.'

Reflecting on the three episodes she appeared in, Sarah has nothing but happy memories. 'They were very funny scenes, especially those where I supposedly had a pigeon under my beret. It was battery-operated by two guys out of sight, first for a scene in the café and then at the wedding when it scooted across the floor with me racing around trying to catch it. It was ridiculously silly but Andy Lazell, the visual effects designer, and his mate were brilliant making it move.'

The Arrival Of The Homing Duck

Helga is ironing Herr Flick's shirt whilst he questions her on what she has discovered about the plot to blow up Hitler.

HERR FLICK: Pay attention to the tail, I hate the wrinkly ones.

HELGA: Yes, Herr Flick. Do you not have a servant to do this?

HERR FLICK: I have advertised in the local paper. 'Single Gestapo gentleman requires willing and obedient peasant for menial domestic tasks.'

HELGA: Have you had many replies?

HERR FLICK: Only one. It came through the window on a brick.

HELGA: Never mind, Herr Flick, I consider it an honour to be pressing the shirt that will shortly contain your fine Gestapo torso.

HERR FLICK: I thought you would.

The Reluctant Millionaires

Having stuffed the money from the bank robbery down his trousers, René retreats to the back room to relieve himself of it. Bending over, with his trousers around his ankles, Gruber walks in.

GRUBER: René!

RENÉ: Lieutenant Gruber, shut the door, quickly.

GRUBER: Could it be that I have hit the jackpot?

RENÉ: Lieutenant Gruber, it is vital that you do not tell anybody what you have seen.

GRUBER: René, long underwear is nothing to be ashamed of.

RENÉ: I was talking about the money.

GRUBER: Oh yes, I see. My, my, you do have a big bundle there.

Another occasion wasn't so amusing. While out in the Norfolk countryside she was bitten by a horsefly above her white sock and suffered a reaction. 'I was apparently allergic to insect bites and was rushed back to casualty to have antihistamine.'

Despite suffering insect bites and having pigeons under her hat, Sarah wishes Agent Grace's stay in Nouvion had been extended beyond three episodes. 'Unfortunately, Jeremy began writing a different storyline which headed off in another direction. I lived in hope that she might return – and Arthur was keen – but, sadly, she didn't.'

Although her time in the French town was brief, it remains one of her favourite jobs. 'I knew Martin, Sue Hodge was a friend and Arthur was very friendly, too. There was a family-like atmosphere which made the job even more enjoyable.'

Before appearing in *'Allo 'Allo!*, Sarah had worked on stage and TV, including roles in, among others, *The Fourth Arm*, *A Married Man*, *Goodbye Mr Chips*, *Dempsey and Makepeace*, *Mr Palfrey of Westminster* and *The Bill*. After hanging up her beret, she continued working in series such as *Howards' Way*, *House of Eliott* and *Birds of a Feather*. She now works primarily as a voice-over artist, including narrating audio books, radio and TV commercials and corporate videos. Among her TV projects, she narrated *Medicine's Strangest Cases*, five one-hour programmes for Channel 5.

THE BRITISH AIRMEN

Throughout the sitcom's run, Michelle Dubois, leader of the region's French Resistance, and her team of merry helpers tried desperately to repatriate Flying Officers Carstairs and Fairfax, played by Nicholas Frankau and John D. Collins respectively; even a reluctant René, his wife, Edith, and café staff played their part in the increasingly madcap schemes dreamt up by Michelle to return the clueless airmen to Blighty.

We learn little of the airmen's backgrounds during the series, other than Carstairs was educated in a grammar school, something he confirms when Fairfax questions him about wearing socks in bed; and Fairfax expresses a desire to work in the Stock Exchange after the war. Other than that, their asinine behaviour and achingly inept approach to their predicament does little to help their plight.

JOHN D. COLLINS
(Flying Officer Fairfax – 63 episodes)

When David Croft informed John D. Collins, who'd just appeared in an episode of *Hi-De-Hi!*, that he was making a pilot programme and would be offering him a part, he failed to mention what it would entail. That became all too apparent when the script dropped through Collins' letterbox the following week.

Sitting in a holiday flat in the Essex seaside resort of Frinton-on-Sea, where he now lives, John tore open the envelope and began reading the *'Allo 'Allo!* pilot script; almost immediately, his heart sank after spotting the words, 'The airmen don't speak French'. He says: 'I couldn't see how you'd have two characters not speaking the language because they couldn't take part in any scenes, other than those between themselves – and that's what happened, really,' John admits.

Despite not seeing much mileage in Flying Officer Fairfax, John put aside any reservations and accepted the role. Thankfully, the airmen's usefulness to the overall plot was aided by the introduction of English-speaking Officer Crabtree in the second series, providing scope for involving the airmen more. 'That was how you could keep them in the show, otherwise Jeremy and David couldn't have sustained it for more than a few episodes, in my opinion. As it was, we ended up being in over 60 episodes.'

Despite their limitations, the airmen were an integral part of the show. Taking a moment to reflect on the role of Fairfax, John smiles before admitting it's not one of his favourite TV roles. 'When you work for a whole week but say just one line, it's not particularly taxing; not that I minded because it was a smashing company and the repeat fees are very welcome.'

Two day trips to France – organized by John – complemented the feeling of togetherness among the cast. 'We hired a coach, caught the ferry and headed to Calais for a fine lunch before returning home. We did it once during the first series and again in the second. We all chipped in towards the cost and good fun was had by all. First time was before any episodes had been transmitted so no one knew us; second time, though, we were better known and numerous people on the ferry approached us – not that it bothered me.'

One worrying incident on 'Allo 'Allo! occurred while on location in Norfolk when John tripped on a step and broke his ankle. 'It was a severe break and the hospital staff stuck plaster on me.' For a while, it looked like John would have to be recast, a potential disaster for Collins, then Martin Dennis, who was part of Croft's production team, realized that for the bulk of the upcoming filming, Collins was dressed as a pantomime cow so suggested one of the crew stepped in. Fortunately, Collins was able to return before the end of the shoot to film a scene in a hot air balloon, where he was only required to wave goodbye; so he was plonked in the basket which conveniently hid his plastered leg.

The London-born actor subsequently played nearly a dozen different characters in six sitcoms produced by Croft, including a bailiff serving divorce papers on Paul Shane's character, Ted, in Hi-De-Hi!. He also popped up as a doctor, waiter and secretary at Number 10 in Are You Being Served?.

'David kept using me in bits and pieces,' says John, who went on to work in the Perry-Croft sitcom, You Rang, M'Lord?, and the railway-based, Oh Doctor Beeching!. John regards the former as much more rewarding than 'Allo 'Allo! because his role developed into a 'proper part'. He confesses, though, that he only got the job by luck after 'everyone else had turned it down!'. He explains: 'There was a character in it, Jerry, who didn't have any lines at all – he just laughed. David came to me and said he'd got this part and would I do it, before warning me that there were no lines, just laughter. I replied, "For you, David, I'll do anything."'

John appeared in the pilot, braying throughout, and was retained when the first series was commissioned. 'The role developed as the series progressed and my character ended up not just with dialogue but marrying the daughter of the house. So there was a lesson there: don't turn anything down, especially if it's for David Croft.'

But John admits he never does reject offers of work. 'I'm not one of those actors who can afford to decline offers. After all, it's best taking the risk, even if it's a job you're not looking forward to, because you don't know what might come of it.'

That work ethic has served him well during a career of more than five decades. Born in London and educated at Harrow, John D. Collins worked as a shop assistant for a year before entering RADA, aged 18, in 1960, after winning Ivor Novello and Robert Donat scholarships.

After graduating from drama school, he began his career in rep, initially at the Nottingham Playhouse, before moving on to other venues. He made his screen debut playing a vicar in a *Play For Today* filmed in Manchester for Granada. A busy career included a ten-year association with the late Spike Milligan as assistant director and actor, and running his own theatre company at Frinton-on-Sea between 1963–64.

Among his many TV credits are *Get Some In!; A Family At War; Some Mothers Do 'Ave 'Em; Only Fools and Horses; Yes, Minister; Peak Practice; Birds Of A Feather; Wycliffe; Trial And Retribution* and *Fortysomething*. He also appeared as Lieutenant Short, a naval officer, in the big screen version of *Dad's Army*.

Considering, again, his time as Flying Officer Fairfax, John agrees that the airmen popped up in the most unusual places before announcing themselves with their frightfully British pronunciation of 'Hello!'. Among the myriad predicaments in which Fairfax and his flying chum found themselves, being squashed inside sewers underneath Nouvion's town square took some beating. 'There was flowing water next to us and someone from the props' department floated artificial turds past us without telling us they were false; they were highly realistic,' laughs John, who was more aware than anyone that there were only so many ways they could utter the word, 'Hello!'. He agrees that the series finished just at the right time. 'I've had more fulfilling jobs. For example, currently I'm on stage two hours a night which is more the kind of thing I want to do. I don't like sitting in the dressing room waiting; we were on the set all week watching the other scenes, hanging around for our turn to come along. But having said all of that, it was a great company with some wonderful people.'

The Policeman Cometh

Helga is standing facing the corner in Herr Flick's quarters.

HERR FLICK: Ten minutes is up, you may now come out of the corner.

HELGA: Yes, Herr Flick.

HERR FLICK: Let that be a lesson to you. Never again will you burn my toast.

HELGA: Yes, Herr Flick. May I sit?

HERR FLICK: Yes. You may continue with your tea. I have kept your egg warm under the cosy.

HELGA: You have a very kind streak in your nature.

HERR FLICK: I nearly failed my Gestapo exams because of it.

HELGA: (Looking at egg) It has a very strong shell.

HERR FLICK: Hit it hard with your spoon. They always break in the end.

HELGA: You are looking pensive, Herr Flick.

HERR FLICK: I am trying to decide what to do with you tonight.

HELGA: I see, Herr Flick.

HERR FLICK: I might take you to the movies.

HELGA: What is showing?

HERR FLICK: Anything we like. Or we could stay here and amuse ourselves. I have a box of sharp needles somewhere. Ah, there they are.

HELGA: What have you in mind, Herr Flick?

HERR FLICK: I have an excellent gramophone and many records of Hitler's speeches. They're quite amusing.

HELGA: Hitler's speeches are quite amusing?

HERR FLICK: Played at double speed he sounds like Donald Duck.

NICHOLAS FRANKAU
(Flying Officer Carstairs – 63 episodes)

One aspect of playing Flying Officer Carstairs that Nicholas Frankau will never forget is the absurd situations in which he found himself – and all in the name of TV. 'The airmen's attempts to escape saw us end up in some crazy predicaments, including standing around in a field donning a pantomime cow costume. There were real cows nearby and one approached quite slowly from behind to investigate; in fact, I was not a hundred percent sure that he wasn't a bull! Fortunately, we escaped unharmed, although we were then seen riding off on a tandem in our costume!' smiles Nicholas, reflecting on the sixty-plus episodes he appeared in. 'I was used to riding them because I'd enjoyed a couple of holidays on tandems. The tandem idea was, I believe, suggested by Gorden Kaye, who knew about my cycling history. Indeed, I used to cycle up from London to Swaffham for the filming.

'Other times, my moustache fell off or we ended up hidden in dustbins or under tables, usually crouching down in tight spaces, so playing Carstairs, though fun, could occasionally be slightly uncomfortable.'

After a seemingly endless run of failed attempts to reach the shores of Blighty, the airmen eventually achieved their goal and weren't required for the latter series which saddened Nicholas. 'We returned for the final episode, though, just as Nouvion was liberated. Overall, we appeared in about ninety-five percent of the first seven series which isn't bad, considering I only expected to be in the pilot episode!'

It was the first time Nicholas had worked with John D. Collins and they soon struck up a friendship. 'We enjoyed each other's company and got on well; we even received requests to attend charity events together. *'Allo 'Allo!* was exciting to work on – everyone got on. Though the writers made Carstairs a grammar school boy, I did, in fact, go to Harrow, just like John. It was clearly a fertile training ground for thick, posh airmen!'

Whenever Nicholas catches a repeat on TV, it still makes him laugh. 'It remains incredibly popular,' says Nicholas. 'But unlike many of the other actors, I wasn't recognized much in the street, other than once immediately after the pilot was shown. I was in between jobs and visiting the dole office when the guy behind the desk said, "I saw you on telly last night."'

Nicholas's involvement with TV began at a very early age, although it wasn't until studying maths at Cambridge University that he decided upon forging a career for himself in the entertainment business. 'With my father being a TV director and grandfather a radio comic, the industry was in my blood,' he explains. 'But I'd also been bitten by the bug when, aged 13, I uttered a line in the film, *Goodbye, Mr Chips*, with Peter O'Toole and Michael Redgrave.'

Playing a pupil late for school, he spent an enjoyable five weeks on the film set during the summer holidays. 'It was thanks to actor Jack May, who appeared in the film and was a family friend, that I got the part. The producer was looking for people to play public schoolboys and Jack suggested me.'

After graduating from Cambridge, he studied at drama school and completed a summer season at Southwold before working with theatre companies up and down the country. His TV debut arrived as a guard in an episode of *Blake's 7*. Other early TV credits included the mini-series, *I Remember Nelson*. After *'Allo 'Allo!*, Nicholas played Sergeant Sennet in the TV series, *The Mixer* – the last thing he did on television. 'But, my final acting job was in 1995, a theatre show at Sonning, directed by Simon Williams.'

By this time, Nicholas was already in the process of switching careers. 'I'd attended a computer course and discovered I could programme computers.' After unearthing this hidden talent in computing, he decided to develop it and secured a job at a computer software company in Cambridge. 'I became immersed in my new career, by which time acting work wasn't coming along – perhaps I wasn't pushing hard enough. I'd also done occasional supply teaching, covering maths in secondary schools in London and Cambridgeshire, but stopped that to settle into my computing career.'

Nicholas is now a software engineer in Cambridge, specialising – ironically, given his acting history – in communication protocols. He says: 'Colleagues know about my time in *'Allo 'Allo!* and have asked me to sign photos, which is flattering. Although I no longer actively seek acting work, if something came along I fancied, who knows? Sometimes I miss the industry but, fortunately, I enjoy using my mathematical brain for computing, too, so am happy with how things have turned out.'

THE ITALIANS

The foppish Captain Bertorelli arrived in Nouvion during Series 4, but we learn little about his background other than he was a gondolier in Venice before the war. His arrival in the town wasn't welcomed by the Germans, especially Colonel Von Strohm, who was told the Italian was his new assistant, acting as a liaison officer. The smooth-talking Italian fancied himself something rotten, and was always grabbing every opportunity to smother the local girls – and even Madame Edith – with kisses.

GAVIN RICHARDS
(Captain Alberto Bertorelli – Series 4, episode 3 – Series 6)

London-born actor Gavin Richards trained at Bristol Old Vic Theatre School before embarking on a career encompassing acting, writing and directing on stage and screen.

In addition to playing the Italian captain, Gavin is best remembered for his portrayal of Terry Raymond in *EastEnders*, a role which lasted over 300 episodes. Other TV credits include *Coronation Street*, playing general manager Harold Fox in episodes of Perry and Croft's holiday camp sitcom, *Hi-De-Hi!*, *Lovejoy*, *Minder*, *Inspector Morse* and *Hannay*, in which he co-starred with Robert Powell.

In the theatre, he earned many plaudits and an Olivier Award nomination for his West End hit, *Accidental Death Of An Anarchist*, in 1980.

Together with his New Zealand-born wife, Tamara Henry, Richards launched his own theatre company, Theatre South, and now lives in Blenheim, in the north east of South Island.

ROGER KITTER
(Captain Alberto Bertorelli – Series 7)

When Gavin Richards left the series, Roger Kitter was brought in to play Captain Bertorelli on stage for a summer season at Blackpool in 1990, joining the likes of Vicki Michelle and Sue Hodge from the TV cast. 'Halfway through the season, I got a call asking if I'd like to play him in the next TV series.

CATCHPHRASES

"What a mistake-a to make-a."
(Captain Bertorelli)

I jumped at the chance, but it meant leaving the summer show early to record the TV series.'

Having seen a few episodes of the sitcom, he knew what was required in terms of the character portrayal. 'It's one thing taking over a character in a stage show but in this case it had been on for years and become established. Without doing an impression, you want to be as close as you can to the way he was played before.'

Roger appeared as the Italian captain for just one season, Series 7, before the character was written out to reflect Italy's departure from the war. But Roger enjoyed his brief spell in the TV programme and his much-longer association with the stage show. 'I ended up touring for five years, working with people from the original cast. The last time I did it was a season at the Pier Theatre, Bournemouth.'

Roger, who's spent over four decades in the entertainment business, started out as an impressionist. For five years, he appeared on London Weekend's sketch show, *Who Do You Do*, before other jobs came along, including stints on *It's Lulu* and *Punchlines*. Occasional acting jobs after playing Bertorelli included roles in *Goodnight Sweetheart* and *Birds Of A Feather*.

Now, Roger has quit performing and works on the other side of the footlights. 'I'm working with a company, Musicality, who put out concerts over the internet.'

The Duel

René is in bed with Edith who is wearing a hairnet, face cream and cotton wool on her eyes. Her alarm goes off.

EDITH: René, wake up. Wake up! It is 5 o'clock. You must not be late for the duel.

RENÉ: But Edith, that is not until seven. Uh! *(He catches sight of her cream-covered face)*

EDITH: I know, but I have to dress and make up and iron your shirt. You are not going to the woods looking a mess. To think that men are prepared to die for me.

RENÉ: It is unbelievable is it not?

(A knocking is heard on the door downstairs)

EDITH: René, go down and see who's at the door.

RENÉ: Who can that be at this hour?

EDITH: It may be somebody wanting to buy tickets.

RENÉ: You have been selling tickets?

EDITH: Well, only for the front row.

PRODUCTION TEAM

(Only those acknowledged in the closing credits of the television episodes are included in this list.)

SCRIPTS

All scripts written by Jeremy Lloyd and David Croft, except: Series 7–9 and Christmas 91, written by Jeremy Lloyd and Paul Adam; Series 5, episode 24 by John Chapman and Ian Davidson; Series 5, episode 25 by Ronald Wolfe and Ronald Chesney.

PRODUCER

David Croft (Pilot; Series 1–6; Christmas 85); Mike Stephens (S7); John B. Hobbs (Christmas 91; S8–S9)

DIRECTOR

David Croft (Pilot; Series 1–2; Christmas 85; Series 3, episode 1; Series 4, episode 5; Series 5, episode 1; Series 6, episodes 1–2); David Croft and Robin Carr (Series 3, episodes 2–6); David Croft and Martin Dennis (S4, episodes 1–4 and 6); Martin Dennis (S5, episodes 2–6, 13–19; S6, episodes 3–8); Richard Boden (S5, episodes 20–26); Susan Belbin (S5, episode 7–12); Mike Stephens (S7, episodes 1, 3, 5, 7, 9); Sue Longstaff (S7, episodes 2, 4, 6, 8, 10); John B. Hobbs (Christmas 91; S8–S9)

FILM CAMERAMAN

William Dudman (Pilot); Max Samett (S1, episodes 2–7; S2, episodes 2–6; Christmas 85; S3, episodes 1–6; S4, episodes 1, 2, 4, 6; S6)

FILM SOUND

Alan Cooper (Pilot); Terry Elms (S1, episodes 2–7); Michael Spencer (S2, episodes 2–6; Christmas 85; S3, episodes 1–6; S4, episodes 1, 2, 4, 6); John A. Parry (S6)

FILM EDITOR

John Dunstan (Pilot; S1, episodes 2–7; S2, episodes 2–6; Christmas 85; S3, episodes 1–6; S4, episodes 1, 2, 4, 6); Rob Poole (S6)

MAKE-UP DESIGNER

Sylvia Thornton (Pilot); Helen Barrett (S1); Benita Barrell (S2; Christmas 85; S3); Lisa Pickering (S4); Ann Rayment (S5); Linda McInnes (S5, episodes 14–16, with Ann Rayment); Charlotte Betsworth (S6); Joan Stribling (S7, episodes 1–6; 7–10 with Jan Phillips); Jan Phillips (S7, episodes 7–10 with Joan Stribling); Suzanne Jansen (Christmas 91 and S8); Jane Walker (S9)

COSTUME DESIGNER

Laura Ergis and Doreen James (Pilot); Jackie Southern (S1; S2 and Christmas 85 as Jacqueline Parry); Anna Stubley (S3); Christian Dyall (S4, S5, episodes 1–12); Sheena Napier (S5, episodes 13–26; S6); Carol Lawrence (S7); Rosemary Cheshire (Christmas 91 and S8); Jill Taylor (S9)

PROPERTIES BUYER

Roger Wood (Pilot); Brenda Barker (S1); John Watts (S2 & Christmas 85); Chris Ferriday (S3); Paul Richmond (S4); Roger Williams (S5, episodes 1–6); Pauline Seager (S5, episodes 7–19; Christmas 91; S8); Phil Taylor (S5, episodes 20–26); Sue Claybyn (S6); Nick Barnett (S7); Jayne Libotte (S9)

VISUAL EFFECTS DESIGNER

Peter Wragg (Pilot); Ted Grumbt/Effects Associates (S1); David Barton (S2, episodes 2 and 3); David Barton and Colin Mapson (S2, episodes 6; Christmas 85); Stephen Lucas (S3, S5, episodes 1–4, 6; S7); Colin Gorry (S4); Robert Thomas (S5, episodes 7–13); David Bezkorowajny (S5, episodes 13–19); Roger Turner (S5, episodes 20–26); Andy Lazell (S6 and S9); Sinclair Brebner (Christmas 91 and S8)

TECHNICAL/RESOURCES COORDINATOR

Jim Cook (S5, episodes 1–12); Richard Philipps (S5, episode 12 with Jim Cook; episodes 13–25); Jeff Jeffery (S5, episode 26); Nick Moore (S6); Steve Lowry (S7, episodes 1, 4–7, 9–10); Richard Hersee (S7, episodes 2–3; Christmas 91; S8; S9); Dinkar Jhalera (S7, episodes 8–9); John Bird (S7, episode 10)

VISION MIXER

Angela Beveridge (Pilot; S1–5; Christmas 85); Hilary West (S6); Sue Collins (S7, episodes 1–4, 6); Anne Stanley (S7, episodes 5, 7–9); Kathryn Randall (Christmas 91; S8, episodes 1, 3–7); Mary Kellehar (S8, episode 2); Carol Abbott (S9)

SENIOR CAMERAMAN
Garth Tucker (Pilot)

CAMERA SUPERVISOR
Ken Major (S1; S2, episodes 1–6; S3; S4, episodes 2–3, 5–6; S5, episodes 1, 10–26; S6; S7, except episode 5); Doug Watson (S4, episode 1); Mike Harrison (S4, episode 4); Stuart Lindley (S5, episodes 2–8); Steve Cockayne (S5, episode 9); Chris Glass (S7, episode 5); Roger Goss (Christmas 91; S8, episodes 1–3, 6–7; S9); Alan Bagley (S8, episodes 4–5); Colin Reid (Christmas 85)

LOCATIONS CAMERA
Roger Goss (S8, episodes 4–5; S9)

ASSISTANT FLOOR MANAGER
Sarah Gowers (S5, episodes 1, 13–19); Charles Garland (S5, episodes 2–6; S6); John Gorringe (S5, episodes 7–12); Francesca Gilpin (S5, episodes 20–26); Mark Mylod (S7); Matthew Napier (Christmas 91 and S8); Michael Towner (S9)

The Nicked Knockwurst

Monsieur Alfonse has been invited to dinner with Edith so she can persuade him to part with some of his money.

RENÉ: Ah, Monsieur Alfonse, welcome to my humble restaurant.
MONSIEUR ALFONSE: Monsieur René, I was burying the Widow Blanquette when I received the invitation. I dropped everything.
(Edith comes down the stairs)
EDITH: Ah, Monsieur Alfonse.
MONSIEUR ALFONSE: Madame Edith, I feel like a man twenty years younger. (Kisses her hand)
RENÉ: So does she but we need his money.

PRODUCTION MANAGER
Susan Belbin (Pilot; S1); Martin Dennis (S1, episodes 2–7; S2; Christmas 85; S3; S5, episode 1); Robin Carr (S3, episode 1 with Martin Dennis); Simon

Spencer (S4; S5, episodes 3–8 with Roy Gould); Ian Strachan (S5, episodes 1–6, 9); Nick Jowitt (S5, episodes 7–12); Mick Evans (S5, episodes 13–19); Roy Gould (S5, episodes 20–26; S6, episodes 1–2, 3–8 with Simon Spencer); Simon Spencer (S7, episode 8, with Suzanna Shaw); Peter R. Lovell (S7, episodes 1–7); Suzanna Shaw (S7, episodes 1–6, 8); Mike Pearce (S7, episode 7; S9); Jez Nightingale (Christmas 91 and S8)

PRODUCTION TEAM
Babara Jones and Penny Thompson (Pilot); Bernadette Darnell, Roy Gould and Martin Dennis (S1, episode 1); Bernadette Darnell and Roy Gould (S1, episodes 2–7); Bernadette Darnell, Jackie Wright, Simon Spencer and Arch Dyson (S2 and Christmas 85); Bernadette Darnell, Roy Gould and Charles Garland (S3); Arch Dyson and Bernadette Darnell (S4)

PRODUCTION ASSISTANT
Bernadette Darnell (S5, episodes 1–6); Penny Thompson (S5, episodes 7–12); Susan Silburn (S5, episodes 13–19); Melanie Hall (S5, episodes 20–26); Nikki Cockcroft (S6); Poonam Megone (S7–S8; Christmas 91); Susan Lawton (S9)

PRODUCTION SECRETARY
Fiona Strachan (S8, episode 7); Simon Sharrod (S9)

VIDEOTAPE EDITOR
Phil Southby (Pilot; S2, episodes 1, 3 & 5; Christmas 85; S3, episodes 2, 4 and 6); Chris Wadsworth (S1, episode 1; S2, episode 2; S3, episodes 1, 3 and 5; S4, episodes 2 and 4; S5; S6, episodes 2–8, Christmas 91; S8, S9); Chris Booth (S1, episodes 2, 4 and 6); Roger Martin (S1, episodes 3, 5 and 7; S2, episode 6; S7); Ed Wooden (S4, episodes 1, 3, 5 and 6); John Bignold (S6, episode 1)

STUDIO SOUND/SOUND SUPERVISOR
Michael McCarthy (Pilot; S1; S2; Christmas 85; S3; S5; S6, episodes 1–2, 4–5); Len Shorey (S4, episode 1, 3 & 4); Tony Philpott (S4, episode 2 and 6); Keith Mayes (S4, episode 5); Hugh Barker (S6, episode 3); Martin Deane (S6, episode 6); Martin Ridout (S6, episode 7–8); Graham Wilkinson (S7); Alan Machin (S8–S9 and Christmas 91)

STUDIO LIGHTING/LIGHTING DIRECTOR
Duncan Brown (Pilot; S1; S2; Christmas 85; S4; S5; S6); Alan Jeffery (S3,

episodes 1–4 and 6); Harry Bradley (S3, episode 5; S7); Henry Barber (S8–S9 and Christmas 91)

DESIGNER
Shelagh Lawson (Pilot); Janet Budden (S1); David Buckingham (S2–5 and Christmas 85); Gary Williamson (S6, episodes 1–6); Gary Freeman and Paul Cross (S6, episode 7); Bob Steer and Paul Cross (S6, episode 8); Roger Harris (S7); John Stout (Christmas 91 and S8); Shaun Moore (S9); Nora Marshall (S9, episode 6)

TECHNICAL ADVISOR
Air Commodore E. S. Chandler A.F.C. (credited on S1, episode 4; S2, episode 3; S3, episode 6; S4, episode 1)

GRAPHIC DESIGNER
Andrew Smee (S7)

CHOREOGRAPHER/DANCE STAGED BY
Kenn Oldfield (S1, episode 7; S3, episode 5; S6, episodes 3 and 5); Tudor Davies (S2, episode 6)

THEME MUSIC
Written by David Croft and Roy Moore

MUSICAL ASSOCIATE
Roy Moore (S2, episode 6; S3, episode 3; credited as Musical Director for S5, episode 23)

STUNT COORDINATOR
Stuart Fell (S6, episodes 3, 4 and 8)

STUNT PERFORMERS
Nick Wilkinson and Bernard Barnsley (S6, episode 3); Denise Ryan (S6, episode 8)

EPISODE GUIDE

Note: David Croft and Jeremy Lloyd didn't formally allocate episode titles for their *'Allo 'Allo!* scripts. Over the years, various versions have popped up on fan and TV sites. The titles chosen for this book are those held by the BBC and are as close as we're going to get to the official episode names.

PILOT

The British Are Coming

Transmitted: 30/12/82

CAST

Gorden Kaye	René Artois
Carmen Silvera	Edith Artois
Vicki Michelle	Yvette
Francesca Gonshaw	Maria
Richard Marner	Colonel Von Strohm
Sam Kelly	Captain Geering
Guy Siner	Lieutenant Gruber
Kim Hartman	Helga Geerhart
Richard Gibson	Otto Flick
Kirsten Cooke	Michelle Dubois
Jack Haig	Monsieur Leclerc
Rose Hill	Madame La Fan
John D. Collins	Flight Lieutenant Fairfax
Nicholas Frankau	Flight Lieutenant Carstairs
Richard Cottan	Claude

Put-upon René is informed by Michelle of the French Resistance that his café has been chosen as a safe-house to shelter shot-down British and Allied airmen; the first two arrive a couple of days early, giving René a headache deciding where to hide them. To add to his woes, he's blackmailed by the local German colonel to conceal stolen valuables, including *The Fallen Madonna With The Big Boobies*, a painting by Van Klomp.

SERIES 1

1. The Fallen Madonna

Transmitted: 7/9/84

CAST	
Gorden Kaye	René Artois
Carmen Silvera	Edith Artois
Vicki Michelle	Yvette
Francesca Gonshaw	Maria
Richard Marner	Colonel Von Strohm
Sam Kelly	Captain Geering
Guy Siner	Lieutenant Gruber
Kim Hartman	Helga Geerhart
Richard Gibson	Otto Flick
Kirsten Cooke	Michelle Dubois
Jack Haig	Monsieur Leclerc
Rose Hill	Madame La Fan
John D. Collins	Flight Lieutenant Fairfax
Nicholas Frankau	Flight Lieutenant Carstairs

Colonel Von Strohm tells René that not only do they need to send the priceless *Fallen Madonna With The Big Boobies* to Hitler but are snitching on the café owner, too, by revealing to the Gestapo that he's harbouring shot-down pilots and aiding their return to Blighty. To save his neck, René persuades Von Strohm to send a copy of the painting so that the Colonel can sell the original after the war, making a fortune in the process. The only trouble is, the French Resistance's forger can't paint so the British airmen must get the picture copied in Britain.

2. Pigeon Post

Transmitted: 14/9/84

CAST

Gorden Kaye	René Artois
Carmen Silvera	Edith Artois
Vicki Michelle	Yvette
Francesca Gonshaw	Maria
Richard Marner	Colonel Von Strohm
Sam Kelly	Captain Geering
Guy Siner	Lieutenant Gruber
Kim Hartman	Helga Geerhart
Richard Gibson	Otto Flick
Kirsten Cooke	Michelle Dubois
Jack Haig	Monsieur Leclerc
Rose Hill	Madame La Fan
John D. Collins	Flight Lieutenant Fairfax
Nicholas Frankau	Flight Lieutenant Carstairs
Denise Kelly	Maquis Leader
Phoebe Scholfield	Henriette (Michelle's Assistant)

Colonel Von Strohm and Captain Geering's uniforms have been borrowed by the British airmen for their attempt to return home, but they run into trouble when captured by the Communist branch of the French Resistance. Although they're eventually released and return safely to Café René with *The Fallen Madonna*, the German uniforms are burnt, leaving no alternative but to request replacements from Britain.

3. Saville Row To The Rescue

Transmitted: 21/9/84

CAST

Gorden Kaye	René Artois
Carmen Silvera	Edith Artois
Vicki Michelle	Yvette
Francesca Gonshaw	Maria
Richard Marner	Colonel Von Strohm
Sam Kelly	Captain Geering
Guy Siner	Lieutenant Gruber
Kim Hartman	Helga Geerhart
Richard Gibson	Otto Flick
Kirsten Cooke	Michelle Dubois
Jack Haig	Monsieur Leclerc
Rose Hill	Madame La Fan
John D. Collins	Flight Lieutenant Fairfax
Nicholas Frankau	Flight Lieutenant Carstairs
John Bluthal	Tailor
Kim Wall	German Sentry
Phoebe Scholfield	Henriette (Michelle's Assistant)
Graham Seed	Pilot

René has been collared into hiding some nitroglycerin for the French Resistance who intend blowing up the local railway line. Meanwhile, the Colonel and Captain – disguised as onion sellers whilst awaiting their new uniforms – are dragged in to Resistance activities. But just when they think their new uniforms have arrived, the tailor landing in the two-seater plane informs them he's only popped over for a fitting.

4. The Execution

Transmitted: 28/9/84

CAST

Gorden Kaye	René Artois
Carmen Silvera	Edith Artois
Vicki Michelle	Yvette
Francesca Gonshaw	Maria
Richard Marner	Colonel Von Strohm
Sam Kelly	Captain Geering
Guy Siner	Lieutenant Gruber
Kim Hartman	Helga Geerhart
Richard Gibson	Otto Flick
Kirsten Cooke	Michelle Dubois
Jack Haig	Monsieur Leclerc
Rose Hill	Madame La Fan
John D. Collins	Flight Lieutenant Fairfax
Nicholas Frankau	Flight Lieutenant Carstairs
Hilary Minster	General Von Klinkerhoffen
Trevor T. Smith	German Guard
Phoebe Scholfield	Henriette (Michelle's Assistant)

While out with the French Resistance reluctantly helping blow up a railway line, René is captured. Accused of being the ring-leader, General Von Klinkerhoffen orders that the café owner is shot at dawn. The German Colonel and Captain try convincing the General that he should be released, but Von Klinkerhoffen is having none of it and demands that René is made an example of by facing the firing squad. But thanks to some dummy bullets he lives to tell the tale – disguised as his twin brother.

5. The Funeral

Transmitted: 5/10/84

CAST

Gorden Kaye	René Artois
Carmen Silvera	Edith Artois
Vicki Michelle	Yvette
Francesca Gonshaw	Maria
Richard Marner	Colonel Von Strohm
Sam Kelly	Captain Geering
Guy Siner	Lieutenant Gruber
Kim Hartman	Helga Geerhart
Richard Gibson	Otto Flick
Kirsten Cooke	Michelle Dubois
Jack Haig	Monsieur Leclerc
Rose Hill	Madame La Fan
John D. Collins	Flight Lieutenant Fairfax
Nicholas Frankau	Flight Lieutenant Carstairs
Kenneth Connor	Monsieur Alfonse
Michael Stainton	German Sergeant

René, masquerading as his twin brother, is back running the café, but when Herr Flick orders the German colonel and captain attend the saboteur's funeral, in an attempt to spot other potential trouble-makers, René has to go along with the farce and turn up at his own funeral. But the event ends in disaster when a runaway coffin tips over and is blown up by a land mine.

6. Red Nick's Colonel

Transmitted: 19/10/84

CAST

Gorden Kaye	René Artois
Carmen Silvera	Edith Artois
Vicki Michelle	Yvette
Francesca Gonshaw	Maria
Richard Marner	Colonel Von Strohm
Sam Kelly	Captain Geering
Guy Siner	Lieutenant Gruber
Kim Hartman	Helga Geerhart
Richard Gibson	Otto Flick
Kirsten Cooke	Michelle Dubois
Jack Haig	Monsieur Leclerc
Rose Hill	Madame La Fan
John D. Collins	Flight Lieutenant Fairfax
Nicholas Frankau	Flight Lieutenant Carstairs
Susan Kyd	Communist Resistance Leader
Pia Henderson	Communist Resistance Girl

The Colonel and Captain are arrested by the Communist Resistance and face execution in revenge for the apparent shooting of René – and it's the café owner, disguised as his twin brother, tasked with carrying out the job. Fortunately, he's able to deceive the Resistance and save the Germans' skins. Meanwhile, the original and forgery of *The Fallen Madonna With The Big Boobies* arrive at Nouvion, but it's the wrong painting which is handed back to Herr Flick.

7. The Dance Of Hitler Youth

Transmitted: 26/10/84

CAST

Gorden Kaye	René Artois
Carmen Silvera	Edith Artois
Vicki Michelle	Yvette
Francesca Gonshaw	Maria
Richard Marner	Colonel Von Strohm
Sam Kelly	Captain Geering
Guy Siner	Lieutenant Gruber
Kim Hartman	Helga Geerhart
Richard Gibson	Otto Flick
Kirsten Cooke	Michelle Dubois
Jack Haig	Monsieur Leclerc
Rose Hill	Madame La Fan
John D. Collins	Flight Lieutenant Fairfax
Nicholas Frankau	Flight Lieutenant Carstairs
Iain Rattray	German Major
Philip Kendall	'London Calling'
Peter Waddington, Gordon Dulieu, David Beckett and Ray Float	German Sentries

The Resistance attempt to retrieve the real painting of *The Fallen Madonna*. Meanwhile, a new radio transmitter is delivered by Monsieur Leclerc to replace the former model which was thrown out of the bedroom window when in danger of being discovered by Herr Flick.

SERIES 2

1. Six Big Boobies

Transmitted: 21/10/85

CAST	
Gorden Kaye	René Artois
Carmen Silvera	Edith Artois
Vicki Michelle	Yvette
Francesca Gonshaw	Maria
Richard Marner	Colonel Von Strohm
Sam Kelly	Captain Geering
Guy Siner	Lieutenant Gruber
Kim Hartman	Helga Geerhart
Richard Gibson	Otto Flick
Kirsten Cooke	Michelle Dubois
Jack Haig	Monsieur Leclerc
Rose Hill	Madame La Fan
John D. Collins	Flight Lieutenant Fairfax
Nicholas Frankau	Flight Lieutenant Carstairs
James Gow	German Soldier

Herr Flick ends up with three versions of *The Fallen Madonna*: two forgeries and the original, which he intends selling after the war to make his fortune; trouble is, he needs to identify which is the genuine article. Helga is tasked with finding someone knowledgeable to spot the real deal – that turns out to be Lieutenant Gruber, who worked as an art gallery assistant in Cologne before the war.

2. The Wooing Of Widow Artois

Transmitted: 28/10/85

CAST

Gorden Kaye	René Artois
Carmen Silvera	Edith Artois
Vicki Michelle	Yvette
Francesca Gonshaw	Maria
Richard Marner	Colonel Von Strohm
Sam Kelly	Captain Geering
Guy Siner	Lieutenant Gruber
Kim Hartman	Helga Geerhart
Richard Gibson	Otto Flick
Kirsten Cooke	Michelle Dubois
Jack Haig	Monsieur Leclerc
Rose Hill	Madame La Fan
John D. Collins	Flight Lieutenant Fairfax
Nicholas Frankau	Flight Lieutenant Carstairs
Rusty Goffe	Pierre Le Grand
Phoebe Scholfield	Henriette (Michelle's Assistant)
James Gow	'London Calling'

René has his work cut out reclaiming the heart of Madame Edith. The supposed passing of the café owner means everything has been bequeathed to her. Now that she is in the money, Edith becomes the subject of much wooing. Meanwhile, Herr Flick decides to send a forgery of *The Fallen Madonna* to Hitler while the original, disguised as a sausage, will be given to René for safe-keeping. But the Colonel, who's asked to carry out the task, has other ideas.

3. The Policeman Cometh

Transmitted: 4/11/85

CAST

Gorden Kaye	René Artois
Carmen Silvera	Edith Artois
Vicki Michelle	Yvette
Francesca Gonshaw	Maria
Richard Marner	Colonel Von Strohm
Sam Kelly	Captain Geering
Guy Siner	Lieutenant Gruber
Kim Hartman	Helga Geerhart
Richard Gibson	Otto Flick
Kirsten Cooke	Michelle Dubois
Jack Haig	Monsieur Leclerc
Rose Hill	Madame La Fan
John D. Collins	Flight Lieutenant Fairfax
Nicholas Frankau	Flight Lieutenant Carstairs
Arthur Bostrom	Officer Crabtree
Phoebe Scholfield	Henriette (Michelle's Assistant)
Gordon Dulieu	German Soldier
David Beckett	German Sergeant

Disguised as a policeman, Crabtree, a British Intelligence agent, arrives on the scene speaking pidgin French. Over at German HQ, the Colonel's plan to blow up the train supposedly carrying *The Fallen Madonna* painting to Hitler backfires meaning he has to take matters into his own hands. Unfortunately, with René driving Gruber's armoured car and Captain Geering in charge of the gun, it's no surprise they miss their target.

4. Swiftly And With Style

Transmitted: 11/11/85

CAST

Gorden Kaye	René Artois
Carmen Silvera	Edith Artois
Vicki Michelle	Yvette
Francesca Gonshaw	Maria
Richard Marner	Colonel Von Strohm
Sam Kelly	Captain Geering
Guy Siner	Lieutenant Gruber
Kim Hartman	Helga Geerhart
Richard Gibson	Otto Flick
Kirsten Cooke	Michelle Dubois
Arthur Bostrom	Officer Crabtree
Jack Haig	Monsieur Leclerc
Rose Hill	Madame La Fan
John D. Collins	Flight Lieutenant Fairfax
Nicholas Frankau	Flight Lieutenant Carstairs
Kenneth Connor	Monsieur Alfonse
Phoebe Scholfield	Henriette (Michelle's Assistant)
Peggy Ann Clifford	French Lady

Good news arrives for the Colonel when it transpires that the RAF blew up the train transporting the sausage containing the painting. Over at the café, René has more important matters on his mind when he's challenged to a duel by Monsieur Alfonse, who proposes to Madame Edith and is determined to win her hand in marriage.

5. The Duel

Transmitted: 18/11/85

CAST	

Gorden Kaye	René Artois
Carmen Silvera	Edith Artois
Vicki Michelle	Yvette
Francesca Gonshaw	Maria
Richard Marner	Colonel Von Strohm
Sam Kelly	Captain Geering
Guy Siner	Lieutenant Gruber
Kim Hartman	Helga Geerhart
Richard Gibson	Otto Flick
Kirsten Cooke	Michelle Dubois
Arthur Bostrom	Officer Crabtree
Kenneth Connor	Monsieur Alfonse
John Louis Mansi	Herr Von Smallhausen
Jack Haig	Monsieur Leclerc
Rose Hill	Madame La Fan
John D. Collins	Flight Lieutenant Fairfax
Nicholas Frankau	Flight Lieutenant Carstairs
Phoebe Scholfield	Henriette (Michelle's Assistant)

René tries everything to wriggle out of duelling with Monsieur Alfonse, but Edith likes the sound of two men fighting over her and brands him a coward. The Colonel, however, hatches a plan for helping the café owner which will result in the undertaker's death. But the event turns into a damp squib when René runs off into the distance.

6. Herr Flick's Revenge

Transmitted: 25/11/85

CAST

Gorden Kaye	René Artois
Carmen Silvera	Edith Artois
Vicki Michelle	Yvette
Francesca Gonshaw	Maria
Richard Marner	Colonel Von Strohm
Sam Kelly	Captain Geering
Guy Siner	Lieutenant Gruber
Kim Hartman	Helga Geerhart
Richard Gibson	Otto Flick
Kirsten Cooke	Michelle Dubois
Arthur Bostrom	Officer Crabtree
Kenneth Connor	Monsieur Alfonse
John Louis Mansi	Herr Von Smallhausen
Jack Haig	Monsieur Leclerc
Rose Hill	Madame La Fan
John D. Collins	Flight Lieutenant Fairfax
Nicholas Frankau	Flight Lieutenant Carstairs
Hilary Minster	General Von Klinkerhoffen
Phoebe Scholfield	Henriette (Michelle's Assistant)
Gary Merry	German Soldier
Philip Kendall	'London Calling'

René is disguised as a female member of the Resistance in order to hide from Monsieur Alfonse, but when the undertaker discovers that the café owner is leader of the Escape Route, he decides to admire Edith from afar and respect René. But the café owner finds himself in hot water when he's arrested, along with the Colonel and Captain, by Herr Flick; the Gestapo leader intends using torture until someone tells him where the painting, which never arrived in Berlin, can be found.

CHRISTMAS SPECIAL

The Gateau From The Château

Transmitted: 26/12/85

CAST

Gorden Kaye	René Artois
Carmen Silvera	Edith Artois
Vicki Michelle	Yvette
Francesca Gonshaw	Maria
Richard Marner	Colonel Von Strohm
Sam Kelly	Captain Geering
Guy Siner	Lieutenant Gruber
Kim Hartman	Helga Geerhart
Richard Gibson	Otto Flick
Kirsten Cooke	Michelle Dubois
Jack Haig	Monsieur Leclerc
Rose Hill	Madame La Fan
John D. Collins	Flight Lieutenant Fairfax
Nicholas Frankau	Flight Lieutenant Carstairs
Hilary Minster	General Von Klinkerhoffen
Phoebe Scholfield	Henriette (Michelle's Assistant)
Joy Allen	Mrs Fairfax
Julie-Christian Young	Operator
Philip Kendall	'London Calling'

With so many incidents occurring around Nouvion, General Von Klinkerhoffen decides to take a more active role in the area; but everyone becomes so frustrated and fed up with his interference that separate plans are drawn up by the Resistance, Colonel Von Strohm aided by Captain Geering and Herr Flick to bump him off. But the plans go awry.

SERIES 3

1. The Nicked Knockwurst

Transmitted: 5/12/86

CAST

Gorden Kaye	René Artois
Carmen Silvera	Edith Artois
Vicki Michelle	Yvette
Francesca Gonshaw	Maria
Richard Marner	Colonel Von Strohm
Sam Kelly	Captain Geering
Guy Siner	Lieutenant Gruber
Kim Hartman	Helga Geerhart
Richard Gibson	Otto Flick
Kirsten Cooke	Michelle Dubois
Arthur Bostrom	Officer Crabtree
Kenneth Connor	Monsieur Alfonse
John Louis Mansi	Herr Von Smallhausen
Jack Haig	Monsieur Leclerc
Rose Hill	Madame La Fan
John D. Collins	Flight Lieutenant Fairfax
Nicholas Frankau	Flight Lieutenant Carstairs
Paul Cooper	German Tailor
Lisa Anselmi	Communist Resistance Leader
Gabrielle Dellal	Communist Girl
Ian Hanham	German Ambush Leader

Although the genuine version of *The Fallen Madonna With The Big Boobies* is hidden in René's cellar, the Germans have been ordered by their hierarchy to raze the town to the ground if the painting hidden inside a sausage stolen by the Communist Resistance – which, in fact, is a forgery – isn't returned; unfortunately, 800,000 francs is the sum required to reclaim it and René is told to raise the funds.

2. Gruber Does Some Mincing

Transmitted: 12/12/86

CAST

Gorden Kaye	René Artois
Carmen Silvera	Edith Artois
Vicki Michelle	Yvette
Francesca Gonshaw	Maria
Richard Marner	Colonel Von Strohm
Sam Kelly	Captain Geering
Guy Siner	Lieutenant Gruber
Kim Hartman	Helga Geerhart
Richard Gibson	Otto Flick
Kirsten Cooke	Michelle Dubois
Arthur Bostrom	Officer Crabtree
Kenneth Connor	Monsieur Alfonse
John Louis Mansi	Herr Von Smallhausen
Jack Haig	Monsieur Leclerc
Rose Hill	Madame La Fan
John D. Collins	Flight Lieutenant Fairfax
Nicholas Frankau	Flight Lieutenant Carstairs
Sherry Louise Plant	Lisette (French Resistance)
Paul Cooper	'London Calling'

The 800,000 francs used to retrieve the painting from the Communist Resistance came from Monsieur Alfonse, but the usual chaos resulted in Gruber's dog grabbing the sausage containing the painting and the undertaker facing the loss of his life savings. Yvette has a plan to solve the monetary crisis by getting Monsieur Leclerc to forge some notes, but the counterfeit francs come back to haunt René.

3. The Sausage In The Wardrobe

Transmitted: 19/12/86

CAST

Gorden Kaye	René Artois
Carmen Silvera	Edith Artois
Vicki Michelle	Yvette
Francesca Gonshaw	Maria
Richard Marner	Colonel Von Strohm
Sam Kelly	Captain Geering
Guy Siner	Lieutenant Gruber
Kim Hartman	Helga Geerhart
Richard Gibson	Otto Flick
Kirsten Cooke	Michelle Dubois
Arthur Bostrom	Officer Crabtree
Jack Haig	Monsieur Leclerc
Rose Hill	Madame La Fan
John D. Collins	Flight Lieutenant Fairfax
Nicholas Frankau	Flight Lieutenant Carstairs
Hilary Minster	General Von Klinkerhoffen
Christopher Wild	German Soldier
Tim Barker	German Soldier
Paul Cooper	'London Calling'
Philip McInnerny	'Wing Commander Hargreaves'

While Maria is taking the priceless painting, hidden inside the sausage, to the Château for Gruber to copy, she's arrested and marched to General Von Klinkerhoffen for questioning. When word gets out that the sausage is now hidden in the General's wardrobe, everyone attempts to retrieve it.

4. Flight Of Fancy

Transmitted: 26/12/86

CAST

Gorden Kaye	René Artois
Carmen Silvera	Edith Artois
Vicki Michelle	Yvette
Francesca Gonshaw	Maria
Richard Marner	Colonel Von Strohm
Sam Kelly	Captain Geering
Guy Siner	Lieutenant Gruber
Kim Hartman	Helga Geerhart
Richard Gibson	Otto Flick
Kirsten Cooke	Michelle Dubois
Arthur Bostrom	Officer Crabtree
Jack Haig	Monsieur Leclerc
Rose Hill	Madame La Fan
John D. Collins	Flight Lieutenant Fairfax
Nicholas Frankau	Flight Lieutenant Carstairs
Sherry Louise Plant	Lisette (French Resistance)
Trevor T. Smith	Orderly
Len Keyes	Old Man
Robert Aldous	French Peasant
Paul Cooper	'London Calling'
Philip McInnerny	'Wing Commander Hargreaves'

While Herr Flick and the Germans find out that none of the sausages they retrieved from the General's quarters contain the painting, René is luckier and passes the genuine work of art to Gruber for copying. But he's not so lucky when roped in to the French Resistance's plan to retrieve an antique plane from a museum so the British airmen can finally set off for Blighty.

5. Pretty Maids All In A Row
Transmitted: 2/1/87

CAST

Gorden Kaye	René Artois
Carmen Silvera	Edith Artois
Vicki Michelle	Yvette
Francesca Gonshaw	Maria
Richard Marner	Colonel Von Strohm
Sam Kelly	Captain Geering
Guy Siner	Lieutenant Gruber
Kim Hartman	Helga Geerhart
Richard Gibson	Otto Flick
Kirsten Cooke	Michelle Dubois
Arthur Bostrom	Officer Crabtree
Kenneth Connor	Monsieur Alfonse
John Louis Mansi	Herr Von Smallhausen
Jack Haig	Monsieur Leclerc
Rose Hill	Madame La Fan
John D. Collins	Flight Lieutenant Fairfax
Nicholas Frankau	Flight Lieutenant Carstairs
Hilary Minster	General Von Klinkerhoffen
Ian Hanham	German Sergeant
Paul Cooper	'London Calling'

René hides *The Fallen Madonna* behind a painting of his mother-in-law, which he hangs in the café. The RAF pilots, meanwhile, don waitress outfits and parade as staff at the caff. But trouble strikes when General Von Klinkerhoffen orders the two new waitresses to work at the Château and requisitions the painting, thinking it's a genuine Van Gogh.

6. The Great Un-Escape

Transmitted: 9/1/87

CAST

Gorden Kaye	René Artois
Carmen Silvera	Edith Artois
Vicki Michelle	Yvette
Francesca Gonshaw	Maria
Richard Marner	Colonel Von Strohm
Sam Kelly	Captain Geering
Guy Siner	Lieutenant Gruber
Kim Hartman	Helga Geerhart
Richard Gibson	Otto Flick
Kirsten Cooke	Michelle Dubois
Arthur Bostrom	Officer Crabtree
Kenneth Connor	Monsieur Alfonse
John Louis Mansi	Herr Von Smallhausen
Jack Haig	Monsieur Leclerc
Rose Hill	Madame La Fan
John D. Collins	Flight Lieutenant Fairfax
Nicholas Frankau	Flight Lieutenant Carstairs
Hilary Minster	General Von Klinkerhoffen
Martin Sadler	British POW
Tim Brown	British POW
Caroline Dennis	French Girl
Nick Burnell	Camp Commandant
Paul Cooper	'London Calling'

The Resistance's latest attempt to hide the airmen sees them – and everyone at the café – digging a tunnel into the nearby prisoner-of-war camp. The Colonel and Captain suspect something is happening and eventually discover the tunnel. While investigating, the Colonel gets stuck inside and Captain Geering's attempts to dislodge him culminate in the earth collapsing behind him. Consequently, everyone ends up stuck at the camp.

SERIES 4

1. Prisoners Of War

Transmitted: 7/11/87

CAST

Gorden Kaye	René Artois
Carmen Silvera	Edith Artois
Vicki Michelle	Yvette
Richard Marner	Colonel Von Strohm
Sam Kelly	Captain Geering
Guy Siner	Lieutenant Gruber
Kim Hartman	Helga Geerhart
Richard Gibson	Otto Flick
Kirsten Cooke	Michelle Dubois
Arthur Bostrom	Officer Crabtree
Kenneth Connor	Monsieur Alfonse
John Louis Mansi	Herr Von Smallhausen
Jack Haig	Monsieur Leclerc
Rose Hill	Madame La Fan
John D. Collins	Flight Lieutenant Fairfax
Nicholas Frankau	Flight Lieutenant Carstairs
Hilary Minster	General Von Klinkerhoffen
Martin Sadler	British POW
Tim Brown	British POW
Paul Cooper	British POW
Nick Burnell	Camp Commandant
Trevor T. Smith	German Soldier
Owen Brenman	Guard

René, Edith, the Resistance and the rest of their cronies, including the General and Captain, hope to resume normal life as soon as possible. In the meantime they adjust to life inside the camp and take part in a concert.

2. Camp Dance

Transmitted: 14/11/87

CAST

Gorden Kaye	René Artois
Carmen Silvera	Edith Artois
Vicki Michelle	Yvette
Richard Marner	Colonel Von Strohm
Sam Kelly (voice only)	Captain Geering
Guy Siner	Lieutenant Gruber
Kim Hartman	Helga Geerhart
Richard Gibson	Otto Flick
Kirsten Cooke	Michelle Dubois
Arthur Bostrom	Officer Crabtree
John Louis Mansi	Herr Von Smallhausen
Jack Haig	Monsieur Leclerc
Rose Hill	Madame La Fan
John D. Collins	Flight Lieutenant Fairfax
Nicholas Frankau	Flight Lieutenant Carstairs
Hilary Minster	General Von Klinkerhoffen
Trevor T. Smith	German Camp Guard
Martin Sadler	Wing Commander
Tim Brown	Squadron Leader
Nick Burnell	Camp Commandant
Peter Bradshaw	'London Calling'

Helga and Gruber rescue René et al from the prisoner-of-war camp, just as Herr Flick and his sidekick break through the tunnel. To their dismay, Germans controlling the camp won't release them, claiming they're British in disguise. Eventually, though, they effect their escape via the tunnel. But one German missing is Hans, the captain; when his glasses are discovered it's feared he's been captured by the Communist Resistance, but it transpires that he ends up in England disguised as an RAF pilot.

3. Good Staff Are Hard To Find

Transmitted: 21/11/87

CAST

Gorden Kaye	René Artois
Carmen Silvera	Edith Artois
Vicki Michelle	Yvette
Richard Marner	Colonel Von Strohm
Guy Siner	Lieutenant Gruber
Kim Hartman	Helga Geerhart
Richard Gibson	Otto Flick
Kirsten Cooke	Michelle Dubois
Arthur Bostrom	Officer Crabtree
Jack Haig	Monsieur Leclerc
Rose Hill	Madame La Fan
John D. Collins	Flight Lieutenant Fairfax
Nicholas Frankau	Flight Lieutenant Carstairs
Hilary Minster	General Von Klinkerhoffen
Gavin Richards	Captain Bertorelli
Sue Hodge	Mimi Labonq
Aimee Delamain	Madame Sablon
Estelle Matthews	Mademoiselle Vendome
Patrick Edwards	German Guard

With Maria, the petite waitress, sent back to Switzerland after disguising herself as a Red Cross parcel at the prisoner-of-war camp, René interviews for a new waitress. But with Edith and Yvette on the interview panel, it won't be some young dish recruited to the payroll. However, it's Michelle who decides on René's new employee: Mimi Labonq, a former gang leader of the Paris Resistance; and she's not the only new face around town: Italian Captain Bertorelli is recruited as a liaison officer, working alongside the reluctant Colonel.

4. The Flying Nun

Transmitted: 28/11/87

CAST

Gorden Kaye	René Artois
Carmen Silvera	Edith Artois
Vicki Michelle	Yvette
Richard Marner	Colonel Von Strohm
Guy Siner	Lieutenant Gruber
Kim Hartman	Helga Geerhart
Richard Gibson	Otto Flick
Kirsten Cooke	Michelle Dubois
Jack Haig	Monsieur Leclerc
Rose Hill	Madame La Fan
John D. Collins	Flight Lieutenant Fairfax
Nicholas Frankau	Flight Lieutenant Carstairs
Arthur Bostrom	Officer Crabtree
Kenneth Connor	Monsieur Alfonse
John Louis Mansi	Herr Von Smallhausen
Sue Hodge	Mimi Labonq
Hilary Minster	General Von Klinkerhoffen
Gavin Richards	Captain Bertorelli
Bill Malin	German Soldier

Herr Flick suspects the Colonel and General of plotting to assassinate Hitler and disguises himself as a temporary typist working for the Colonel. Helped by a listening device, he hopes to discover what is going on. René has his work cut out, too, because explosives are needed to blow open the General's safe to retrieve plans for the invasion of Britain. Unfortunately, the radio isn't working properly and needs a bigger aerial. Michelle devises a plan utilising a kite to raise the aerial and achieve a better signal, but when René lets go of the string a flying nun is spotted!

5. The Sausages In The Trousers

Transmitted: 5/12/87

CAST

Gorden Kaye	René Artois
Carmen Silvera	Edith Artois
Vicki Michelle	Yvette
Richard Marner	Colonel Von Strohm
Guy Siner	Lieutenant Gruber
Kim Hartman	Helga Geerhart
Richard Gibson	Otto Flick
Kirsten Cooke	Michelle Dubois
Arthur Bostrom	Officer Crabtree
John Louis Mansi	Herr Von Smallhausen
Jack Haig	Monsieur Leclerc
Rose Hill	Madame La Fan
John D. Collins	Flight Lieutenant Fairfax
Nicholas Frankau	Flight Lieutenant Carstairs
Hilary Minster	General Von Klinkerhoffen
Sue Hodge	Mimi Labonq
Gavin Richards	Captain Bertorelli
Bill Malin	German Soldier
Trevor T. Smith	German Guard
Paul Cooper	'London Calling'
Stephen Churchett	'Wing Commander Belfridge'

Michelle tells René that explosives must be hidden in his cellar. They'll be delivered by a special agent concealing the dynamite within a special compartment in his trousers; another agent will bring new batteries for the radio. But when Italian salami sausages, explosives, batteries and paintings, all concealed in sausages, are delivered simultaneously, pandemonium breaks out. Meanwhile, Herr Flick is arrested and thrown in the dungeon by the General when discovered disguised as the typist.

6. The Jet-Propelled Mother-in-Law

Transmitted: 12/12/87

CAST

Gorden Kaye	René Artois
Carmen Silvera	Edith Artois
Vicki Michelle	Yvette
Richard Marner	Colonel Von Strohm
Guy Siner	Lieutenant Gruber
Kim Hartman	Helga Geerhart
Richard Gibson	Otto Flick
Kirsten Cooke	Michelle Dubois
Arthur Bostrom	Officer Crabtree
Kenneth Connor	Monsieur Alfonse
John Louis Mansi	Herr Von Smallhausen
Jack Haig	Monsieur Leclerc
Rose Hill	Madame La Fan
John D. Collins	Flight Lieutenant Fairfax
Nicholas Frankau	Flight Lieutenant Carstairs
Hilary Minster	General Von Klinkerhoffen
Sue Hodge	Mimi Labonq
Gavin Richards	Captain Bertorelli
Howard Leader	Sergeant
Trevor T. Smith	Guard
James Gow	Soldier

René is arrested and marched to the Colonel's office to explain why dynamite and batteries were discovered within the sausages, while the Resistance head for a local vineyard hoping to locate a spy camera dropped by the RAF.

SERIES 5

1. Desperate Doings In The Dungeon

Transmitted: 3/9/88

CAST

Gorden Kaye	René Artois
Carmen Silvera	Edith Artois
Vicki Michelle	Yvette
Richard Marner	Colonel Von Strohm
Guy Siner	Lieutenant Gruber
Kim Hartman	Helga Geerhart
Richard Gibson	Otto Flick
Kirsten Cooke	Michelle Dubois
Arthur Bostrom	Officer Crabtree
Kenneth Connor	Monsieur Alfonse
John Louis Mansi	Herr Von Smallhausen
Jack Haig	Monsieur Leclerc
Rose Hill	Madame La Fan
John D. Collins	Flight Lieutenant Fairfax
Nicholas Frankau	Flight Lieutenant Carstairs
Sue Hodge	Mimi Labonq
Hilary Minster	General Von Klinkerhoffen
Gavin Richards	Captain Bertorelli
James Gow	German Guard
Trevor T. Smith	German Guard

A plan is conceived to photograph the General's safe so Monsieur Leclerc can confirm if it's one he can crack so photos of the invasion plans can be taken; needing a film, René and his gang have no alternative but to steal one from the Colonel's camera. Meanwhile, Gestapo HQ is worried about the disappearance of Herr Flick, who is held in the General's cellar. Plans to secure his rescue, however, go awry and René ends up chained in the dungeon donning basque and suspenders.

2. The Camera In The Potato

Transmitted: 10/9/88

CAST

Gorden Kaye	René Artois
Carmen Silvera	Edith Artois
Vicki Michelle	Yvette
Richard Marner	Colonel Von Strohm
Guy Siner	Lieutenant Gruber
Kim Hartman	Helga Geerhart
Richard Gibson	Otto Flick
Kirsten Cooke	Michelle Dubois
Arthur Bostrom	Officer Crabtree
Kenneth Connor	Monsieur Alfonse
Jack Haig	Monsieur Leclerc
Rose Hill	Madame La Fan
John D. Collins	Flight Lieutenant Fairfax
Nicholas Frankau	Flight Lieutenant Carstairs
John Louis Mansi	Herr Von Smallhausen
Sue Hodge	Mimi Labonq
Hilary Minster	General Von Klinkerhoffen
Paul Cooper	'London Calling'
Martin Sadler	Voice of Gibson
Patrick Edwards	Solidier in Café
David Lloyd	Soldier in Château

The camera being used to photograph the safe is disguised as a potato. It's the responsibility of René, Mimi and Yvette to obtain the pictures and they head for the château, pretending to deliver food to the General's kitchen. But events take an unexpected course when the café owner loses his way and ends up in Gruber's bedroom.

3. Dinner With The General

Transmitted: 17/9/88

CAST

Gorden Kaye	René Artois
Carmen Silvera	Edith Artois
Vicki Michelle	Yvette
Richard Marner	Colonel Von Strohm
Guy Siner	Lieutenant Gruber
Kim Hartman	Helga Geerhart
Richard Gibson	Otto Flick
Kirsten Cooke	Michelle Dubois
Arthur Bostrom	Officer Crabtree
Kenneth Connor	Monsieur Alfonse
John Louis Mansi	Herr Von Smallhausen
Sue Hodge	Mimi Labonq
Hilary Minster	General Von Klinkerhoffen
Jack Haig	Monsieur Leclerc
Rose Hill	Madame La Fan
John D. Collins	Flight Lieutenant Fairfax
Nicholas Frankau	Flight Lieutenant Carstairs
Gavin Richards	Captain Bertorelli
Patrick Edwards	German Guard

Photos of the safe are developed and presented to Monsieur Leclerc to see if it can be opened to retrieve the invasion plans. It's decided that the Resistance, disguised as firemen, will break into the château grounds and drop a smoke bomb down the chimney to cause a diversion, allowing time for Leclerc to blow the safe. But the bomb is thrown down the wrong chimney, causing chaos at the château.

4. The Dreaded Circular Saw

Transmitted: 24/9/88

CAST

Gorden Kaye ....René Artois
Carmen Silvera ....Edith Artois
Vicki Michelle ....Yvette
Richard Marner ....Colonel Von Strohm
Guy Siner ....Lieutenant Gruber
Kim Hartman ....Helga Geerhart
Richard Gibson ....Otto Flick
Kirsten Cooke ....Michelle Dubois
Arthur Bostrom ....Officer Crabtree
John Louis Mansi ....Herr Von Smallhausen
Sue Hodge ....Mimi Labonq
Hilary Minster ....General Von Klinkerhoffen
Jack Haig ....Monsieur Leclerc
Rose Hill ....Madame La Fan
Gavin Richards ....Captain Bertorelli
Moira Foot ....Denise Laroque
Carole Ashby ....Louise (Communist Resistance)

(It would appear that Rose Hill's scene was cut from the DVD release.)

When the safe is blown, instead of finding invasion plans, René and the others happen upon two paintings which they discover are originals. In order to escape the chaos at the château, René and Leclerc don German uniforms, only to be captured by the Communist Resistance. When Michelle breaks the news to Edith, Yvette and Mimi, a rescue plan is devised.

5. Otherwise Engaged

Transmitted: 1/10/88

CAST

Gorden Kaye	René Artois
Carmen Silvera	Edith Artois
Vicki Michelle	Yvette
Richard Marner	Colonel Von Strohm
Guy Siner	Lieutenant Gruber
Kim Hartman	Helga Geerhart
Richard Gibson	Otto Flick
Arthur Bostrom	Officer Crabtree
Kenneth Connor	Monsieur Alfonse
John Louis Mansi	Herr Von Smallhausen
Sue Hodge	Mimi Labonq
Hilary Minster	General Von Klinkerhoffen
Jack Haig	Monsieur Leclerc
Rose Hill	Madame La Fan
John D. Collins	Flight Lieutenant Fairfax
Nicholas Frankau	Flight Lieutenant Carstairs
Gavin Richards	Captain Bertorelli
Moira Foot	Denise Laroque
	(Communist Resistance)
Carole Ashby	Louise (Communist Resistance)
Phoebe Scholfield	Communist Resistance Girl

Captured René and Leclerc strike lucky when it transpires that Denise, leader of the Communist Resistance, was an old flame of the café owner's. The only trouble is, she thinks her old sweetheart is her destiny and intends marrying him. It's a worried René who is freed to return to the café until his wedding day.

6. A Marriage Of Inconvenience

Transmitted: 8/10/88

CAST

Gorden Kaye	René Artois
Carmen Silvera	Edith Artois
Vicki Michelle	Yvette
Richard Marner	Colonel Von Strohm
Guy Siner	Lieutenant Gruber
Kim Hartman	Helga Geerhart
Richard Gibson	Otto Flick
Kirsten Cooke	Michelle Dubois
Arthur Bostrom	Officer Crabtree
Kenneth Connor	Monsieur Alfonse
Sue Hodge	Mimi Labonq
Jack Haig	Monsieur Leclerc
Rose Hill	Madame La Fan
John D. Collins	Flight Lieutenant Fairfax
Nicholas Frankau	Flight Lieutenant Carstairs
Gavin Richards	Captain Bertorelli

(It would appear John D. Collins and Nicholas Frankau's scene was cut from the DVD release.)

While the two valuable paintings, including *The Fallen Madonna With The Big Boobies*, are hidden among the beams of the old saw mill – which doubles as Communist Resistance HQ – Denise is still intent on marrying René. Edith has other ideas, though, and concocts a plan to kidnap Denise and swap places at the altar.

7. No Hiding Place

Transmitted: 15/10/88

CAST

Gorden Kaye	René Artois
Carmen Silvera	Edith Artois
Vicki Michelle	Yvette
Richard Marner	Colonel Von Strohm
Guy Siner	Lieutenant Gruber
Kim Hartman	Helga Geerhart
Richard Gibson	Otto Flick
Kirsten Cooke	Michelle Dubois
Arthur Bostrom	Officer Crabtree
Kenneth Connor	Monsieur Alfonse
John Louis Mansi	Herr Von Smallhausen
Sue Hodge	Mimi Labonq
Jack Haig	Monsieur Leclerc
Rose Hill	Madame La Fan
John D. Collins	Flight Lieutenant Fairfax
Nicholas Frankau	Flight Lieutenant Carstairs
John Rutland	Clock Repairer
Christopher Gray	German Soldier
Richard Bonehill	German Guard
Moira Foot	Denise Laroque
Carole Ashby	Louise (Communist Resistance)
Phoebe Scholfield	Communist Resistance Girl

While Edith is disappointed that her attempted marriage to René, with Crabtree pretending to be a vicar, isn't legal, everyone is worried when they hear Denise, who'd been held prisoner at the bottom of a mine shaft, has escaped. When members of the Communist Resistance, desperate for revenge after Denise's failed marriage ceremony, rush to the caff spraying bullets, rumours spread that René has been shot. Instead, he disguises himself as an old man to escape. But when no one offers him protection, he's intent on running away – until being recaptured.

8. The Arrival Of The Homing Duck

Transmitted: 22/10/88

CAST

Gorden Kaye	René Artois
Carmen Silvera	Edith Artois
Vicki Michelle	Yvette
Richard Marner	Colonel Von Strohm
Guy Siner	Lieutenant Gruber
Kim Hartman	Helga Geerhart
Richard Gibson	Otto Flick
Kirsten Cooke	Michelle Dubois
Arthur Bostrom	Officer Crabtree
Kenneth Connor	Monsieur Alfonse
John Louis Mansi	Herr Von Smallhausen
Sue Hodge	Mimi Labonq
Hilary Minster	General Von Klinkerhoffen
Jack Haig	Monsieur Leclerc
Rose Hill	Madame La Fan
John D. Collins	Flight Lieutenant Fairfax
Nicholas Frankau	Flight Lieutenant Carstairs
Gavin Richards	Captain Bertorelli
Patrick Edwards	German Guard
John Readman	Italian Soldier

René has returned to the café having been released by his intended, Denise Laroque, because she has a pressing engagement at the party conference in Lyon. Michelle barges into the café to announce that German generals are meeting at the château to discuss the invasion of Britain. As the maps will be on display, René's café is chosen to supply the catering; it's up to René and his staff to photograph the plans – the snaps will be dispatched to England by long-distance duck!

9. Watch The Birdie
Transmitted: 29/10/88

CAST

Gorden Kaye	René Artois
Carmen Silvera	Edith Artois
Vicki Michelle	Yvette
Richard Marner	Colonel Von Strohm
Guy Siner	Lieutenant Gruber
Kim Hartman	Helga Geerhart
Richard Gibson	Otto Flick
Kirsten Cooke	Michelle Dubois
Arthur Bostrom	Officer Crabtree
Kenneth Connor	Monsieur Alfonse
John Louis Mansi	Herr Von Smallhausen
Sue Hodge	Mimi Labonq
Hilary Minster	General Von Klinkerhoffen
Gavin Richards	Captain Bertorelli
Jack Haig	Monsieur Leclerc
Rose Hill	Madame La Fan
John D. Collins	Flight Lieutenant Fairfax
Nicholas Frankau	Flight Lieutenant Carstairs
Tim Brown	Tailor
Ken Morley	General Von Flockenstuffen
Paul Cooper	'London Calling'

With a camera concealed under a false apron, René is responsible for grabbing a picture of the plans while Edith causes a distraction. If that wasn't enough to worry about, military officials from London inform René that a French general attending the conference is a collaborator and must be eliminated. But schemes never run smoothly in Nouvion and the long-distance duck, responsible for carrying the film to England, escapes.

10. René – Under An Assumed Nose

Transmitted: 5/11/88

CAST

Gorden Kaye	René Artois
Carmen Silvera	Edith Artois
Vicki Michelle	Yvette
Richard Marner	Colonel Von Strohm
Guy Siner	Lieutenant Gruber
Kim Hartman	Helga Geerhart
Richard Gibson	Otto Flick
Kirsten Cooke	Michelle Dubois
Arthur Bostrom	Officer Crabtree
Kenneth Connor	Monsieur Alfonse
Sue Hodge	Mimi Labonq
Hilary Minster	General Von Klinkerhoffen
Gavin Richards	Captain Bertorelli
Jack Haig	Monsieur Leclerc
Rose Hill	Madame La Fan
John D. Collins	Flight Lieutenant Fairfax
Nicholas Frankau	Flight Lieutenant Carstairs
Paul Cooper	'London Calling'
Dick Harris	Stormtrooper
Richard Bonehill	German Guard

While Michelle admits that the photos René struggled to take of the invasion maps weren't good enough, Gruber has more bad news for the café owner. It's believed that René was behind the suspected plot to assassinate the generals and, therefore, is to be shot. Until his innocence is proven, the Lieutenant suggests René goes into hiding – but that's easier said than done.

11. The Confusion Of The Generals

Transmitted: 12/11/88

CAST

Gorden Kaye	René Artois
Carmen Silvera	Edith Artois
Vicki Michelle	Yvette
Richard Marner	Colonel Von Strohm
Guy Siner	Lieutenant Gruber
Kim Hartman	Helga Geerhart
Richard Gibson	Otto Flick
Kirsten Cooke	Michelle Dubois
Arthur Bostrom	Officer Crabtree
John Louis Mansi	Herr Von Smallhausen
Sue Hodge	Mimi Labonq
Hilary Minster	General Von Klinkerhoffen
Gavin Richards	Captain Bertorelli
Jack Haig	Monsieur Leclerc
Rose Hill	Madame La Fan
John D. Collins	Flight Lieutenant Fairfax
Nicholas Frankau	Flight Lieutenant Carstairs
Ken Morley	General Von Flockenstuffen
Fred Bryant	German General
Patrick Edwards	German Guard

Gruber has good news for René: he's convinced Von Klinkerhoffen that the café owner isn't responsible for the attempt to blow up the generals, so René can sleep easy again, especially when, later, the French General is arrested for conspiring to kill. General Von Klinkerhoffen, meanwhile, decides to hold his next meeting at the café with the generals dressed as onion-sellers to avoid further problems. Unfortunately, a new batch of British airmen also arrive, ready to be taken to the coast, choosing the same diguise.

12. Who's For The Vatican?

Transmitted: 19/11/88

CAST

Gorden Kaye	René Artois
Carmen Silvera	Edith Artois
Vicki Michelle	Yvette
Richard Marner	Colonel Von Strohm
Guy Siner	Lieutenant Gruber
Kim Hartman	Helga Geerhart
Richard Gibson	Otto Flick
Kirsten Cooke	Michelle Dubois
Arthur Bostrom	Officer Crabtree
Kenneth Connor	Monsieur Alfonse
Sue Hodge	Mimi Labonq
Hilary Minster	General Von Klinkerhoffen
Gavin Richards	Captain Bertorelli
Jack Haig	Monsieur Leclerc
Rose Hill	Madame La Fan
Trevor T. Smith	German Soldier
John Readman	Italian Soldier
Carole Ashby	Louise (Communist Resistance)
Moira Foot	Denise Laroque
Jacqueline Ashman	Michelle's Assistant

René thinks he'll be blamed for the fiasco in the café whereby the German generals, disguised as onion-sellers, were shipped to the coast, bound for England. But when news breaks that the truck, carrying the Germans, hit a bomb crater and never reached the coastline, René is in the clear. Blame shifts to the Colonel: destined for the Russian Front, Von Strohm and Gruber decide hastily to seek safety at the Vatican. However, this requires cash so they pressurize René into retrieving the paintings from the sawmill. But with Resistance funds low, Michelle wants the originals and tells René to switch them for forgeries before passing them over. Trouble is, René, Mimi, the Colonel, Gruber, Bertorelli and the Italian soldiers all get captured in the process.

13. Ribbing The Bonk
Transmitted: 26/11/88

CAST

Gorden Kaye	René Artois
Carmen Silvera	Edith Artois
Vicki Michelle	Yvette
Richard Marner	Colonel Von Strohm
Guy Siner	Lieutenant Gruber
Kim Hartman	Helga Geerhart
Richard Gibson	Otto Flick
Kirsten Cooke	Michelle Dubois
Arthur Bostrom	Officer Crabtree
Kenneth Connor	Monsieur Alfonse
Sue Hodge	Mimi Labonq
Hilary Minster	General Von Klinkerhoffen
Gavin Richards	Captain Bertorelli
Jack Haig	Monsieur Leclerc
Rose Hill	Madame La Fan
John D. Collins	Flight Lieutenant Fairfax
Nicholas Frankau	Flight Lieutenant Carstairs
Moira Foot	Denise Laroque
Carole Ashby	Louise (Communist Resistance)
Jackie D. Broad	Large Communist Resistance Girl
Eddie Caswell	Fruit Seller
Owen Brenman	'London Calling'

With the Germans and Bertorelli captured by the Communist Resistance, René intervenes to prevent them being shot – but at a cost. The Communists set a ransom for their release: a million francs for the Germans – and ten tins of beans for the Italian captain. René and Monsieur Leclerc return to the café to make the ransom demand. But with General Von Klinkerhoffen refusing to pay, and Michelle having arranged for the RAF to bomb the sawmill to eliminate the enemy, there is no option but for René and his team to rob the bank in order to save Mimi – unfortunately left behind – who is concealing the original paintings; but that's where their problems begin.

14. The Reluctant Millionaires

Transmitted: 3/12/88

CAST

Gorden Kaye	René Artois
Carmen Silvera	Edith Artois
Vicki Michelle	Yvette
Richard Marner	Colonel Von Strohm
Guy Siner	Lieutenant Gruber
Kim Hartman	Helga Geerhart
Richard Gibson	Otto Flick
Kirsten Cooke	Michelle Dubois
Arthur Bostrom	Officer Crabtree
Kenneth Connor	Monsieur Alfonse
Sue Hodge	Mimi Labonq
Hilary Minster	General Von Klinkerhoffen
Gavin Richards	Captain Bertorelli
Jack Haig	Monsieur Leclerc
Moira Foot	Denise Laroque
Carole Ashby	Louise (Communist Resistance)

(It would appear John D. Collins and Nicholas Frankau's scene was cut from the DVD release.)

Herr Flick is livid because the money stolen from the bank by René et al came from the Gestapo's slush fund. At the café, Michelle has plans for the cash: she wants it paid into the Resistance's current account. René decides to split the money, but then Officer Crabtree turns up and informs everyone that the million francs were, in fact, Gestapo money. Panicking, René passes the money to Gruber so the Gestapo don't find it on him.

15. A Duck For Launch

Transmitted: 10/12/88

CAST

Gorden Kaye	René Artois
Carmen Silvera	Edith Artois
Vicki Michelle	Yvette
Richard Marner	Colonel Von Strohm
Guy Siner	Lieutenant Gruber
Kim Hartman	Helga Geerhart
Richard Gibson	Otto Flick
Kirsten Cooke	Michelle Dubois
Arthur Bostrom	Officer Crabtree
Kenneth Connor	Monsieur Alfonse
John Louis Mansi	Herr Von Smallhausen
Sue Hodge	Mimi Labonq
Gavin Richards	Captain Bertorelli
Rose Hill	Madame La Fan
John D. Collins	Flight Lieutenant Fairfax
Nicholas Frankau	Flight Lieutenant Carstairs
Moira Foot	Denise Laroque
Carole Ashby	Louise (Communist Resistance)
Christopher Gray	German Soldier
Owen Brenman	Voice of 'Kingfisher'

Herr Flick is determined to bring the miscreants responsible for stealing the Gestapo funds to justice. As the money was, in fact, counterfeit, to find the culprits, Von Smallhausen and Flick dress as market traders and wait to pounce on anyone passing forged notes; unfortunately, it's Monsieur Alfonse who finds himself arrested. Meanwhile, another branch of the French Resistance obtains the photos of the invasion plans and it's René who has to send them to England by duck, but his feathery friend is reluctant to leave.

16. The Exploding Bedpan

Transmitted: 17/12/88

CAST

Gorden Kaye	René Artois
Carmen Silvera	Edith Artois
Vicki Michelle	Yvette
Richard Marner	Colonel Von Strohm
Guy Siner	Lieutenant Gruber
Kim Hartman	Helga Geerhart
Richard Gibson	Otto Flick
Kirsten Cooke	Michelle Dubois
Arthur Bostrom	Officer Crabtree
Kenneth Connor	Monsieur Alfonse
John Louis Mansi	Herr Von Smallhausen
Sue Hodge	Mimi Labonq
Gavin Richards	Captain Bertorelli
Rose Hill	Madame La Fan
Moira Foot	Denise Laroque
Lucinda Smith	Nurse
Stephen Reynolds	Surgeon
Owen Brenman	French radio voice
Julie-Christian Young	Cockney girl voice

Monsieur Alfonse is interrogated by the Gestapo for passing forged bank notes. After Von Smallhausen fails to extract information from the undertaker, Helga takes over; but she intends helping Alfonse escape and lifts her skirt in order to reach a hacksaw she's hiding on her person. Catching a momentary flash of her black suspenders is enough to send Alfonse's dicky ticker into overdrive and he ends up being rushed to hospital. An exploding bedpan, René doubling as a patient and a host of other events are employed to rescue Monsieur Alfonse.

17. Going Like A Bomb

Transmitted: 24/12/88

CAST

Gorden Kaye	René Artois
Carmen Silvera	Edith Artois
Vicki Michelle	Yvette
Richard Marner	Colonel Von Strohm
Guy Siner	Lieutenant Gruber
Kim Hartman	Helga Geerhart
Kirsten Cooke	Michelle Dubois
Arthur Bostrom	Officer Crabtree
Kenneth Connor	Monsieur Alfonse
Sue Hodge	Mimi Labonq
Gavin Richards	Captain Bertorelli
Jack Haig	Monsieur Leclerc
Rose Hill	Madame La Fan
John D. Collins	Flight Lieutenant Fairfax
Nicholas Frankau	Flight Lieutenant Carstairs
Moira Foot	Denise Laroque
Carole Ashby	Louise (Communist Resistance)

Herr Flick remains frustrated having not traced the missing money, which is now stuffed down the Italian captain's trousers. Other developments in Nouvion see Michelle telling René and his team that the Germans have developed a new land mine and two of them, minus explosives, have been stolen to use in yet another attempt to return the British airmen to their homeland.

18. Money To Burn

Transmitted: 31/12/88

CAST

Gorden Kaye	René Artois
Carmen Silvera	Edith Artois
Vicki Michelle	Yvette
Richard Marner	Colonel Von Strohm
Guy Siner	Lieutenant Gruber
Kim Hartman	Helga Geerhart
Richard Gibson	Otto Flick
Kirsten Cooke	Michelle Dubois
Arthur Bostrom	Officer Crabtree
John Louis Mansi	Herr Von Smallhausen
Sue Hodge	Mimi Labonq
Hilary Minster	General Von Klinkerhoffen
Gavin Richards	Captain Bertorelli
Jack Haig	Monsieur Leclerc
Rose Hill	Madame La Fan
John D. Collins	Flight Lieutenant Fairfax
Nicholas Frankau	Flight Lieutenant Carstairs
Jacqueline Ashman	French Resistance Girl
John Readman	Italian Soldier

Monsieur Leclerc has been arrested by Herr Flick on suspicion of holding stolen money. If it's not returned, he'll be shot. But Herr Flick's forged notes are burnt to a cinder when Madame Fanny turns on the oven where they are hidden; but that's not the only thing she's cooked: the spy camera inside a potato is roasted, too. Just as it looks like Leclerc's time is up, the RAF come to the rescue with an unexpected drop.

19. Puddings Can Go Off

Transmitted: 7/1/89

CAST

Gorden Kaye	René Artois
Carmen Silvera	Edith Artois
Vicki Michelle	Yvette
Richard Marner	Colonel Von Strohm
Guy Siner	Lieutenant Gruber
Kim Hartman	Helga Geerhart
Richard Gibson	Otto Flick
Kirsten Cooke	Michelle Dubois
Arthur Bostrom	Officer Crabtree
Kenneth Connor	Monsieur Alfonse
John Louis Mansi	Herr Von Smallhausen
Sue Hodge	Mimi Labonq
Hilary Minster	General Von Klinkerhoffen
Jack Haig	Monsieur Leclerc
Rose Hill	Madame La Fan
John D. Collins	Flight Lieutenant Fairfax
Nicholas Frankau	Flight Lieutenant Carstairs
Phoebe Scholfield	Henriette (Michelle's Assistant)

The French Resistance is hiding 1,000 kilos of explosives extracted from the two land mines at René's café, disguised as 500 Christmas puddings. Berlin expects the Gestapo to find the explosives so Herr Flick, noticing much subversive activity has been occurring at the café, holes himself up inside the church tower so he and Von Smallhausen can keep a close eye on matters – but they have trouble with the bells!

20. Land Mines For London

Transmitted: 14/1/89

CAST	
Gorden Kaye	René Artois
Carmen Silvera	Edith Artois
Vicki Michelle	Yvette
Richard Marner	Colonel Von Strohm
Guy Siner	Lieutenant Gruber
Kim Hartman	Helga Geerhart
Richard Gibson	Otto Flick
Kirsten Cooke	Michelle Dubois
Arthur Bostrom	Officer Crabtree
John Louis Mansi	Herr Von Smallhausen
Sue Hodge	Mimi Labonq
Gavin Richards	Captain Bertorelli
Jack Haig	Monsieur Leclerc
Rose Hill	Madame La Fan
John D. Collins	Flight Lieutenant Fairfax
Nicholas Frankau	Flight Lieutenant Carstairs
John Readman	Italian Soldier
Sion Tudor Owen	German Pilot
Steven Bronowski	German Pilot
James Charles	German Corporal
Chris Andrews	German Soldier

Herr Flick has identified that the stolen land mines are hidden at a builder's yard adjacent to the café. Along with Von Smallhausen, they hide inside the empty mines but end up being transported, unknowingly, to a German airfield where they're loaded onto a plane, ready for a bombing raid over England.

21. Flight To Geneva

Transmitted: 21/1/89

CAST

Gorden Kaye	René Artois
Carmen Silvera	Edith Artois
Vicki Michelle	Yvette
Richard Marner	Colonel Von Strohm
Guy Siner	Lieutenant Gruber
Kim Hartman	Helga Geerhart
Richard Gibson	Otto Flick
Kirsten Cooke	Michelle Dubois
Arthur Bostrom	Officer Crabtree
Kenneth Connor	Monsieur Alfonse
John Louis Mansi	Herr Von Smallhausen
Sue Hodge	Mimi Labonq
Hilary Minster	General Von Klinkerhoffen
Jack Haig	Monsieur Leclerc
Michael Percival	Yoop Hoop De Hoop (Art Expert)
Howard Leader	Ticket Seller
Neil West	Train's Guard
John Leeson	Train's Cook

René's nerves are shot to pieces. He decides it's time to elope with Yvette, taking the paintings with him, but the Colonel tells René that Berlin want them else the Russian Front beckons for Von Strohm and his cronies. Still intent on hiding in the mountains until the war is over, René steals gold bars deposited by the General in the police station's safe and rushes to catch the Geneva Express; but he should never have relied on Monsieur Leclerc to give letters to Yvette and Edith and finds the train full of unexpected passengers.

22. Train Of Events

Transmitted: 28/1/89

CAST

Gorden Kaye	René Artois
Carmen Silvera	Edith Artois
Vicki Michelle	Yvette
Richard Marner	Colonel Von Strohm
Guy Siner	Lieutenant Gruber
Kim Hartman	Helga Geerhart
Richard Gibson	Otto Flick
Arthur Bostrom	Officer Crabtree
John Louis Mansi	Herr Von Smallhausen
Sue Hodge	Mimi Labonq
Hilary Minster	General Von Klinkerhoffen
Gavin Richards	Captain Bertorelli
Jack Haig	Monsieur Leclerc
John Readman	Italian Soldier
Patrick Edwards	German Soldier

René's plans to elope with Yvette are thrown into disarray when a mix up sees Edith turn up instead of the sexy waitress. The Germans, meanwhile, are still attempting to get their hands on the genuine paintings. Utter chaos reigns before everyone returns to their everyday lives in Nouvion. The Colonel, Gruber and Helga are happy, though, because they've finally got hold of the original paintings, which they've hidden inside a statue – but then General Von Klinkerhoffen comes calling.

23. An Enigma Variation

Transmitted: 4/2/89

CAST

Gorden Kaye	René Artois
Carmen Silvera	Edith Artois
Vicki Michelle	Yvette
Richard Marner	Colonel Von Strohm
Guy Siner	Lieutenant Gruber
Kim Hartman	Helga Geerhart
Richard Gibson	Otto Flick
Kirsten Cooke	Michelle Dubois
Arthur Bostrom	Officer Crabtree
Kenneth Connor	Monsieur Alfonse
John Louis Mansi	Herr Von Smallhausen
Sue Hodge	Mimi Labonq
Hilary Minster	General Von Klinkerhoffen
Gavin Richards	Captain Bertorelli
Jack Haig	Monsieur Leclerc
Rose Hill	Madame La Fan
Ken Morley	General Von Flockenstuffen
Fred Bryant	German General
Paul Cooper	'London Calling'

René is blackmailed by the Colonel into retrieving the valuable paintings, which are hidden inside a statue at the Château. Reluctantly, René and his team pretend to be a musical quartet hired to entertain at the officers' dance; but on hearing that they're going to be performing at the Château, Michelle adds another item to their shopping list: she wants an Enigma machine.

24. Wedding Bloss

Transmitted: 11/2/89

CAST

Gorden Kaye	René Artois
Carmen Silvera	Edith Artois
Vicki Michelle	Yvette
Richard Marner	Colonel Von Strohm
Guy Siner	Lieutenant Gruber
Kim Hartman	Helga Geerhart
Richard Gibson	Otto Flick
Kirsten Cooke	Michelle Dubois
Arthur Bostrom	Officer Crabtree
Kenneth Connor	Monsieur Alfonse
John Louis Mansi	Herr Von Smallhausen
Sue Hodge	Mimi Labonq
Hilary Minster	General Von Klinkerhoffen
Gavin Richards	Captain Bertorelli
Jack Haig	Monsieur Leclerc
Rose Hill	Madame La Fan
John D. Collins	Flight Lieutenant Fairfax
Nicholas Frankau	Flight Lieutenant Carstairs
Howard Leader	German Guard

When Edith announces that she's marrying Monsieur Alfonse, René starts panicking because he fears he'll lose the café. In desperation, he declares his love for Edith and says he'll book the registry office so they can tie the knot once again. But Monsieur Alfonse acts as registrar and it transpires the wedding isn't official, letting René off the hook.

25. Down The Drain

Transmitted: 18/2/89

CAST

Gorden Kaye	René Artois
Carmen Silvera	Edith Artois
Vicki Michelle	Yvette
Richard Marner	Colonel Von Strohm
Guy Siner	Lieutenant Gruber
Kim Hartman	Helga Geerhart
Richard Gibson	Otto Flick
Kirsten Cooke	Michelle Dubois
Arthur Bostrom	Officer Crabtree
Kenneth Connor	Monsieur Alfonse
John Louis Mansi	Herr Von Smallhausen
Sue Hodge	Mimi Labonq
Hilary Minster	General Von Klinkerhoffen
Gavin Richards	Captain Bertorelli
Jack Haig	Monsieur Leclerc
Rose Hill	Madame La Fan
John D. Collins	Flight Lieutenant Fairfax
Nicholas Frankau	Flight Lieutenant Carstairs
David Lloyd	German Soldier

(It would appear Richard Gibson, Kim Hartman, John Louis Mansi and Gavin Richards all had their scenes cut from the DVD release.)

While the Germans continue searching for the missing Enigma machine, Michelle takes it to the café instructing René to put it inside a barrel and throw it down a drain; a British submarine will be waiting to collect it when it emerges at the sewer outlet. But when the RAF bomb the pumping station, cutting off the water supply, it seems a hopeless cause until it's discovered that wine does an equally efficient job of flushing the barrel away. Then René realizes that it's not the Enigma machine he's washed away!

26. All In Disgeese

Transmitted: 25/2/89

CAST

Gorden Kaye	René Artois
Carmen Silvera	Edith Artois
Vicki Michelle	Yvette
Richard Marner	Colonel Von Strohm
Guy Siner	Lieutenant Gruber
Kim Hartman	Helga Geerhart
Richard Gibson	Otto Flick
Kirsten Cooke	Michelle Dubois
Arthur Bostrom	Officer Crabtree
Kenneth Connor	Monsieur Alfonse
John Louis Mansi	Herr Von Smallhausen
Sue Hodge	Mimi Labonq
Hilary Minster	General Von Klinkerhoffen
Gavin Richards	Captain Bertorelli
Jack Haig	Monsieur Leclerc
Rose Hill	Madame La Fan
John D. Collins	Flight Lieutenant Fairfax
Nicholas Frankau	Flight Lieutenant Carstairs
Philip Fox	British Agent
James Gow	British Agent
Robbin John	German Guard

The Enigma machine is back in the hands of the Resistance and experts, dressed as policemen, will be dropped by parachute to examine it. General Von Klinkerhoffen learns that he'll be posted to the Russian Front if the machine isn't retrieved. René is blamed, and Gruber warns him that if it's not found within 30 hours, he'll be shot. But just when it looks like René has had his chips, Edith comes to the rescue.

SERIES 6

1. Desperate Doings In The Graveyard

Transmitted: 2/9/89

CAST

Gorden Kaye	René Artois
Carmen Silvera	Edith Artois
Vicki Michelle	Yvette
Richard Marner	Colonel Von Strohm
Guy Siner	Lieutenant Gruber
Kim Hartman	Helga Geerhart
Richard Gibson	Otto Flick
Kirsten Cooke	Michelle Dubois
Arthur Bostrom	Officer Crabtree
Kenneth Connor	Monsieur Alfonse
John Louis Mansi	Herr Von Smallhausen
Sue Hodge	Mimi Labonq
Hilary Minster	General Von Klinkerhoffen
Gavin Richards	Captain Bertorelli
Derek Royle	Ernest Leclerc
Rose Hill	Madame La Fan
John D. Collins	Flight Lieutenant Fairfax
Nicholas Frankau	Flight Lieutenant Carstairs
Rikki Howard	Elaine (French Resistance)

Michelle arrives at the café to announce that a communication centre is being built underneath the empty grave which supposedly holds the body of René. Continual digging raises suspicion and Monsieur Alfonse is interrogated by Herr Flick about the curious graveyard activities. But Gruber and Helga are in for the shock of their lives when they head to the cemetary.

2. The Gestapo For The High Jump

Transmitted: 9/9/89

CAST

Gorden Kaye	René Artois
Carmen Silvera	Edith Artois
Vicki Michelle	Yvette
Richard Marner	Colonel Von Strohm
Guy Siner	Lieutenant Gruber
Kim Hartman	Helga Geerhart
Richard Gibson	Otto Flick
Kirsten Cooke	Michelle Dubois
Arthur Bostrom	Officer Crabtree
John Louis Mansi	Herr Von Smallhausen
Sue Hodge	Mimi Labonq
Hilary Minster	General Von Klinkerhoffen
Gavin Richards	Captain Bertorelli
Derek Royle	Ernest Leclerc
Rose Hill	Madame La Fan
Rikki Howard	Elaine Cerise
Phoebe Scholfield	Henriette (Michelle's Assistant)
John Readman	Italian Soldier

Helga delivers parachutes to Herr Flick and Von Smallhausen so they can leap from a plane dressed as RAF airmen in order to infiltrate the Resistance. Despite being in shock after seeing the ghostly apparition at the cemetary, Gruber manages to warn René about Herr Flick's plans. But the Gestapo are in for a shock themselves when witches and monsters appear on the scene.

3. The Nouvion Oars

Transmitted: 16/9/89

CAST

Gorden Kaye	René Artois
Carmen Silvera	Edith Artois
Vicki Michelle	Yvette
Richard Marner	Colonel Von Strohm
Guy Siner	Lieutenant Gruber
Kim Hartman	Helga Geerhart
Richard Gibson	Otto Flick
Kirsten Cooke	Michelle Dubois
Arthur Bostrom	Officer Crabtree
Kenneth Connor	Monsieur Alfonse
John Louis Mansi	Herr Von Smallhausen
Sue Hodge	Mimi Labonq
Hilary Minster	General Von Klinkerhoffen
Derek Royle	Ernest Leclerc
Rose Hill	Madame La Fan
John D. Collins	Flight Lieutenant Fairfax
Nicholas Frankau	Flight Lieutenant Carstairs
Richard Seymour	German Soldier
David Griffin	Submarine Commander
Tim Brown	Submarine Officer

The communication aerial is reinstalled in the attic bedroom of Madame La Fan and a message sent to London confirming the airmen are ready to be picked up. When a submarine arrives in the estuary, the Resistance set about helping the airmen escape. Meanwhile, General Von Klinkerhoffen orders Helga to marry Herr Flick as a means of obtaining secret information.

4. The Nicked Airmen

Transmitted: 23/9/89

CAST

Gorden Kaye	René Artois
Carmen Silvera	Edith Artois
Vicki Michelle	Yvette
Richard Marner	Colonel Von Strohm
Guy Siner	Lieutenant Gruber
Kim Hartman	Helga Geerhart
Richard Gibson	Otto Flick
Kirsten Cooke	Michelle Dubois
Arthur Bostrom	Officer Crabtree
Kenneth Connor	Monsieur Alfonse
John Louis Mansi	Herr Von Smallhausen
Sue Hodge	Mimi Labonq
Hilary Minster	General Von Klinkerhoffen
Gavin Richards	Captain Bertorelli
Derek Royle	Ernest Leclerc
Rose Hill	Madame La Fan
John D. Collins	Flight Lieutenant Fairfax
Nicholas Frankau	Flight Lieutenant Carstairs
David Lloyd	German Soldier
Trevor T. Smith	German Soldier

After failing to make it to the submarine, the airmen are captured. René and Edith pray that they don't spill the beans about being harboured at the café. But they have more immediate worries when they're arrested, too, and taken to the Colonel. It transpires that the airmen are to be questioned in Berlin but with a little help from Gruber, they'll hopefully be freed. On the marriage front, Helga risks the wrath of Herr Flick – who has endured sleepless nights since her proposal – by suddenly withdrawing her offer of marriage.

5. The Airmen De-Nicked

Transmitted: 30/9/89

CAST

Gorden Kaye	René Artois
Carmen Silvera	Edith Artois
Vicki Michelle	Yvette
Richard Marner	Colonel Von Strohm
Guy Siner	Lieutenant Gruber
Kim Hartman	Helga Geerhart
Richard Gibson	Otto Flick
Kirsten Cooke	Michelle Dubois
Arthur Bostrom	Officer Crabtree
John Louis Mansi	Herr Von Smallhausen
Sue Hodge	Mimi Labonq
Gavin Richards	Captain Bertorelli
Derek Royle	Ernest Leclerc
Rose Hill	Madame La Fan
John D. Collins	Flight Lieutenant Fairfax
Nicholas Frankau	Flight Lieutenant Carstairs
Phoebe Scholfield	Henriette (Michelle's Assistant)
Trevor T. Smith	German Soldier
Howard Leader	German Soldier
Ian McLaren	German Guard

With the airmen still held prisoner, the Resistance have a fresh plan to free them, involving Madame La Fan's wheelchair and stolen German uniforms. A reluctant René is again in the thick of the action as the team manages to rescue the airmen but end up being handcuffed to the prisoners.

6. The Crooked Fences

Transmitted: 7/10/89

CAST

Gorden Kaye	René Artois
Carmen Silvera	Edith Artois
Vicki Michelle	Yvette
Richard Marner	Colonel Von Strohm
Guy Siner	Lieutenant Gruber
Kim Hartman	Helga Geerhart
Richard Gibson	Otto Flick
Kirsten Cooke	Michelle Dubois
Arthur Bostrom	Officer Crabtree
Kenneth Connor	Monsieur Alfonse
John Louis Mansi	Herr Von Smallhausen
Sue Hodge	Mimi Labonq
Gavin Richards	Captain Bertorelli
Derek Royle	Ernest Leclerc
Rose Hill	Madame La Fan
John D. Collins	Flight Lieutenant Fairfax
Nicholas Frankau	Flight Lieutenant Carstairs
Sarah Sherborne	Agent Grace
Iain Mitchell	Catholic Priest

Worried about his future, Herr Flick decides to flee. In need of an injection of cash, he opts to sell the Fallen Madonna. The Colonel and Gruber are worried about their futures, too: when the General eventually discovers the airmen are missing, they'll need to scarper so plan selling the famous painting as well, in an attempt to raise funds. To help, René is asked to arrange a 'fence'.

7. Crabtree's Podgeon Pist

Transmitted: 14/10/89

CAST

Gorden Kaye	René Artois
Carmen Silvera	Edith Artois
Vicki Michelle	Yvette
Richard Marner	Colonel Von Strohm
Guy Siner	Lieutenant Gruber
Kim Hartman	Helga Geerhart
Richard Gibson	Otto Flick
Kirsten Cooke	Michelle Dubois
Arthur Bostrom	Officer Crabtree
Kenneth Connor	Monsieur Alfonse
John Louis Mansi	Herr Von Smallhausen
Sue Hodge	Mimi Labonq
Hilary Minster	General Von Klinkerhoffen
Gavin Richards	Captain Bertorelli
Derek Royle	Ernest Leclerc
Rose Hill	Madame La Fan
John D. Collins	Flight Lieutenant Fairfax
Nicholas Frankau	Flight Lieutenant Carstairs
Sarah Sherborne	Agent Grace
Iain Mitchell	Catholic Priest

Madame La Fan and Ernest Leclerc are getting married and Michelle uses the occasion to aid the airmen's escape. The Resistance have captured a barrage balloon and it will be delivered the same time as the marquee being used for the wedding reception. The helium fuel will be supplied in canisters disguised as marrows. Then, when the wind is favourable, the balloon will be launched behind the café.

8. Rising To The Occasion

Transmitted: 21/10/89

CAST

Gorden Kaye	René Artois
Carmen Silvera	Edith Artois
Vicki Michelle	Yvette
Richard Marner	Colonel Von Strohm
Guy Siner	Lieutenant Gruber
Kim Hartman	Helga Geerhart
Richard Gibson	Otto Flick
Kirsten Cooke	Michelle Dubois
Arthur Bostrom	Officer Crabtree
Kenneth Connor	Monsieur Alfonse
John Louis Mansi	Herr Von Smallhausen
Sue Hodge	Mimi Labonq
Hilary Minster	General Von Klinkerhoffen
Gavin Richards	Captain Bertorelli
Derek Royle	Ernest Leclerc
Rose Hill	Madame La Fan
John D. Collins	Flight Lieutenant Fairfax
Nicholas Frankau	Flight Lieutenant Carstairs
Ken Morley	General Von Flockenstuffen
Sarah Sherborne	Agent Grace
Phoebe Scholfield	Henriette (Michelle's Assistant)
Jackie D. Broad	Large French Resistance Girl
Carole Ashby	Louise (Communist Resistance)
Estelle Matthews	Communist Girl

It's all go in Nouvion. René is informed that a large bomb has been planted in the sewer under the café and General Von Flockenstuffen arrives on the scene worried by news that Von Klinkerhoffen is intending blowing up the town. Meanwhile, Herr Flick, his sidekick and the Colonel are taken hostage by the Communist Resistance while at the wedding reception the barrage balloon is inflated too early – and it's not the airmen who take to the air.

SERIES 7

1. A Quiet Honeymoon

Transmitted: 5/1/91

CAST

Gorden Kaye	René Artois
Carmen Silvera	Edith Artois
Vicki Michelle	Yvette
Richard Marner	Colonel Von Strohm
Guy Siner	Lieutenant Gruber
Kim Hartman	Helga Geerhart
Richard Gibson	Otto Flick
Kirsten Cooke	Michelle Dubois
Arthur Bostrom	Officer Crabtree
Kenneth Connor	Monsieur Alfonse
John Louis Mansi	Herr Von Smallhausen
Sue Hodge	Mimi Labonq
Hilary Minster	General Von Klinkerhoffen
Roger Kitter	Captain Bertorelli
Robin Parkinson	Ernest Leclerc
Rose Hill	Madame La Fan
John D. Collins	Flight Lieutenant Fairfax
Nicholas Frankau	Flight Lieutenant Carstairs
Ken Morley	General Von Flockenstuffen
Joyce Windsor	Nurse
Howard Leader	German Soldier

With General Von Klinkerhoffen – who is suspected of going mad – retained in hospital, General Von Flockenstuffen, who takes a shine to Gruber, seizes control of the district. Later, Madame La Fan and Monsieur Leclerc are shot down in their floating bed and make their way back to the café after stealing a bike. But they're arrested for their crimes and Edith sets about planning their escape.

2. An Almighty Bang

Transmitted: 12/1/91

CAST

Gorden Kaye	René Artois
Carmen Silvera	Edith Artois
Vicki Michelle	Yvette
Richard Marner	Colonel Von Strohm
Guy Siner	Lieutenant Gruber
Kim Hartman	Helga Geerhart
Richard Gibson	Otto Flick
Arthur Bostrom	Officer Crabtree
Kenneth Connor	Monsieur Alfonse
John Louis Mansi	Herr Von Smallhausen
Sue Hodge	Mimi Labonq
Hilary Minster	General Von Klinkerhoffen
Roger Kitter	Captain Bertorelli
Robin Parkinson	Ernest Leclerc
Ken Morley	General Von Flockenstuffen
Rose Hill	Madame La Fan
John D. Collins	Flight Lieutenant Fairfax
Nicholas Frankau	Flight Lieutenant Carstairs

General Von Flockenstuffen comes up with a hairbrained plan to head for England and kidnap Churchill, hoping it will earn him myriad brownie points from Berlin. Realising the foolishness of the idea, the Colonel, Gruber, Helga and Bertorelli instigate a plan to secure the release of General Von Klinkerhoffen from hospital. His first task on returning to duty is to send Von Flockenstuffen, who accidentally blows himself up in René's wine cellar, for treatment.

3. Fleeing Monks

Transmitted: 19/1/91

CAST

Gorden Kaye	René Artois
Carmen Silvera	Edith Artois
Vicki Michelle	Yvette
Richard Marner	Colonel Von Strohm
Guy Siner	Lieutenant Gruber
Kim Hartman	Helga Geerhart
Richard Gibson	Otto Flick
Kirsten Cooke	Michelle Dubois
Arthur Bostrom	Officer Crabtree
Kenneth Connor	Monsieur Alfonse
John Louis Mansi	Herr Von Smallhausen
Sue Hodge	Mimi Labonq
Hilary Minster	General Von Klinkerhoffen
Roger Kitter	Captain Bertorelli
Robin Parkinson	Ernest Leclerc
Rose Hill	Madame La Fan
John D. Collins	Flight Lieutenant Fairfax
Nicholas Frankau	Flight Lieutenant Carstairs
Carole Ashby	Louise (Communist Resistance)
Roger Hammond	Monk
David Valentine-Webb	British Airman in Plane

René is to be awarded a collaboration medal because General Von Klinkerhoffen thinks he was instrumental in the capture of Von Flockenstuffen. But it's the worst thing that could happen to the café owner, who soon becomes the most hated man in Nouvion. If he refuses the medal, he's in danger of being shot so decides to get away. Using a monk's habit, intended for the British airmen, he jumps onto the waiting RAF plane with Yvette – or so he thinks.

4. Up the Crick Without A Piddle

Transmitted: 26/1/91

CAST	
Gorden Kaye	René Artois
Carmen Silvera	Edith Artois
Vicki Michelle	Yvette
Richard Marner	Colonel Von Strohm
Guy Siner	Lieutenant Gruber
Kim Hartman	Helga Geerhart
Richard Gibson	Otto Flick
Kirsten Cooke	Michelle Dubois
Arthur Bostrom	Officer Crabtree
John Louis Mansi	Herr Von Smallhausen
Sue Hodge	Mimi Labonq
Hilary Minster	General Von Klinkerhoffen
Roger Kitter	Captain Bertorelli
Robin Parkinson	Ernest Leclerc
Rose Hill	Madame La Fan
John D. Collins	Flight Lieutenant Fairfax
Nicholas Frankau	Flight Lieutenant Carstairs
Sam Kelly	Hans Geering
Tim Marriott	British Aircrew
Eric Dodson	RAF Officer
Steve Edwin	RAF Officer
John James Evans	Winston Churchill
Harriet Thorpe	Restaurant Waitress

René and Edith – not Yvette, much to the café owner's dismay – arrive in England and are taken for questioning by the RAF, only to meet Hans Geering who's been neutralized and now works as an intelligence officer. But when René and Edith hear that Madame Fanny and Monsieur Leclerc, who are minding the café in their absence, are drinking away the profits, Edith returns home. René intends to remain in Blighty for the duration but his plans are ruined.

5. The Gestapo Ruins A Picnic

Transmitted: 2/2/91

CAST

Gorden Kaye	René Artois
Carmen Silvera	Edith Artois
Vicki Michelle	Yvette
Richard Marner	Colonel Von Strohm
Guy Siner	Lieutenant Gruber
Kim Hartman	Helga Geerhart
Richard Gibson	Otto Flick
Kirsten Cooke	Michelle Dubois
Arthur Bostrom	Officer Crabtree
Kenneth Connor	Monsieur Alfonse
John Louis Mansi	Herr Von Smallhausen
Sue Hodge	Mimi Labonq
Hilary Minster	General Von Klinkerhoffen
Roger Kitter	Captain Bertorelli
Robin Parkinson	Ernest Leclerc
Rose Hill	Madame La Fan
John D. Collins	Flight Lieutenant Fairfax
Nicholas Frankau	Flight Lieutenant Carstairs
Roger Hammond	Monk

René no longer being given a collaboration medal by the Germans means he's out of danger. Life returns to normal until the Germans, annoyed by a Resistance propaganda poster, decide to resurrect the local paper, installing René as editor. The plan is to use the rag to spread their own propaganda and various stories are manufactured in an attempt to show cordial relationships with the French.

6. The Spirit Of Nouvion

Transmitted: 9/2/91

CAST

Gorden Kaye	René Artois
Carmen Silvera	Edith Artois
Vicki Michelle	Yvette
Richard Marner	Colonel Von Strohm
Guy Siner	Lieutenant Gruber
Kim Hartman	Helga Geerhart
Richard Gibson	Otto Flick
Kirsten Cooke	Michelle Dubois
Arthur Bostrom	Officer Crabtree
Kenneth Connor	Monsieur Alfonse
John Louis Mansi	Herr Von Smallhausen
Sue Hodge	Mimi Labonq
Roger Kitter	Captain Bertorelli
Robin Parkinson	Ernest Leclerc
Rose Hill	Madame La Fan
Lino Omoboni	Italian soldier

Since the Germans appointed René editor of the local paper, life has been hectic. Herr Flick, meanwhile, tells Helga that their relationship is over because Himmler has heard about his extra-curricular activities and isn't pleased. Helga takes the news badly and throws water over him. The Resistance break into Herr Flick's safe to steal the painting – *The Fallen Madonna With The Big Boobies* – but the Colonel has the same idea ... and they're in for a shock.

7. Leg It To Spain!

Transmitted: 16/2/91

CAST

Gorden Kaye	René Artois
Carmen Silvera	Edith Artois
Vicki Michelle	Yvette
Richard Marner	Colonel Von Strohm
Guy Siner	Lieutenant Gruber
Kim Hartman	Helga Geerhart
Richard Gibson	Otto Flick
Kirsten Cooke	Michelle Dubois
Arthur Bostrom	Officer Crabtree
Kenneth Connor	Monsieur Alfonse
John Louis Mansi	Herr Von Smallhausen
Sue Hodge	Mimi Labonq
Hilary Minster	General Von Klinkerhoffen
Roger Kitter	Captain Bertorelli
Robin Parkinson	Ernest Leclerc
Rose Hill	Madame La Fan
John D. Collins	Flight Lieutenant Fairfax
Nicholas Frankau	Flight Lieutenant Carstairs
Paul Cooper	'London Calling'

Having stolen the painting from Herr Flick's safe, René has to give it to the Colonel; in turn, the Colonel – much to his chagrin – ends up passing it on to the General. But Herr Flick is determined to discover its whereabouts and wants Helga to help him find it; trouble is, he has to woo her back first – which is no easy task.

8. Prior Engagements

Transmitted: 23/2/91

CAST

Gorden Kaye	René Artois
Carmen Silvera	Edith Artois
Vicki Michelle	Yvette
Richard Marner	Colonel Von Strohm
Guy Siner	Lieutenant Gruber
Kim Hartman	Helga Geerhart
Richard Gibson	Otto Flick
Kirsten Cooke	Michelle Dubois
Arthur Bostrom	Officer Crabtree
Kenneth Connor	Monsieur Alfonse
John Louis Mansi	Herr Von Smallhausen
Sue Hodge	Mimi Labonq
Hilary Minster	General Von Klinkerhoffen
Roger Kitter	Captain Bertorelli
Robin Parkinson	Ernest Leclerc
Rose Hill	Madame La Fan
John D. Collins	Flight Lieutenant Fairfax
Nicholas Frankau	Flight Lieutenant Carstairs
Louis Sheldon	German Soldier

Continuing their propaganda campaign, the General decides that a reluctant Bertorelli should propose to the Spirit of Nouvien: Madame Edith. Herr Flick grasps the opportunity of using the engagement ceremony at the Château to reclaim *The Fallen Madonna*. And the French Resistance exploit the occasion to help the airmen – hidden in wine vats in the Château – escape.

9. Soup And Sausage

Transmitted: 2/3/91

CAST

Gorden Kaye	René Artois
Carmen Silvera	Edith Artois
Vicki Michelle	Yvette
Richard Marner	Colonel Von Strohm
Guy Siner	Lieutenant Gruber
Kim Hartman	Helga Geerhart
Richard Gibson	Otto Flick
Kirsten Cooke	Michelle Dubois
Arthur Bostrom	Officer Crabtree
Kenneth Connor	Monsieur Alfonse
John Louis Mansi	Herr Von Smallhausen
Sue Hodge	Mimi Labonq
Hilary Minster	General Von Klinkerhoffen
Roger Kitter	Captain Bertorelli
Robin Parkinson	Ernest Leclerc
John D. Collins	Flight Lieutenant Fairfax
Nicholas Frankau	Flight Lieutenant Carstairs
Louise Gold	Private Elsa Bigstern

The airmen's latest escape plan backfires and they're stuck in the drains below the town square. René and his team are tasked with feeding them while Michelle comes up with a way of getting them out of their predicament. But it isn't easy for René – not even his ice cream van idea succeeds.

10. René Of The Gypsies

Transmitted: 16/3/91

CAST

Gorden Kaye	René Artois
Carmen Silvera	Edith Artois
Vicki Michelle	Yvette
Richard Marner	Colonel Von Strohm
Guy Siner	Lieutenant Gruber
Kim Hartman	Helga Geerhart
Richard Gibson	Otto Flick
Kirsten Cooke	Michelle Dubois
Arthur Bostrom	Officer Crabtree
Kenneth Connor	Monsieur Alfonse
John Louis Mansi	Herr Von Smallhausen
Sue Hodge	Mimi Labonq
Hilary Minster	General Von Klinkerhoffen
Roger Kitter	Captain Bertorelli
Robin Parkinson	Ernest Leclerc
John D. Collins	Flight Lieutenant Fairfax
Nicholas Frankau	Flight Lieutenant Carstairs
Louise Gold	Private Elsa Bigstern
Ruben Lee	Gypsy
Stanley Lebor	Gypsy Leader
Robert East	Wing Commander Blenkinsop

With the airmen still stuck in the drains below the town square, it's decided that René and Edith will ask local gypsies pitched just outside Nouvion to come over to celebrate the Summer Solstice. While they're entertaining in the square, René, Michelle and the gang can attempt to release the airmen. But when the gypsies pull out, it's up to René and the rest to don gypsy outfits.

CHRISTMAS SPECIAL

A Bun In The Oven

Transmitted: 24/12/91

CAST

Gorden Kaye	René Artois
Carmen Silvera	Edith Artois
Vicki Michelle	Yvette
Richard Marner	Colonel Von Strohm
Guy Siner	Lieutenant Gruber
Kim Hartman	Helga Geerhart
Richard Gibson	Otto Flick
Kirsten Cooke	Michelle Dubois
Arthur Bostrom	Officer Crabtree
Kenneth Connor	Monsieur Alfonse
John Louis Mansi	Herr Von Smallhausen
Sue Hodge	Mimi Labonq
Hilary Minster	General Von Klinkerhoffen
Robin Parkinson	Ernest Leclerc
Rose Hill	Madame La Fan
Michael Cotterill	The Pope
Paul Cooper	'London Calling'

It's September 13th, 1943, nearly two years since we last saw René and the citizens of Nouvion. The British airmen have finally managed to reach Britain after being picked up by a trawler, and Captain Bertorelli left after Mussolini threw in the towel. The war is going badly for the Germans and the Allied invasion is imminent. René has expunged any bad memories from his mind and no longer has a care in the world until Yvette announces she's pregnant and he's the father. The Germans, meanwhile, are trying to raise cash so they can flee to Spain – if only they could get their hands on *The Fallen Madonna*, which they've now lost to Herr Flick.

SERIES 8

1. Arousing Suspicions

Transmitted: 5/1/92

CAST

Gorden Kaye	René Artois
Carmen Silvera	Edith Artois
Vicki Michelle	Yvette
Richard Marner	Colonel Von Strohm
Guy Siner	Lieutenant Gruber
Kim Hartman	Helga Geerhart
Richard Gibson	Otto Flick
Kirsten Cooke	Michelle Dubois
Arthur Bostrom	Officer Crabtree
Kenneth Connor	Monsieur Alfonse
John Louis Mansi	Herr Von Smallhausen
Sue Hodge	Mimi Labonq
Hilary Minster	General Von Klinkerhoffen
Robin Parkinson	Ernest Leclerc
Rose Hill	Madame La Fan
Kate Kenny	German Soldier
Marek Anton	German Soldier
Paul Cooper	'London Calling'

The Resistance plan to launch a radio station in Nouvion and make a propaganda broadcast. An Edison machine is dropped by the RAF, but the parachute containing the wax cylinders – required for pre-recording messages – gets stuck in the Château chimney. René and his gang replace visiting Flamenco dancers in order to gain access to the Château.

2. A Woman Never Lies

Transmitted: 12/1/92

CAST	
Gorden Kaye	René Artois
Carmen Silvera	Edith Artois
Vicki Michelle	Yvette
Richard Marner	Colonel Von Strohm
Guy Siner	Lieutenant Gruber
Kim Hartman	Helga Geerhart
Richard Gibson	Otto Flick
Kirsten Cooke	Michelle Dubois
Arthur Bostrom	Officer Crabtree
Kenneth Connor	Monsieur Alfonse
John Louis Mansi	Herr Von Smallhausen
Sue Hodge	Mimi Labonq
Hilary Minster	General Von Klinkerhoffen
Robin Parkinson	Ernest Leclerc
Rose Hill	Madame La Fan
George Garratt	Spanish Flamenco Dancer
Huw Tipler	Guard
David Taylor	Guard

While performing at the Château as flamenco dancers, Monsieur Alfonse is mistaken, by Gruber, for Juan Garcia, the man who was to take the photo of him, holding *The Fallen Madonna With The Big Boobies*, to a Spanish art dealer to have the painting valued. When the Resistance see the photo they decide to blackmail Gruber by threatening to send it to the General. Not wanting the General to discover they have the original painting, Gruber and the Colonel decide to ambush a wages truck to pay the 10 million franc ransom demand.

3. Hitler's Last Heil

Transmitted: 19/1/92

CAST

Gorden Kaye	René Artois
Carmen Silvera	Edith Artois
Vicki Michelle	Yvette
Richard Marner	Colonel Von Strohm
Guy Siner	Lieutenant Gruber
Kim Hartman	Helga Geerhart
Richard Gibson	Otto Flick
Kirsten Cooke	Michelle Dubois
Arthur Bostrom	Officer Crabtree
Kenneth Connor	Monsieur Alfonse
John Louis Mansi	Herr Von Smallhausen
Sue Hodge	Mimi Labonq
Hilary Minster	General Von Klinkerhoffen
Robin Parkinson	Ernest Leclerc
Rose Hill	Madame La Fan
David Rowlands	Doctor
Michael Jayes	Catholic Priest
David Janson	Hitler
Michael Sheard	Field Marshal Goering
John Hoye	Guard
Jonathan Gleeson	Guard
Julian Moss	Guard
Kit Hillier	Guard
Samantha O'Brien	Kitchen Girl

While visiting troops on the coast to boost morale, Hitler and Goering stop off at Nouvion. The Resistance try to kill them – not realising they're substitutes – but before they can, Helga, inadvertently, does the job for them. To cover up their deaths the General orders the Colonel and Gruber to take their places for the drive through the town. Meanwhile, Michelle is planning to blow up their car but when Mimi climbs into a drain to place a bomb under the vehicle it's not them who are eliminated but René's birthday present.

4. Awful Wedded Wife

Transmitted: 26/1/92

CAST

Gorden Kaye	René Artois
Carmen Silvera	Edith Artois
Vicki Michelle	Yvette
Richard Marner	Colonel Von Strohm
Guy Siner	Lieutenant Gruber
Kim Hartman	Helga Geerhart
Richard Gibson	Otto Flick
Kirsten Cooke	Michelle Dubois
Arthur Bostrom	Officer Crabtree
Kenneth Connor	Monsieur Alfonse
John Louis Mansi	Herr Von Smallhausen
Sue Hodge	Mimi Labonq
Hilary Minster	General Von Klinkerhoffen
Robin Parkinson	Ernest Leclerc
Rose Hill	Madame La Fan
Annabel Lambe	French Resistance
Michael Jayes	Catholic Priest
Paul David Betts	Guard
James Bingham	Guard
Carole Ashby	Louise (Communist Resistance)
Elizabeth Ash	Communist Resistance Girl
Sarah Hauenstein	Communist Resistance Girl

The Resistance failed to blow up Hitler and Goering so plan another attack when they return to Berlin. But the General intends organising his own explosion, once their car is out of his jurisdiction, to cover up the death of the original substitutes. Both plans are foiled by a Communist Resistance ambush with Gruber and the Colonel captured. Meanwhile, René has a narrow escape just when it looks like he'll have to wed again.

5. Firing Squashed

Transmitted: 2/2/92

CAST

Gorden Kaye	René Artois
Carmen Silvera	Edith Artois
Vicki Michelle	Yvette
Richard Marner	Colonel Von Strohm
Guy Siner	Lieutenant Gruber
Kim Hartman	Helga Geerhart
Richard Gibson	Otto Flick
Kirsten Cooke	Michelle Dubois
Arthur Bostrom	Officer Crabtree
Kenneth Connor	Monsieur Alfonse
John Louis Mansi	Herr Von Smallhausen
Sue Hodge	Mimi Labonq
Hilary Minster	General Von Klinkerhoffen
Robin Parkinson	Ernest Leclerc
Rose Hill	Madame La Fan
Carole Ashby	Louise (Communist Resistance)
Elizabeth Ash	Communist Resistance Girl
Christine Moore	Communist Resistance Girl
Amanda Gibson-Lees	Communist Resistance Girl
Tim Faulkner	Soldier
Friedrich Solms-Baruth	Soldier

Hitler and Goering – alias Gruber and the Colonel – are still in captivity and the Communist Resistance plan using Michelle's Edison machine to broadcast a surrender from Hitler. But the French Resistance want a piece of the action so intend getting their hands on Hitler and Goering. Both schemes fail and the prisoners escape seeking refuge in René's café.

6. A Fishful Of Francs

Transmitted: 9/2/92

CAST

Gorden Kaye	René Artois
Carmen Silvera	Edith Artois
Vicki Michelle	Yvette
Richard Marner	Colonel Von Strohm
Guy Siner	Lieutenant Gruber
Kim Hartman	Helga Geerhart
Richard Gibson	Otto Flick
Kirsten Cooke	Michelle Dubois
Arthur Bostrom	Officer Crabtree
Kenneth Connor	Monsieur Alfonse
John Louis Mansi	Herr Von Smallhausen
Sue Hodge	Mimi Labonq
Hilary Minster	General Von Klinkerhoffen
Robin Parkinson	Ernest Leclerc
Rose Hill	Madame La Fan
Carole Ashby	Louise (Communist Resistance)
Elizabeth Ash	Communist Resistance Girl
Jack Hedley	General Von Karzibrot
Mark Carey	Soldier
David Hopkins	Soldier

Gruber and the Colonel are free but their troubles return when the French Resistance resume their blackmail demands over the incriminating photo of Gruber with the painting. The money is to be placed in a dogfish but when it escapes, only to be caught and sold to a fishmonger, who will end up having it for tea? Meanwhile, the General is still trying to get the Hitler and Goering substitutes out of his jurisdition but this time chooses two peasants for the job: René and Edith.

7. A Swan Song

Transmitted: 1/3/92

CAST

Gorden Kaye	René Artois
Carmen Silvera	Edith Artois
Vicki Michelle	Yvette
Richard Marner	Colonel Von Strohm
Guy Siner	Lieutenant Gruber
Kim Hartman	Helga Geerhart
Richard Gibson	Otto Flick
Kirsten Cooke	Michelle Dubois
Arthur Bostrom	Officer Crabtree
Kenneth Connor	Monsieur Alfonse
John Louis Mansi	Herr Von Smallhausen
Sue Hodge	Mimi Labonq
Hilary Minster	General Von Klinkerhoffen
Robin Parkinson	Ernest Leclerc
Rose Hill	Madame La Fan
Jack Hedley	General Von Karzibrot
Miles Richardson	British Soldier
Darren Matthews	British Soldier
David Rowlands	Doctor
Brian Weston	British Soldier

René and Edith, disguised as Hitler and Goering, are captured by a German Officer, who's anti-Hitler and wants to kill them; but they're saved by a British ambush and eventually released once it's discovered that they're not the genuine articles. Having retrieved the 10 million francs from the dogfish, Herr Flick blackmails Gruber and the Colonel into parting with the painting in exchange for the cash. As the Resistance have already sent the incriminating photo to the General, they agree and plan an escape to Spain. The swap is made but not without the double-cross. Only the 'boobie' is passed on. Back at the café there's good news: Yvette isn't pregnant but Madame Lenare from the hat shop is. Who is the father this time?

SERIES 9

1. Gone With The Windmill

Transmitted: 9/1/92

CAST

Gorden Kaye	René Artois
Carmen Silvera	Edith Artois
Vicki Michelle	Yvette
Richard Marner	Colonel Von Strohm
Guy Siner	Lieutenant Gruber
Kim Hartman	Helga Geerhart
David Janson	Otto Flick
Kirsten Cooke	Michelle Dubois
Arthur Bostrom	Officer Crabtree
Kenneth Connor	Monsieur Alfonse
John Louis Mansi	Herr Von Smallhausen
Sue Hodge	Mimi Labonq
Hilary Minster	General Von Klinkerhoffen
Peter Clapham	German Officer
Jeremy Lloyd	German Officer
Carole Ashby	Louise (Communist Resistance)
Sarah Hauenstein	Communist Resistance Girl
Taryn Dielle	Tart
Natalie Tomlinson	Tart
Jeremy Beckman	Soldier

Gruber and the Colonel fail to reach Spain and ask René for help to avoid them being accused of desertion. Edith devises a plan where it appears the Resistance set them up when instead they had the painting all along. To back up the scheme, they pretend to be held captive in a nearby windmill, the same one as the General plans blowing up in target practice. René tries warning them but is caught by the Communist Resistance who decide to feign his death in order to keep him as their slave. Meanwhile, Herr Flick reveals his new face to aid his escape to Argentina when the British forces land.

2. A Tour De France

Transmitted: 16/1/92

CAST

Gorden Kaye	René Artois
Carmen Silvera	Edith Artois
Vicki Michelle	Yvette
Richard Marner	Colonel Von Strohm
Guy Siner	Lieutenant Gruber
Kim Hartman	Helga Geerhart
David Janson	Otto Flick
Kirsten Cooke	Michelle Dubois
Arthur Bostrom	Officer Crabtree
Kenneth Connor	Monsieur Alfonse
John Louis Mansi	Herr Von Smallhausen
Sue Hodge	Mimi Labonq
Hilary Minster	General Von Klinkerhoffen
Carole Ashby	Louise (Communist Resistance)
Anne Michelle	Communist Resistance Girl
Cheryl Fergison	Communist Resistance Girl
Linda Styan	Communist Resistance Girl
Debi Thomson	Communist Resistance Girl
Sarah Hauenstein	Communist Resistance Girl

With René presumed dead, Gruber and the Colonel ask Edith for *The Fallen Madonna*. Unfortunately, she doesn't know its whereabouts. They also want Helga to retrieve the 'boobie' from Herr Flick, but she demands a cut of the proceeds first. A memorial service is planned for René who's struggling in his new role as love slave to the Communist Resistance. Having had enough, he escapes wrapped in an elk bedspread and narrowly misses being killed by the General, Colonel and Gruber out shooting. When the day of the memorial arrives, Edith and friends hold a séance. But as they attempt to reach the dead, an elk arrives!

3. Dead Man Marching

Transmitted: 23/11/92

CAST

Gorden Kaye	René Artois
Carmen Silvera	Edith Artois
Vicki Michelle	Yvette
Richard Marner	Colonel Von Strohm
Guy Siner	Lieutenant Gruber
Kim Hartman	Helga Geerhart
David Janson	Otto Flick
Kirsten Cooke	Michelle Dubois
Arthur Bostrom	Officer Crabtree
Kenneth Connor	Monsieur Alfonse
John Louis Mansi	Herr Von Smallhausen
Sue Hodge	Mimi Labonq
Robin Parkinson	Ernest Leclerc
Rose Hill	Madame La Fan
David Rowlands	Doctor
Max Diamond	Peasant
Peter Dukes	Peasant
Jon Hurn	Peasant
Nancy Olive Moore	Cleaning Lady

René is back at the café but with the Germans believing he's dead, Michelle suggests he heads for England to help with the invasion plans. But when news arrives that the plane picking him up is delayed for a week, René has had enough of playing dead and gives himself up, citing amnesia caused by the blast led to him wandering the countryside for weeks.

4. Tarts And Flickers

Transmitted: 30/11/92

CAST

Gorden Kaye	René Artois
Carmen Silvera	Edith Artois
Vicki Michelle	Yvette
Richard Marner	Colonel Von Strohm
Guy Siner	Lieutenant Gruber
Kim Hartman	Helga Geerhart
David Janson	Otto Flick
Kirsten Cooke	Michelle Dubois
Arthur Bostrom	Officer Crabtree
Kenneth Connor	Monsieur Alfonse
John Louis Mansi	Herr Von Smallhausen
Sue Hodge	Mimi Labonq
Hilary Minster	General Von Klinkerhoffen
Robin Parkinson	Ernest Leclerc
Rose Hill	Madame La Fan
Paul David Betts	Soldier
Peter Dayson	Soldier
Paul Cooper	'London Calling'

The Resistance have obtained copies of the German defence plans and need to devise a way of sending them to England. Over at the Château, the General is planning to assassinate the Führer. He decides to send him a copy of *The Fallen Madonna* with a bomb attached and forces a reluctant Colonel and Gruber to help with his scheme.

5. A Fishy Send-Off

Transmitted: 7/12/92

CAST

Gorden Kaye	René Artois
Carmen Silvera	Edith Artois
Vicki Michelle	Yvette
Richard Marner	Colonel Von Strohm
Guy Siner	Lieutenant Gruber
Kim Hartman	Helga Geerhart
David Janson	Otto Flick
Kirsten Cooke	Michelle Dubois
Arthur Bostrom	Officer Crabtree
Kenneth Connor	Monsieur Alfonse
John Louis Mansi	Herr Von Smallhausen
Sue Hodge	Mimi Labonq
Hilary Minster	General Von Klinkerhoffen
Robin Parkinson	Ernest Leclerc
Rose Hill	Madame La Fan
Matthew Woolcott	German Soldier
David Hopkins	German Officer
Ian Soundy	Sentry
James Pertwee	Soldier on Coast
Dennis Arnell	Onlooker

René and the gang are entering a float in the Fishmonger's Parade to the Coast. They intend using it to sail to England with the German defence plans. But when the Allied invasion starts, the retreating German troops commandeer the float. The General's plan to blow up Hitler fails when Herr Flick finds out and informs officials at the train station. But when he tries stealing what he believes is the real painting, it accidentally detonates.

6. A Winkle In Time

Transmitted: 14/12/92

CAST

Gorden Kaye	René Artois
Carmen Silvera	Edith Artois
Vicki Michelle	Yvette
Richard Marner	Colonel Von Strohm
Guy Siner	Lieutenant Gruber
Kim Hartman	Helga Geerhart
David Janson	Otto Flick
Kirsten Cooke	Michelle Dubois
Arthur Bostrom	Officer Crabtree
Kenneth Connor	Monsieur Alfonse
John Louis Mansi	Herr Von Smallhausen
Sue Hodge	Mimi Labonq
Hilary Minster	General Von Klinkerhoffen
Robin Parkinson	Ernest Leclerc
Rose Hill	Madame La Fan
John D. Collins	Flight Lieutenant Fairfax
Nicholas Frankau	Flight Lieutenant Carstairs
Giles Watling	British Officer
James Barron	British Oficer
Paul Cooper	'London Calling'

Everyone in Nouvion is excited about the Allied troops arriving, except the Germans. The Colonel and Gruber try escaping dressed as British airmen, and Herr Flick is planning his escape in a midget submarine made out of two baths. Unfortunately, Von Smallhausen's tunnel to the river ends up in René's café, just as the Germans are surrendering to the British.

Fast-forward many years after the war and Gruber and Helga return to the café. Gruber has become a millionaire art dealer and married Helga: They've even employed the Colonel as their chauffeur.

A wheelchair-bound René has handed over the running of the café to his son, a baby found on his doorstep. As they chat, René's statue is damaged and out falls the priceless painting of the Fallen Madonna. When Helga produces the missing 'boobie', which Herr Flick gave her as a going-away present, René grabs the painting and elopes with Yvette.

The Best Of 'Allo 'Allo!

Transmitted: 17/8/94

At the Café de La Place, René and Edith drink champagne to celebrate Edith's birthday. They reminisce about the war years and ponder on how they started working for the Resistance.

The Return Of 'Allo 'Allo!

Transmitted: 28/4/07

René is writing his memoirs at Café René and old friends and foes pop in to say 'hello'.

THE STAGE SHOW

The sustained success of the *'Allo 'Allo!* television series gave rise to an equally popular stage show which ran, initially, between 1986 and 1992, including sell-out nationwide and international tours and several London runs. Since then, the show has been revisited several times, including a 1996 summer season at Bournemouth's Pier Theatre and a 2007 trip down under for Gorden Kaye, Sue Hodge and Guy Siner; they revived their characters again, this time in Brisbane, the most populous city in Queensland. But that's not all: in 2008, an adaptation of the original show kicked off at the Gordon Craig Theatre in Stevenage, Hertfordshire, before embarking on an eagerly-awaited national tour with Vicki Michelle, once again, playing Yvette while Jeffrey Holland, of *Hi-De-Hi!* fame, cast as René; and let's not forget the many amateur productions performed throughout the UK on a regular basis.

Considering the sitcom's popularity, it was only a matter of time before Messrs Lloyd and Croft were approached about adapting their wartime comedy for the stage. That moment arrived when theatre producer Mark Furness contacted the writers. David Croft, when interviewed by Michael Leech for the souvenir brochure sold during the initial tour of principal English and Scottish venues, acknowledged that he knew *'Allo 'Allo!* would work on stage. 'I've done a lot of West End work as an actor, singer and lyricist, and I've toured a lot so I think you rapidly get a feeling for what will go on stage.'

Rather than rework two or three popular TV episodes, Croft pointed out that the story was fresh. 'What Jeremy and I have provided is a new comedy, an extension of the TV stories. All the well-known characters are there of course, but the theatre audience is actually getting more than they would from TV.' He admitted, however, that it wasn't an easy show to mount, technically. 'I think there are 17 sets in the show. But the director, Peter Farago, has had a lot of London experience, and the bookings have been sensational, so we must be doing something right!'

Gruber Does Some Mincing

Helga is in Herr Flick's quarters.
HERR FLICK: Now, pay attention, I will shortly be inviting you to the Gestapo club. Are you pleased?
HELGA: Of course, Herr Flick. To be in the club with the Gestapo will be a great honour.

He was right, the bookings were sensational from the moment the show opened at Birmingham's Alexandra Theatre in July 1986, which augured well for the rest of the tour. Guy Siner, who reprised his role for the stage show, says: 'I have wonderful memories. Night after night, theatre after theatre, it broke box office records.' In particular, he remembers the opening night in Birmingham. 'It was extraordinary because we walked on stage and saw the whole front row filled with people in costume – fans who'd booked their seats early and dressed for the occasion; there were three Grubers, half a dozen Michelles – it was utterly extraordinary. There were gales of laughter and the reaction took your breath away.'

Afterwards, Guy shared his thoughts with co-writer David Croft. 'I said, "That was something, wasn't it?" He told me that he'd been in the business for decades and had never heard laughter like it. There was wave after wave and it made us realize that we had a hit on our hands.'

Kim Hartman concurs with Guy. 'We were peeping through the curtains before the show started and it was daunting in a way; I remember feeling nervous after that because it seemed we had so much to live up to.' But as soon as the opening show started, the reaction from the audience soothed any first-night nerves. 'The audience was amazing and I can't begin to tell you how exciting it was,' says Kim. 'I've always enjoyed working in live theatre but the atmosphere was tremendous with people literally rocking in their seats. You'd walk out of the theatre at the end of the night and be floating on air.'

Eventually, the production reached London's Prince of Wales Theatre in November 1986, a first for Kim. 'I'd never worked in the West End before and suddenly there we were at the Prince of Wales after an enormously successful national tour; I think the Liverpool Empire was filled for the first time since the Beatles had performed there, decades before.'

The rapturous welcome the cast were given as they moved from place to place delighted everyone, including Sue Hodge, who enjoyed transferring Mimi to the stage. 'I loved the theatre show because unlike TV you get that larger-than-life performance; and what joy to hear 1,500 people not letting you get the next line out because they're uncontrollable, screaming with laughter.' Reflecting on the show's financial success, Sue says: 'There was a long Prince of Wales' run in 1986 and the Palladium in 1988, which had only been booked for three months initially but because it was taking £300,000 gross a week, was extended to six months.'

Jeremy Lloyd and David Croft took a week to pen the stage script with Croft, initially, keen to write it as a musical. Eventually, they opted for straight comedy, based on the sitcom's comedic style. Their search for a director took them to Peter Farago, an experienced theatre director, although such a project meant a departure from his normal line of work. 'I had never done a commercial piece of comedy of this nature before,' admits Peter. 'I was trained in repertory theatre and so my track record was to do with, among others, "The Classics".' He had run Birmingham Rep for some nine years and was making the move to being a freelance director so it was a project which interested him.

Just because a comedy series is a runaway success on television doesn't mean it will automatically be as popular if adapted for another medium, such as film or stage. But considering Lloyd and Croft's vast experience, the odds were favourable that 'Allo 'Allo! would succeed. 'David and Jeremy had a great deal of experience of turning their sitcoms into stage shows,' says Peter. 'David tended not to undertake projects he didn't think could succeed. I think it was a very canny commercial calculation on his and the theatre producer's behalf because the television series was at or getting towards its peak of popularity and, therefore, there was enough of an audience who would want to come and see a live version.'

Reflecting on the *'Allo 'Allo!* script, Peter Farago believes that out of all the shows written by the Lloyd-Croft and Perry-Croft partnerships, it's the one most like a stage farce in structure and, therefore, likely to transfer successfully. 'If it had been *Dad's Army*, I would have been less certain – partly because most of the actors are dead, and I wouldn't have been personally convinced that a lookalike version on stage would have been a success. The quality of the writing in *Dad's Army* is much more naturalistic, much more subtle and, therefore, personally I wouldn't have wanted to direct it because I wouldn't have been certain if it could be successful on any level. Clearly, I was wrong because the show has been revived in the last five or so years for the stage and very successfully. But back then, I would have said "no" because I wouldn't have known how to do it on the stage because it seemed quintessentially a filmic show. To me, *'Allo 'Allo!* didn't seem like that, so when asked to do it, I thought it would be very interesting, especially as I hadn't done anything like it before.'

The overwhelming success was a shock to the system for everyone, including David and Jeremy. 'The show previewed in Birmingham at the Alexandra Theatre, and I remember walking across on the first night and thinking something strange was going on because there seemed to be French maids, French police officers and Gestapo officers hanging around,' recalls Peter. 'It was such an unlikely event and the only other time I experienced something like that was when I went to see *The Rocky Horror Show*, which was a long time before. The theatre was packed and when Gorden Kaye came on for his first monologue, the roof almost fell in. It was extraordinary.'

Many theatre critics slated the production. When it opened at London's Prince of Wales Theatre, the reviewer in the *Daily Telegraph* wrote 'wonderful on TV but dreadful on stage' while adding it had a 'clumsy climax'. The *Guardian* was equally critical. The writer hadn't seen the TV series so arrived at the theatre fresh, but didn't enjoy his evening. He wrote: 'I left two and a half hours later extremely jaundiced' and commented on the 'crude and ill-written rubbish'.

But the critics' views weren't shared by the audiences who loved the show, and before long plans were afoot to take the production abroad. 'It was an obvious next step,' admits Peter. 'It's not brain surgery: if you have a commercial production which you've toured successfully because there seemed to be an endless audience for it, it seemed a good idea to take it to places where the series was successful, such as Australia and New Zealand.'

For the long Australian tour in 1990, the company were without Gorden Kaye, who had been involved in the tragic accident on the eve of departing;

fortunately, a replacement was found just in time, with Max Gillies donning the apron of René Artois. 'Max was well-known Down Under for political satire, impressions and his own TV series,' says Arthur Bostrom. 'Being well-known in his own right made a huge difference; he had great presence on stage and was lovely to work with, although it wasn't ideal and he could never have replaced Gorden. But as a compromize it worked, which was essential because we were out there four and a half months.'

Despite acknowledging the overwhelming success of the show, Sam Kelly – who played Captain Geering – had a couple of reservations about the stage show when compared to the small screen version. 'It went extremely well and was very funny. But, in my opinion, it was a bit rude and too long; occasionally the script went slightly over the top.'

Guy Siner disagrees with Sam on this point. 'It certainly went a bit further than the TV series but I don't think it was a mistake – quite the reverse. One of the reasons it worked so well is that on stage you had hundreds of years of theatrical experience. These weren't actors who'd become successful in a television series and suddenly were transferred on to a stage and told to get on with it. No, you had consummate theatre actors with years of experience. It was a theatrical piece and David and Jeremy wrote for that; I thought it was wonderful and wouldn't have changed any of it.'

Arthur Bostrum agrees with Guy. 'There were always double entendres, although it was never knowingly rude. There weren't any crude lines but there may have been crude implications – and there's a big difference.'

Working with Lloyd and Croft proved extremely beneficial for director, Peter Farago, who admits he learnt more about comedy through directing 'Allo 'Allo! than any other project. 'Without doubt, it was one of the major staging posts in my career and was something I'll always remember.'

Watching the writers work was, for Peter, an intriguing experience. 'Seeing them work together, on the hoof as it were, was very interesting because Jeremy would spew out 15 jokes and David would edit them down to the one that was the best. David, though, had no desire to direct his stage shows because he thought there were better theatre directors than him. But his knowledge of the script and how that script would work with a live audience was impeccable. So it became one of the most significant learning experiences in my career.'

VENUES

The show has toured regularly, in various shapes and forms, from 1986. Here are some of the venues which hosted the comedy.

1986
Between July and October 1986, the show was performed at Birmingham's Alexandra Theatre, Norwich's Theatre Royal, Leeds' Grand Theatre and Opera House, Bristol's Hippodrome, Nottingham's Theatre Royal, Glasgow's Theatre Royal, Edinburgh's King's Theatre, Aberdeen's His Majesty's Theatre, Wimbledon's New Wimbledon Theatre before, in November 1986, transferring to London's Prince of Wales Theatre.

1988
The show was performed at the London Palladium.

1992
Between February and March, the show was staged at London's Dominion Theatre and the Grand Theatre and Opera House, Leeds.

1996
Covering the summer (June – September), the show was seen at Woking's New Victoria Theatre, Bradford's Alhambra Theatre, Norwich's Theatre Royal, Llandudno's North Wales Theatre and Bournemouth's Pier Theatre, finishing its run at the Dorset seaside town on September 9, 1996.

EPISODE LISTING – AT A GLANCE

Note: David Croft and Jeremy Lloyd didn't allocate episode titles for their *'Allo 'Allo!* scripts. Over the years, various versions have popped up on fan and TV sites. The titles chosen for this book are those held by the BBC and are as close as we're going to get to official episode names.

PILOT
The British Are Coming.....................................(30/12/82)

SERIES 1
1. The Fallen Madonna ....(7/9/84)
2. Pigeon Post..(14/9/84)
3. Saville Row To The Rescue ....(21/9/84)
4. The Execution ....(28/9/84)
5. The Funeral ....(5/10/84)
6. Red Nick's Colonel ....(19/10/84)
7. The Dance Of Hitler Youth ....(26/10/84)

SERIES 2
1. Six Big Boobies ....(21/10/85)
2. The Wooing Of Widow Artois ....(28/10/85)
3. The Policeman Cometh...................................(4/11/85)
4. Swiftly And With Style ....(11/11/85)
5. The Duel..(18/11/85)
6. Herr Flick's Revenge ....(25/11/85)

CHRISTMAS SPECIAL
The Gateau From The Château ....(26/12/85)

SERIES 3
1. The Nicked Knockwurst ....(5/12/86)
2. Gruber Does Some Mincing ....(12/12/86)
3. The Sausage In The Wardrobe ....(19/12/86)
4. Flight Of Fancy...(26/12/86)

5. Pretty Maids All In A Row............................(2/1/87)
6. The Great Un-Escape..................................(9/1/87)

SERIES 4
1. Prisoners Of War...(7/11/87)
2. Camp Dance...(14/11/87)
3. Good Staff Are Hard To Find.......................(21/11/87)
4. The Flying Nun...(28/11/87)
5. The Sausages In The Trousers ....(5/12/87)
6. The Jet-Propelled Mother-In-Law ....(12/12/87)

SERIES 5
1. Desperate Doings In The Dungeon..............(3/9/88)
2. The Camera In The Potato ....(10/9/88)
3. Dinner With The General............................(17/9/88)
4. The Dreaded Circular Saw...........................(24/9/88)
5. Otherwise Engaged ....(1/10/88)
6. A Marriage of Inconvenience.......................(8/10/88)
7. No Hiding Place...(15/10/88)
8. The Arrival Of The Homing Duck...............(22/10/88)
9. Watch The Birdie ....(29/10/88)
10. René – Under An Assumed Nose...............(5/11/88)
11. The Confusion Of The Generals ....(12/11/88)
12. Who's For The Vatican?............................(19/11/88)
13. Ribbing The Bonk.....................................(26/11/88)
14. The Reluctant Millionaires........................(3/12/88)
15. A Duck For Launch...................................(10/12/88)
16. The Exploding Bedpan...............................(17/12/88)
17. Going Like A Bomb ....(24/12/88)
18. Money To Burn ....(31/12/88)
19. Puddings Can Go Off.................................(7/1/89)
20. Land Mines for London ....(14/1/89)
21. Flight To Geneva.......................................(21/1/89)
22. Train Of Events ....(28/1/89)
23. An Enigma Variation..................................(4/2/89)
24. Wedding Bloss ....(11/2/89)
25. Down The Drain...(18/2/89)
26. All In Disgeese...(25/2/89)

SERIES 6

1. Desperate Doings In The Graveyard............(2/9/89)
2. The Gestapo For The High Jump.................(9/9/89)
3. The Nouvion Oars...(16/9/89)
4. The Nicked Airmen......................................(23/9/89)
5. The Airmen De-Nicked................................(30/9/89)
6. The Crooked Fences.....................................(7/10/89)
7. Crabtree's Podgeon Pist..............................(14/10/89)
8. Rising To The Occasion...............................(21/10/89)

SERIES 7

1. A Quiet Honeymoon ....(5/1/91)
2. An Almighty Bang ....(12/1/91)
3. Fleeing Monks ....(19/1/91)
4. Up the Crick Without A Piddle ....(26/1/91)
5. The Gestapo Ruins A Picnic.........................(2/2/91)
6. The Spirit Of Nouvion ....(9/2/91)
7. Leg It To Spain! ....(16/2/91)
8. Prior Engagements ....(23/2/91)
9. Soup And Sausage..(2/3/91)
10. René Of The Gypsies ....(16/3/91)

CHRISTMAS SPECIAL

A Bun In The Oven ....(24/12/91)

SERIES 8

1. Arousing Suspicions.....................................(5/1/92)
2. A Woman Never Lies ....(12/1/92)
3. Hitler's Last Heil...(19/1/92)
4. Awful Wedded Wife ....(26/1/92)
5. Firing Squashed ....(2/2/92)
6. A Fishful Of Francs......................................(9/2/92)
7. A Swan Song...(1/3/92)

'ALLO 'ALLO!

SERIES 9

The Best Of 'Allo 'Allo!

The Return Of 'Allo 'Allo!

NUMBER OF APPEARANCES

Note: The programmes The Best Of 'Allo 'Allo! *and* The Return Of 'Allo 'Allo! *are not included. Only cast and regular supporting performers listed.*

APPEARANCES   ACTOR

APPEARANCES	ACTOR
85	Gorden Kaye
85	Carmen Silvera
85	Vicki Michelle
85	Richard Marner
85	Guy Siner
85	Kim Hartman
82	Kirsten Cooke
78	Richard Gibson
78	Rose Hill
74	Arthur Bostrom
64	John D. Collins
64	Nicholas Frankau
63	John Louis Mansi
62	Sue Hodge
61	Kenneth Connor
60	Hilary Minster
51	Jack Haig
33	Gavin Richards
23	Sam Kelly (plus one 'voice only')
22	Robin Parkinson
21	Francesca Gonshaw
17	Paul Cooper (including 15 as 'London Calling')
15	Phoebe Scholfield
15	Carole Ashby
10	Roger Kitter
9	Moira Foot
8	Derek Royle
7	David Janson
6	Ken Morley

'ALLO 'ALLO! TIMELINE

Pilot
Our first visit to Café René in the French town of Nouvion.

Series 1, episode 4
- René is supposedly shot by a firing squad only to return as his own twin brother.

Series 2, episode 3
- Officer Crabtree, a British agent, arrives on the scene with his pidgin French. He masquerades as a French policeman.

Series 4, episode 2
- We discover Maria will not be returning to the café as she has been shipped to Switzerland disguised as a Red Cross parcel.
- Captain Geering is missing, presumed captured by the Communist Resistance. However, it transpires that he has fled to England disguised as an RAF pilot.

Series 4, episode 3
- The Italian captain, Bertorelli, has been recruited as liaison officer working alongside Colonel Von Strohm.
- A new recruit in the café, Mimi Labonq, is René's new waitress.

Series 6, episode 1
- Ernest Leclerc arrives as the new pianist. He was in prison but whilst visiting him, his twin brother Roger decided to switch places because he regarded prison food better that Edith's. Ernest doesn't take long to rekindle his love for Fanny and is soon proposing.

Series 6, episode 8
- Fanny and Ernest Leclerc tie the knot.

Series 7, episode 1
- Roger Kitter replaces Gavin Richards as Captain Bertorelli and Robin Parkinson replaces Derek Royle, who died, as Ernest Leclerc.

Series 7, episode 4
- Sam Kelly is seen again as Captain Geering when Edith and René arrive in England.

Series 8, episode 1

- The British airmen return to England at last having been disguised as squids and netted by an English trawler.
- Bertorelli has gone due to Mussolini throwing in the towel.
- Yvette announces she is pregnant and that René is the father.

Series 8, episode 8

- The doctor admits that he made a mistake and that Yvette isn't pregnant after all.

Series 9, episode 1

- René is presumed dead having been caught up in the bombing of a windmill.
- Herr Flick reveals his new face after plastic surgery. He plans to escape to Argentina when the British invade.

Series 9, episode 6

- The Allied Forces arrive in Nouvion after defeating the Nazis.

MERCHANDISE

During the life of the sitcom, various items of merchandise were released in an attempt to satisfy the insatiable appetite of 'Allo 'Allo! fans – and to exploit, financially, of course, the show's indubitable success. These include:

BOOKS

Title: 'Allo 'Allo! – The War Diaries of René Artois: Volume 1
Author: John Haselden
ISBN: 0563206888 978-0563206880
Publisher: BBC Books; **Publication Date:** 1988
Notes: René Artois's memoirs, recounting his role in the French Resistance.

Title: 'Allo 'Allo! – The War Diaries of René Artois: Volume 2
Author: John Haselden and Jeremy Lloyd
ISBN: 0563208422 978-0563208426
Publisher: BBC Books; **Publication Date:** 1989
Notes: René Artois's memoirs, recounting his role in the French Resistance.

Title: *'Allo 'Allo! – The Complete War Diaries of René Artois*
Author: René Fairfax and John Haselden
ISBN: 0563363274 978-0563363279
Publisher: BBC Books; **Publication Date:** 1991
Notes: Volumes 1 and 2 of René Artois's memoirs recounting his role in the French Resistance.

Title: *'Allo 'Allo!* (Acting Edition)
Author: David Croft and Jeremy Lloyd
ISBN: 0573018782 978-0573018787
Publisher: Samuel French Ltd; **Publication Date:** 2000
Notes: A comedy based on the TV series in script form.

AUDIOBOOK
Title: *'Allo 'Allo! – The War Diaries of René Artois*
Author: John Haselden
ISBN: 0563381159 978-0563381150
Publisher: BBC Audiobooks Ltd/BBC Gold
Publication Date: 1996
Notes: Gorden Kaye recalls the exploits of René Artois.

DVDs
Title: *'Allo 'Allo!* (Series 1 and 2)
Release Date: 2002; **ASIN:** B000067A8U
Notes: Three discs. **Released by:** BBC

Title: *'Allo 'Allo!* (Series 3 and 4)
Release Date: 2004; **ASIN:** B000163X5C
Notes: Three discs. **Released by:** BBC

Title: *'Allo 'Allo!* (Series 5, Vol. 1)
Release Date: 2006; **ASIN:** B000I2IZQ6
Notes: Two discs. **Released by:** BBC

Title: *'Allo 'Allo!* (Series 5, Vol. 2)
Release Date: 2006; **ASIN:** B000JJ7C08
Notes: Two discs. **Released by:** BBC

Title: *'Allo 'Allo!* (Series 6 and 7)
Release Date: 2008; **ASIN:** B000YHMTG2
Notes: Three discs. **Released by:** BBC

Title: *'Allo 'Allo!* (Series 8 and 9)
Release Date: 2008; **ASIN:** B001D0TCBE
Notes: Three discs. **Released by:** BBC

Title: *'Allo 'Allo!* (The Complete Series)
Release Date: 2009; **ASIN:** B002L7O7QS
Notes: Sixteen discs. **Released by:** BBC

BIBLIOGRAPHY

Croft, David, *You Have Been Watching... The Autobiography of David Croft*
(London: BBC Books, 2004)
Hayward, Anthony & Deborah, *TV Unforgettables*
(Enfield, Middlesex: Guinness, 1993)
Lloyd, Jeremy, *Listen Very Carefully, I Shall Say This Only Once – An Autobiography*
(London: BBC Books, 1993)
Webber, Richard, *Are You Being Served?*
(London: Orion, 1998)
Webber, Richard, *Dad's Army – A Celebration*
(London: Virgin, 1997)
Webber, Richard, *The Complete A–Z of Everything Carry On*
(London: HarperCollins, 2005)

Additionally, **www.comedy.co.uk** and **www.en.wikipedia.org** were useful sources of reference.